ON THE ROAD TO SIANGYANG

Studies in Chinese Christianity

G. Wright Doyle and Carol Lee Hamrin,
Series Editors
A Project of the Global China Center
www.globalchinacenter.org

The Rev. Peter Matson (1868–1943)

On the Road to Siangyang

Covenant Mission in Mainland China 1890–1949

JACK R. LUNDBOM

☙PICKWICK *Publications* · Eugene, Oregon

ON THE ROAD TO SIANGYANG
Covenant Mission in Mainland China 1890–1949

Studies in Chinese Christianity

Pickwick Publications
An Imprint of Wipf and Stock Publishers
199 W. 8th Ave., Suite 3
Eugene, OR 97401

www.wipfandstock.com

ISBN 13: 978-1-4982-3529-7

Cataloguing-in-Publication Data

Lundbom, Jack R.

On the road to Siangyang : Covenant mission in mainland China 1890–1949 / Jack R. Lundbom.

xvi + 292 p. ; 23 cm. Includes bibliographical references and index.

ISBN: 978-1-4982-3529-7

1. China—Christianity. 2. China—Church history—20th century. 3. Christianity—China. I. Title. II. Series.

BR1287 L86 2015

Manufactured in the U.S.A.   12/29/2015

Dedicated to the memory of Peter and Edla Matson, Isaac and Anna
Jacobson, Oscar and Ruth Anderson, Ed and Millie Nelson,
Viola Larson, and other Covenant missionaries, who,
for nearly 60 years labored together with other
missionaries and Chinese Christians to
bring the Gospel to the people
of Central China

If you hear contradictory things about China,
they're all true

Contents

Permissions

THE AUTHOR AND PUBLISHER are grateful to the following for permission to quote from previous publications and translations of others:

From members of the Anderson family—Edward Anderson, Doris Jackson, Marian Ekstrand, and Vivian Johnson—to publish Oscar Anderson's account of his capture by Ho Lung's Red Army in C. Oscar Anderson and Ruth M. Anderson, *Two Lives of Faith* (ed. J. Edward Anderson et al; Denver: World Press, 1974), 52–58, 61–82.

From Viola Larson to publish her personal account of the murder of three Covenant Missionaries, "The Martyr of Three Missionaries in Central China, Province of Hupeh, January 7, 1948."

From Cao Jing to publish her translation of "A Brief Introduction of Christianity in Nanzhang County."

From the F. M. Johnson Archves and Special Collections in Brandel Library, North Park University, for historical pictures relating to the Covenant China mission.

From Zhang Jiang, for pictures taken on a trip to China in October, 2014.

Preface

THE STORY OF COVENANT missionary work in China is a fascinating one. It was a story widely known among Mission Covenant people in the pre-World War II era, but one that faded or was forgotten—except by the missionaries—during 30 years of communist rule in China, particularly during the Cultural Revolution of 1966–1976. Today there is renewed interest in China missions generally, with the country having opened up and China missionaries or their children having returned to former mission fields for visits.[1] Even more important is evidence all throughout China that the seed sown by Christian missionaries has yielded a rich harvest, more than anyone could have imagined. Having survived for years underground, the Christian church has largely—but not entirely—come above ground and experienced enormous growth in the past 35 years, a growth that continues today. One can only imagine what the Church in China will look like 35 years from now, and in years following.

This book expands four lectures on the Covenant Mission to Mainland China, 1890–1949, delivered to Covenant adult classes and retirement audiences during 2008–2014. After an introduction to the Covenant missionary work, three chapters focus on its stated aims: 1) preaching, evangelism, and the establishment of a Chinese Church; 2) medical and benevolence work; and 3) educational work, all of which characterized Protestant missions generally. A final chapter gives a modern, twenty-first century look at cities where Christianity, at some point, has made its mark in China, and Covenant mission work has been carried on—cities I have visited with my wife Linda, my daughter Jeanie, or Chinese students and friends who have accompanied me. Chapter 5 reports in addition the dedication of a new church in Nanzhang in 2007, at which time representatives of the Evangelical Covenant Church were present.

---

1. Dr. Mildred Nordlund and Ruth Edlund visited China in 1980; see M. Nordlund, "A China Experience."

In chapters recounting the history of the Covenant China mission I have used older spellings of place names to keep continuity with the earlier written material. In Chapter 5, however, which reports my visits to China in the twenty-first century, I use modern (pinyin) spellings that will be more familiar to the present-day reader. A table with the two spellings appears in Appendix 5.

The author is grateful to many who supplied information and documents at their disposal for the research and writing of this book, among whom I am happy to mention the following:

Rev. Craig Anderson—for material on Judith Peterson and Ann Kulberg Carlson's letters in her unpublished "Mission to China" booklet;

Minglan Hammerlind Wong—for material on Elsa Hammerlind;

Evangelist Leng Jia-quan of the Nanzhang Church—for a "Brief Introduction of Christianity in Nanzhang County" and personal conversation about Christianity in China during the Cultural Revolution;

Pastor Ding Jiang-hua of the Jingzhou-Shasi Church—for an Anniversary Booklet of the church and personal conversation about the Covenant China Mission;

Shing Hua Tang of the Jingzhou-Shasi Church—for records and pictures of the Covenant schools in Jingzhou and personal conversation about the Covenant China Mission;

Pastor Zhang Jiang, my traveling companion to Mainland China in October, 2014—for pictures taken on this trip;

Brian Backstrand—for sharing unpublished correspondence of Otelia Hendrickson;

Ernie and Vivian Anderson Johnson—for information and pictures from their visit to China, and to Vivian for books from the library of her father, C. Oscar Anderson, and for personal conversation about China and the Covenant China mission;

J. Edward Anderson—for personal conversation about China and the Covenant China Mission;

Marian Anderson Ekstrand—for personal conversation about China and the Covenant China Mission;

Rev. Norman E. Dwight—for information about the Fancheng Church and former Covenant residences at Kuling;

Viola Larson—for her unpublished account of "The Martyr of Three Missionaries" and personal conversation about China, Peter Matson, and the Covenant China Mission;

Rev. Paul S. Backlund—for personal conversation about China and the Covenant China Mission.

Rev. Carl A. and Lillian Branstrom—for personal conversation about China and the Covenant China Mission;

Edward G. and Mildred Nelson—for Edward's book, *China in Your Blood*, and many conversations with both about China and the Covenant China Mission;

Professor Virginia M. Ohlson—for information about the American Nurses' Association Tour of The People's Republic of China in November-December, 1977;

Rev. Ralph P. Hanson—for personal conversation about the Covenant China Mission;

Professor F. Burton Nelson—for personal conversation about the Covenant China Mission;

Rev. Quentin and Virginia Larson—for the unpublished autobiography of Leonard J. Larson, "Son of Prayer";

Vernoy Johnson—for the unpublished biography, "The Momentous Years: A Biography of Ruth Alice Hedberg Johnson and Alfred Joseph Johnson," and personal conversation about China and the Covenant China Mission;

Gordon Johnson, who held a position in China affairs with the U.S. Department of State—for personal conversation about China;

Doris Johnson—for personal conversation about China and the Covenant China Mission;

Jeannine Nordlund—for sharing her travel diary from a visit with her husband Ted to Hankou in May, 2005;

Dr. Arland Hultgren and Bruce Eldevik of Luther Theological Seminary, St. Paul, MN—for material on the Norwegian Lutheran Mission in China in the Luther Seminary library;

Professor Maria E. Erling, Lutheran Theological Seminary at Gettysburg—for information on China Missions;

Professor Ted Zimmerman, Lutheran Theological Seminary, Hong Kong—for information on the Lutheran Mission in Hupeh Province, and the legendary "St Paul" airplane that evacuated many China missionaries in 1948–49;

Anna-Kajsa Anderson, archivist at the F. M. Johnson Archives and Special Collections in Brandel Library, North Park University, Chicago—for access to Covenant China records; also Steve Spencer, Brandel Librarian, for locating books on the Covenant China mission in the F. M. Johnson Archives;

Betty Bolden, Special Collections Librarian at the Burke Library, Union Theological Seminary, Columbia University Libraries—for supplying information about Kuling;

Lucy Chung, Director of the United Library of Garrett-Evangelical Theological Seminary—for China records in the Garrett library;

Sui-Tung Tang, Librarian at the Lutheran Theological Seminary, Hong Kong—for records of the Lutheran United Mission in China and other China mission records;

And above all to Cao Jing—my traveling companion on two visits to Mainland China, for translating the "Brief Introduction of Christianity in Nanzhang County," and for providing much information about Xiangyang and Hubei Province.

I am grateful for Wright Doyle and Carol Hamrin's acceptance of this book into Pickwick's "Studies in Chinese Christianity" series. Wright read the entire manuscript, making a number of helpful suggestions. A special thanks to him.

August 15, 2015
Jack R. Lundbom

Abbreviations

CIM	China Inland Mission
CPC	Communist Party of China
CRH	Chinese High Speed Rail
KMT	The Kuomintang (Nationalist Party in China)
LTS	Lutheran Theological Seminary, Hong Kong
NRSV	The New Revised Standard Version
NT	New Testament
OT	Old Testament
PRC	People's Republic of China
RMB	Renminbi ("people's currency"), the official currency of the People's Republic of China. The *yuan* is the basic unit of the renminbi, and is used interchangeably with it
RSV	The Revised Standard Version
SMF	Svenska Missionsförbundet (The Mission Covenant Church of Sweden)
VJ Day	Victory in Japan Day

1

The American Mission Covenant
Goes to China

EXPANDED VISION IN A MISSION-MINDED CHURCH

THE AMERICAN MISSION COVENANT (*Missionsförbundet i Amerika*), today the Evangelical Covenant Church, has been—and still is—a small Protestant denomination, yet for nearly 60 years it carried on a significant mission work in Central China. This book will tell something about that mission, and about the men and women who evangelized, brought medical and benevolence assistance, and educated young and old with the larger purpose that the Christian gospel might transform this ancient land and its people. Their labor has borne fruit, and one chapter in the book will report visits the author has made to China in the first two decades of the twenty-first century, where evidence abounds that Christianity is fast growing in China. The yield is not yet great, but there is a yield, and it remains to be seen what this will mean for China in the days and years ahead. The Apostle Paul said to the young church at Corinth: "I planted, Apollos watered, but God gave the growth" (1 Cor 3:6).

The American Covenant Church was mission-minded from the beginning. Within five years after its organization in 1885, missionary enterprises were launched in Alaska and China. Alaska was the oldest field, work beginning there in 1887. China was targeted as a mission field three years later.

At the Covenant Annual Meeting on September 8, 1890, held in Galesburg, Illinois, Karl Petter Wallén and Per Matson were ordained and commissioned, and Mrs. Mia Wallen was later dedicated, for missionary

1

service in China.[1] Matson went on to become the Covenant's premier China missionary, choosing the field, beginning the work there, and setting the tone of Covenant missions for 60 years to come.

PETER MATSON, PIONEER CHINA MISSIONARY

Peter Matson was born in Lindesnäs, Dalarna, Sweden, on March 27, 1868, emigrating to America with his parents when he was 11 years old.[2] The family settled on a farm in Alexandria, Minnesota.[3] On a summer day in 1888, when the day's work was done, Matson knelt by a haystack and promised the Lord that he would give half his income to missions or become a missionary himself.[4] His mother, not without tears, praised God for the privilege of giving her first-born to the missionary cause.[5] After study in 1888–90 at the "Skogsbergh's School" in Minneapolis and "Risberg's School" at the Chicago Theological Seminary, he was called by the Covenant for missionary service to China.

On October 1, 1890, Matson sailed with the Wallens out of San Francisco for China. When they arrived in Japan, Mrs. Wallen was worn out from seasickness, so she and her husband decided to remain a week in Yokohama. Matson went on ahead to Shanghai, arriving there on October 28, just two weeks ahead of the first contingent of missionaries from the Swedish Mission Covenant,[6] who arrived in Shanghai on November 13. The Wallens arrived in Shanghai on November 4.

Upon arrival in Shanghai, Matson met up with a Mr. Dyer of the British and Foreign Bible Society, who took him to the headquarters of the China Inland Mission (CIM) on Woosung Road in Hongkew, the northern district of Shanghai.[7] He recalled his feelings at the time: "I was all alone,

1. See *Protokoll öfver Sv. Ev. Missions-Förbundets i Amerika Sjette årsmöte hållet i Galesburg, Ill, den 3–9 September 1890*, 30; cf. Olsson, *By One Spirit*, 437.

2. John Peterson, "Our Pioneer Missionary in China," 19.

3. On Matson's remembrances of his early childhood in Sweden and America, when even as a young boy he had a desire "to go to heathen lands with the gospel of salvation," see P. Matson, "Recollections from China," 40.

4. Warner Sallman, who painted the famous "Head of Christ," did an oil of "Peter Matson Praying at a Minnesota Haystack" (1943), which hung for many years in the Covenant World Missions Office in Chicago. For a picture of this artwork, see *Our Covenant* 18 (1943), opposite p. 33.

5. P. Matson, "Recollections from China," 43.

6. The Swedish Mission Covenant (*Svenska Missionsförbundet*) was organized among Pietistic minded members of the Swedish Lutheran Church in 1878.

7. In my article, "All Great Works of God Begin in Secret," 295, I mistakenly took

nobody knew of my coming, I did not even have a letter of introduction. Fortunately I had my certificate of ordination and, of course, my passport."[8] He explained his circumstances to the CIM director, a Mr. Stevenson:

> It was not only that I was a newcomer myself, I represented a new mission that nobody ever heard of. The first question was, "Where are you going to work?" The only answer I could give was that there had been some correspondence with E. Folke,[9] and the understanding was that we should work in connection with him. But he was in Shansi, a four week journey from Shanghai, entirely out of reach of a newcomer who did not know one word of the language.[10]

After talking with Mr. Stevenson, it was decided that he and the Wallens, who had not yet arrived, should study Chinese at the CIM language school in Anking.[11] Matson was also advised to shave the front part of his head and shed Western dress for Chinese dress, which he did.

While waiting for the Wallens to arrive, Matson stayed at the CIM home and received his first lessons in the Chinese language from Frederick William Baller (1852–1922), who at the time was head of the Anking Language School and considered one of the best Mandarin speakers among missionaries in China. Baller took Matson through the tones and aspirants, the initials and finals—the same old road all newcomers have to tread, and was kind enough to say, "You seem to have no difficulty at all."[12] Matson eventually became very good in the Chinese language, and it was said that he knew it better than the average Chinese.[13] Many Covenant missionaries learned the language from him.[14]

"Hongkew" (today "Hongkou") in one of my sources to be Hankow, when in fact it was a northern district of Shanghai.

8. P. Matson, "Chinese Reminiscences," 19.

9. Erik Folke, a Swede and graduate of Uppsala University, went out as a China missionary under the China Inland Mission in 1887; cf. Olsson, *By One Spirit*, 433. For a picture of Erik Folke and his wife, see *Hemåt* (1893) 25.

10. P. Matson, "Chinese Reminiscences," 19.

11. In Matson's writings this city is referred to as Ganking, which may simply be a different spelling or pronunciation. Anking (Anqing) was located on the north bank of the Yangtze River in southwest Anhwei (Anhui) Province.

12. P. Matson, *Sowing in Tears, Reaping in Joy*, 12–13.

13. The view of Alfred Johnson in V. Johnson, *The Momentous Years: A Biography of Ruth Alice Hedberg Johnson and Alfred Joseph Johnson*, chap. 5.

14. Viola Larson recalled her instruction in Chinese by Matson on her first trip to China in 1935.

A week later the Wallens arrived and Mr. Baller took the three of them to Anking, which was 300 miles up the Yangtze. All were dressed in Chinese clothes and traveled Chinese class on the steamer. The Wallens were given the one cabin to be had, and Matson and Baller spread their bedding on the open deck. The deck was filled with Chinese, and there was hardly enough space to lie down. The air was thick with opium fumes. Four months were spent at the language school,[15] where Chinese teachers read with each person individually two hours a day.

SEARCH FOR A MISSION FIELD

In the spring and summer of 1891 were the "Yangtze riots," generating considerable anti-foreign feeling in the country. In a small town below Hankow,[16] in June, mission stations were burned and two Englishmen were killed, one a missionary and the other a customs official.[17] More anti-foreign feeling would come into the open and erupt in violence by the end of the decade. Nevertheless, Western missionaries were everywhere present in China, seeking to plant the Christian gospel. The American Mission Covenant had come to Central China for the same reason, and in May, 1892, Peter Matson would open a mission station in Fancheng at the north end of Hupeh Province.

Early in March, 1891, letters came from the Covenant Mission office in Chicago advising Matson and the Wallens to give up the idea of going to Shansi, and to locate rather in the neighborhood of newly arrived Swedish Covenant missionaries, who would subsequently establish a station in Wuchang in the winter of 1891. Two matters now had to be attended to. Matson realized he must make a trip to Shanghai and consult with J. Hudson Taylor of the CIM, since the original plan was to work in connection with Erik Folke, who was associated with CIM, and now after having the privilege of studying at the CIM language school it seemed only right to explain to Taylor this new step being contemplated.

---

15. P. Matson, *Sowing in Tears, Reaping in Joy*, 14; and *Our China Mission*, 37.

16. Hankow (Hankou) was one of three cities, the other two being Wuchang and Han-yang, which combined to form Wuhan, the capital of Hupeh (Hubei) Province. By 1900 Hankow had become the commercial center, Wuchang the home of officials and literary persons, and Han-yang a combination of the two in addition to housing the vast iron works established by Chang Chih-tung. The three cities lie at the confluence of the Yangtze and Han Rivers; cf. *The Chinese Recorder* 28 (1897) 434. Wuhan was sometimes referred to as "the Chicago of China."

17. P. Matson, *Sowing in Tears, Reaping in Joy*, 15–16.

Matson also had to talk with the newly arrived Swedish Covenant missionaries in Wuchang. Wallen, being a family man, favored locating in nearby Hankow,[18] but Matson did not envision a cooperative union with the Swedish Mission Covenant, wanting rather to venture into new territory where the gospel had not been preached. Matson, then, had to speak with both parties, which he did, and after doing so went in search of another field in which to establish his mission.

Matson had a warm encounter with J. Hudson Taylor in Shanghai. Before Matson left, just before midnight, the two knelt together in Taylor's office and Taylor laid his hands on Matson's head and prayed God's blessing upon him. While in Shanghai, Matson also met a number of Scandinavian Alliance missionaries who had gone out under Fredrick Franson, and had fellowship with them.[19]

When Matson went to Wuchang to see the Swedish Covenant missionaries he was given accommodation at Chinese premises rented by missionaries Mr. and Mrs. Sköld, Mr. Lund, Mr. Engdahl, and Mr. Vikholm. All were newcomers, although Lund had been three years with CIM.

Matson was now ready to go out in search of another field in which to establish the Covenant mission, so in April, 1891 he and Mr. Lund went up the Yangtze to the port city of Shasi to see what the possibilities were of opening a work in this busy, strategic place.[20] The CIM occupied a small Chinese house in Shasi. There he met Mr. McNair, the missionary in charge, who was about to leave on an extended tour south of the Yangtze. Matson decided to go with him. On this trip, which went through mountains and extended as far west as the port city of Ichang, they sold many gospels and tracts in places never before visited by a missionary.

Matson returned to much unrest in Wuchang, due to the "Yangtze riots" in the spring and summer of 1891. He and others had to take turns standing watch through the night, as an attack might come at any moment. Then in August and September Matson made another trip in the company of a Wesleyan missionary, visiting places in southeastern Hupeh. On his return he found the Wallen and Sköld families as refugees in Hankow. The Consuls had ordered all foreign families away from Wuchang. Single men

---

18. P. Matson, "The Siang Fan District," 20–21; and *Sowing in Tears, Reaping in Joy,* 17.

19. P. Matson, "Chinese Reminiscences," 24–25; on Fredrik Franson, see Olsson, *By One Spirit,* 432–39.

20. For Matson's own account of his search for a field in 1891, and his decision to take over the lease of the CIM premises in Fancheng in early 1892, see *Sowing in Tears, Reaping in Joy,* 15–22; and *Our China Mission,* 38–44.

were allowed to stay at their own risk, so Matson remained in the city, although he said the tension in Wuchang was now worse than ever.

UP THE HAN TO FANCHENG

Matson now embarked on a trip that would decide the question of where the Covenant mission would be located. It was November, 1891 and Matson began the trip with a Mr. Gulston of the China Inland Mission. Their destination was Fancheng at the northern end of Hupeh Province, a twin city to Siangyang, which lay on the other side of the Han River. Mr. Lund of the Swedish Mission Covenant had traveled through northern Hupeh and recommended Fancheng to Matson.[21] The two men hired two coolies to travel with them, needing help in carrying their bedding and a supply of books and tracts. Along the way they went into marketplaces to sell books and preach the gospel.

At Anluh, which is roughly half way between Hankow and Fancheng, the two men met up with Dr. Howard Taylor, son of J. Hudson Taylor, and a Mr. Joyce who had been one of Matson's school mates at Anking. They, too, were headed for Fancheng, and invited Matson and Gulston to join them in the boat ride up the Han. Matson used the opportunity to speak with Taylor about Fancheng. It seemed like a strategic place to begin work, being on the main road from western China to Peking, and situated on the Han River, which provided communication with Hankow year round. Moreover, it was just across the river from the official city of Siangyang, the political center of northern and western Hupeh. The CIM had rented a house in the city and worked there for two or three years, but without success, so they had given up the place and moved farther up the river to Laohokow. Taylor advised Matson to write to his father, assuring him that his father would have no objection to Matson entering the field they had vacated.

Matson and Gulston continued up river to Laohokow, where Sunday was spent with workers of the CIM. Mr. Gulston had been in poor health on the journey, and at Laohokow became quite ill, so Matson had to leave him there and return alone to Fancheng. At Fancheng he met his friend Mr. Annand of the Scotch Bible Society, and with him Matson made his first visit to the city that would become the main head station of the Covenant mission. Siangyang had the reputation of being strongly anti-foreign; nevertheless, Matson said: "We walked the main street right through the city, selling books and tracts and talking to the crowds the best we could." When some rowdies began cursing and pelting them with stones and bricks,

21. P. Matson, "Pioneer Days in Fancheng," 53.

Matson left the city with a hunchbacked Chinese carrying his bedding and books. When the burden became too heavy for the Chinese man, Matson took part of the load himself.

Matson then went south to Icheng and Kingmen, where the Covenant would eventually open mission stations, and reported selling books by the hundred and having great crowds following him. At Icheng he sold single gospels and sheet calendars with a Christian message. His vocabulary at the time was very limited, but two phrases he could use—*pah ko chi'en ih pen* ("eight cash a copy") and *liang ko ch'ien ih chang* ("two cash a sheet"). Matson returned to the inn that night with about one thousand copper coins in the recesses of his old-fashioned Chinese sleeves.[22]

EVANGELISM AND THE DISTRIBUTION OF BIBLES AND TRACTS

Evangelism at this point was done largely by personal witness and a distribution of the written word. Marcus Cheng, the premier Chinese evangelist, stressed the importance of both the oral and written word in evangelism. The only thing more effective, he said, was one's daily life being a testimony to the truth.[23] Matson, like other missionaries, distributed gospels and tracts in Chinese, which for years had been available from various tract societies.

Translations of Bible portions and tracts written in the Chinese language began with Dr. Robert Morrison, the first Protestant missionary to China.[24] By 1810 this pioneer missionary had printed 1000 copies of the Acts of the Apostles on wooden boards, and in September, 1811 he sent back to England a translation of Luke's Gospel along with a copy of a recently published tract.[25] A tract of 1812, said to have been Morrison's first, was entitled, "A Summary of the Divine Doctrine respecting the Redemption and Salvation of the World."[26]

The Religious Tract Society of London, founded in 1799, had already by the end of 1823 circulated 102,000 tracts in the Chinese language. They had titles such as: "A Christian Hymn Book," "An Outline of the Old Testament History," and "A Treatise on the Life of our Blessed Lord Jesus."[27]

22. P. Matson, and C. O. Anderson, "The Icheng District," 41.

23. Cheng, "Literary Work."

24. Broomhall, *Robert Morrison: A Master-Builder.*

25. Ibid., 67.

26. *The Chinese Recorder* 38 (1907) 368.

27. "The Religious Tract Society of London in China," *The Chinese Recorder* 38 (1907) 368–69; Darroch, "The Influence of the Religious Tract Societies in China,"

Hudson Taylor was converted through reading a tract of this society.[28] In Matson's time tracts would have been available from the East Chinese Tract Society in Shanghai (1884),[29] the Central China Tract Society in Hankow (1884),[30] The North China Tract Society in Peking (1883),[31] and other distributors. By 1912 there were nine Religious Tract Societies in China, and an American Tract Society in New York.[32] Tracts issued by the Hankow Tract Society had titles such as: "Week of prayer topics"; "Introduction to the New Testament"; "John 3:16"; "Pictorial tracts"; and "Scripture extracts."

The publication of tracts, Bible portions, and entire Bibles increased dramatically in the years following. The Tract Society also published 53 Bible commentaries; one entitled, "The Conference Commentary," contained commentary on every book of the Bible. By 1930–31 the Religious Tract Society of China reported a circulation of 13,609,689 publications.[33] Chinese Bibles could be had from the British and Foreign Bible Society, the American Bible Society, and the National Bible Society of Scotland. In 1930 alone these societies distributed 13,901,462 Bibles, New Testaments, and portions of the Bible, mostly Gospels, and the great majority of these were distributed not by representatives of the Bible Societies, but by missionaries and their Chinese co-workers.[34]

CORRESPONDENCE WITH J. HUDSON TAYLOR

On Matson's return to Shasi he met up with a Chinese Christian from the neighboring province of Hunan, and the two of them went out daily to different parts of the city and nearby market places distributing books and "telling people the old, old story." At Shasi he hoped to get a steamer to Hankow to be there in time for Christmas, but was disappointed, having to wait 10 days for the next steamer. He arrived in Hankow on New Years Day, 1892.

398–399.

    28. Darroch, "The Influence of Religious Tract Societies in China," 399.

    29. Darroch, "Evangelistic Tracts and Literature," 331; Darroch, "The Influence of Religious Tract Societies in China," 399.

    30. "The Religious Tract Society of London in China," 371; Darroch, "Evangelistic Tracts and Literature," 332–33.

    31. "The Religious Tract Society of London in China," 371; Darroch, "Evangelistic Tracts and Literature," 333–36.

    32. Darroch, "The Influence of Religious Tract Societies in China," 399, 403.

    33. P. Matson, *Our China Mission*, 71.

    34. Ibid., 70–71.

Uppermost now in Matson's mind, after talking to Howard Taylor, was getting in touch with his father, J. Hudson Taylor, about the possibility of taking over the CIM premises at Fancheng. Matson therefore sent J. Hudson Taylor a letter on January 5, 1892, asking him whether the CIM would consider the Covenant entering the field at Fancheng and taking over the lease CIM had on their vacated premises. Taylor responded favorably in a letter of January 16, but said he wanted first to consult with Mr. Gulston and see, too, if a Miss Black wanted to return to the station.

After receiving this encouraging reply Matson made another trip to Fancheng in February, this one together with Wallen. Despite a hostile reception, many opportunities were afforded to sell books and tell people the good news about Christ. It did not help that Wallen was in foreign dress. Matson said he used to carry a Chinese umbrella to ward off missiles, but on this trip it proved of little avail. One umbrella after another was battered to shreds, leaving him with the bare handle in his hands.[35]

Correspondence between Matson and Hudson Taylor continued. A final answer came to Matson in a letter dated April 16. It said:

> Dear Mr. Matson:
>
> I am sorry that from sickness and other causes I have been unable to answer your kind letter of April 4th (received April 7th) sooner. We have at last the consent of all concerned to our retiring from Fancheng, and shall be glad for you to take over our premises, as you propose. I cannot myself give you the needful information as to kind of agreement etc., but will make enquiries and have you informed as soon as possible. May you and Mr. and Mrs. Wallen have much blessing in working the place. I am sure Mr. King of Laohokow, and the Misses Black will give you any information or advice in their power.
>
> Yours in Christ Jesus.
>
> J. Hudson Taylor[36]

That decided the matter. Matson took over the lease that CIM held on the houses they were occupying, and wrote home to the Covenant Board in Chicago saying that they were opening a mission station in Fancheng.

---

35. P. Matson, *Sowing in Tears, Reaping in Joy*, 21; and *Our China Mission*, 44.

36. P. Matson, "Pioneer Days in Fancheng," 53–54; cf. "China Reminiscences," 27–28.

UP THE HAN AGAIN WITH NORWEGIAN LUTHERANS

On May 11, 1892, Matson picked up his few belongings and sailed up the Han in a houseboat with three Norwegian Lutherans: Halvor Ronning of the Hauge Synod, Daniel Nelson of the Norwegian-American Lutheran Church, and J. B. Brandtzaeg of the Norwegian China Mission Society, on a tour of investigation.[37] Matson recalls that he was the youngest of the three, only 24 years of age; the others were over 30.

It turned out that Norwegians, too, were interested at the time in opening a mission in Hupeh Province.[38] The men all dressed in Chinese clothes to make themselves less conspicuous. James Scherer, Professor of Missions at the Lutheran Theological Seminary in Chicago reports:

> Coming to the twin cities of Fancheng and Siangyang, the men climbed a small mountain for a spectacular overview and for a time of prayer. They were filled with thanks for God's guidance, and joyous in their anticipation of the work which could be done in spreading the gospel in this unevangelized area. According to one account, they heaped together some stones as a memorial to their first visit to the place of their future labors. Matson chose Siangyang for the Mission Covenant; Brandtzaeg decided on Laohokow; Nelson and Ronning selected Fancheng and its surrounding territory, taking over the work already begun in a small way by the China Inland Mission[39]

The agreement with Hudson Taylor allowed Matson to occupy the rented CIM premises at Fancheng, and in May, 1892 he took up residence in the city.[40] A decision had been reached that the Lutherans would work north of Fancheng, and the Mission Covenant would work south. Both would carry on work in Fancheng, but the Mission Covenant would have its main station across the river in Siangyang.

37. P. Matson, "Pioneer Days in Fancheng," 54–55; and "China Reminiscences, 28.

38. Syrdal, "American Lutheran Mission Work in China," 31–32.

39. Scherer, "The Lutheran Missionary Pioneers: Who Were They?" 352; P. Matson gives his own report in "Pioneer Days in Fancheng," 55.

40. P. Matson, *Sowing in Tears, Reaping in Joy*, 22; *Our China Mission*, 45; "The Siang Fan District," 22.

2

Preaching, Evangelism, and Establishing a Chinese Church

China in the last decade of the nineteenth century saw the Qing dynasty in a weakened state. In the First Sino-Japanese War of 1894–95 it lost control of Korea, which devastated the Manchu population and became background for the rise of Sun Yat Sen and the First Revolution of 1911. Anti-foreign sentiments also continued during the decade, coming out in the open in the Boxer Rebellion of 1899–1901, when the lives of many Christian missionaries were taken.

BEGINNING OF THE COVENANT HUPEH MISSION (1892–1900)

Fancheng

In May, 1892 Peter Matson took up residence in Fancheng at the former premises of the China Inland Mission (CIM).[1] At first he was quite lonely, reporting that he was the only foreigner in this part of Hupeh Province. Most of his time was spent with books and his Chinese language teacher. In the afternoons he would go out to sell gospels and tracts and do some street preaching.[2]

---

1. P. Matson, *Our China Mission*, 45.
2. Ibid.

In the summer of 1892, while he was still alone in Fancheng, Matson was brutally stoned and nearly beaten to death.[3] A cholera epidemic was raging in the city, and Matson was suspected of having poisoned the wells. Matson tells the story in his own words:

> One day I happened into an open space in front of a temple where theatricals were going on. Thousands were gathered together, and before I knew it the cry was raised, "Kill, kill, beat him to death, the foreign devil." A shower of stones and bricks came down upon me. I tried to reason with them, but those at a distance could not hear, and the yelling and stone-throwing got worse every second. Behind me was a narrow lane. Through this I beat a hasty retreat to the street. After came the mob running, but they jammed each other in the narrow passage and I succeeded in getting a good lead on them. Unfortunately the people in the street got wind of the trouble and made ready to give me a hot reception. In a few minutes the whole town seemed to be after me. Coolies and rowdies of every description stood with their carrying poles ready to strike as I passed by. How I got out of it all is a miracle to me to this day. I finally reached my house somehow, but no sooner was the door shut behind me than the mob filled the street and began to yell that they were going to tear down the house over my head and take my life. This they no doubt would have done had not God interfered by sending, in the last minute, two friendly officials with a company of soldiers who managed to disperse the rabble.[4]

He survived the incident, but for several days had to stay in his room, hardly able to walk across the floor.[5] Matson had been pelted with stones before, in November, 1891 on his first visit to Siangyang with Mr. Annand of the Scottish Bible Society.

---

3. P. Matson, "The Siang Fan District," 23; Olsson, *By One Spirit*, 441.

4. P. Matson, *Our China Mission*, 46.

5. Ibid., 45–46.

The First Three Covenant Missionaries to China, the Rev. K. P. Wallen and Mia Wallen with child (seated), the Rev. Peter Matson (standing)"

Early Covenant Missionaries (l. to r.): John Sjöquist, K. P. Wallen holding baby, and Peter Matson (standing); Mia Wallen holding baby, and Christine Matson (seated (1894)"

Peter Matson married Kristina Svensson from the Swedish Covenant Mission in Hankow on May 18, 1893. She came to Fancheng and the two were joined by the Rev. and Mrs. Wallen, their two small children, and newly-arrived John Sjöquist. The old house where Peter had been living alone was rebuilt, and the missionaries moved in during the summer of 1893.[6] The following year news came that good friends Vikholm and Johanson from the Swedish Covenant Mission had been brutally murdered by a mob in a suburb of Sungpu, which was in the Macheng district of Hupeh.[7] More tragedy followed. The heat and poor sanitary conditions led to the death of the Matsons' firstborn in July, 1894.[8] Both of these tragedies, and the subsequent loss of another infant child in 1899,[9] were very hard on Christine, leaving her a semi-invalid until her death in 1922.

A building was purchased in 1894 and the front of it used as a street chapel;[10] in the back was a school. Matson and his missionary comrades preached daily at the chapel.[11] Lutheran missionaries made a similar arrangement in a house purchased in Fancheng in 1894.[12] At first practically no one would come to Matson's meetings, except some of the very poorest in hopes of receiving charity. Women were more superstitious and fearful than the men. Over time, however, Matson and the other missionaries succeeded in living down the bad rumors and winning the people's confidence.[13]

6. Ibid., 47.

7. E. C. Matson, *Peter Matson: Covenant Pathfinder in China*, 66; *The Chinese Recorder* 24 (1893) 397, 399–400. The tragedy took place on July 1, 1893.

8. The baby boy was born in Fancheng on April 13, 1894; see *The Chinese Recorder* 25 (1894) 310.

9. Swanson, "Missionary Peter Matson," 34.

10. Street-chapels located on the busiest street of a city were used by all missions; cf. Grainger, "The Street-Chapel," 593–99.

11. P. Matson, *Our China Mission*, 48.

12. Syrdal, "American Lutheran Mission Work in China," 37, 108, says the arrangement of a chapel and a school in the same building was made also at the outstations.

13. P. Matson, "The Siang Fan District," 23–24, which reports also the continuance of his early missionary efforts.

Street Scene in Fancheng (1900)

Interior of Fancheng Mission Chapel (1900)

Peter Matson's 26 school children in Fancheng (1897)

Alma Carlson and Christine Matson (l. to r.) with Christine's Girls' School children
in Fancheng (1900)

Although Matson preached and gave personal witness to his faith, his method of evangelism was indirect. He is said to have waited until people came to him and asked about the claims of Christ, at which point he would tell them. Four years passed before a single convert was won.[14] In the spring of 1894 Matson baptized his first convert; in the spring of 1895 there was a second; and in 1896 a third.[15] Only by 1897 did any significant number of Chinese begin to attend Matson's meetings and become baptized.[16]

Covenant missionary work in China was broadly conceived. Matson "wanted a mission which through evangelism, education, and benevolence slowly spread the Gospel and the savor of Christ throughout an entire culture. It was the doctrine of the leaven rather than of the bugle blast."[17] Evangelism consisted of preaching, witnessing to people one on one, and what was called "women's work," i.e., work specifically among women: presenting them with the gospel message; enrolling them in study groups and catechumen classes; teaching them to read; organizing them into women's societies, and instructing them on how to care for babies and small children. Benevolence consisted largely of medical work in hospitals and dispensaries, although it included caring for the ever-present poor and refugees displaced by war or civil unrest, and in the last years at Nanchang included the opening of an orphanage. Education took place in primary and secondary schools for boys and girls; in a theological seminary for young men at

14. T. W. Anderson, "Foreword," 7. This probably refers to the years 1890–94 when Matson first came to China and began itinerant preaching while in search of a mission field, and before he and Christine went home to get financial matters straightened out with the Covenant Board; cf. P. Matson, *Our China Mission*, 49.

15. Dahlstrom, "The Covenant Missionary Society in China," 41–42.

16. Other missionaries engaged in evangelism at Fancheng during this first decade were Matson's wife Christine (1893–1900); the Rev. K. P. and Mia Wallen (1893–1897); John Sjöquist (1893–1896); Annie Sanders (1895–97); Alma Carlson (1897–1899); and Albert and Beda André (1899–1901). Christine Matson was a pioneer of women's work and the education of girls, which earlier had been entirely neglected in China; the Rev. and Mrs. K. P. Wallen did evangelism and dispensary work until they went home and resigned in early 1897; John Sjöquist, before going home to get medical training, was engaged in evangelism; Alma Carlson devoted herself to dispensary and women's work, but in 1899 married Rev. T. H. Himle of the Norwegian Hauge Synod Mission and left the Covenant Mission; Annie Sanders participated in ministry to women and helped Christine at the girls' school, but in 1897–98 she left to return to the Scandinavian Alliance Mission from which she had come; Albert André spent his time in evangelism and Beda André among women. During much of the first decade the ranks were depleted, which left the Matsons alone in the field except for short periods when Alma Carlson came to serve in the dispensary and minister among women, and Annie Sanders came to help Christine at the girls' school. When the Andrés arrived to labor as evangelists in 1899, wider contacts were made.

17. Olsson, *By One Spirit*, 445.

Kingchow; and in Bible teaching for women carried on in homes by Bible women and by missionaries in Bible schools for young women. This broad emphasis coincided with the aim of Protestant missions generally.[18]

A few years after ministry began in Fancheng a house was purchased in Siangyang where the main station of the Covenant would be located. Again, the front apartment of the house was used as a street chapel where Matson would preach several times a week, and in the rear of the house Matson opened up a school. A Confucian scholar was found to teach the traditional subjects (mainly reading and writing), and Matson offer instruction in the Bible. Children attending the school would also be present for the preaching services.

In 1894 financial matters at the Fancheng mission had become critical. They had neither food nor coal, and Matson was forced to borrow money from Chinese usurers at exorbitant rates of interest. In May of 1895, therefore, Matson borrowed money for Christine and himself to make a trip to the States where he would present his needs to the Covenant constituency and seek to drum up support for the China Mission.[19] Another baby boy, Paul, was born to the Matsons in August, 1895.[20] The Matsons returned to China in 1896, buoyed up by interest shown at the Annual Covenant Meeting in St. Paul. Peter had succeeded in presenting the needs of the China mission to the hearts of Covenanters.[21] After their return to Fancheng, a daughter, Esther, was born on October 7, 1897. Sadly, two years later, in 1899, the Matson's second boy died.[22]

In the summer of 1900 came the Boxer Rebellion, which resulted in the death of hundreds of missionaries and other foreigners in the country, as well as of thousands of Chinese Christians. In the Province of Shansi, where the CIM had 88 workers, more than half the number were killed (47), with only 41 escaping.[23] The "Boxers" were a guild named "I Ho Ch'üan"

18. Latourette, *The Chinese: Their History and Culture*, vol. I, 484, says that Protestant missionaries, besides presenting the Christian message to millions in public meetings, personal conversations, and distributing religious literature (in 1924 alone ten million copies of portions of the Bible were circulated), "founded and maintained some of the best educational institutions in the country" and "gave much attention to hospitals and to education in Western medicine." Roman Catholics, who preceded Protestants in China, had no hospitals or schools; cf. Dahlstrom, "The Covenant Missionary Society in China," 27.

19. Olsson, *By One Spirit*, 441–443.

20. P. Matson, *Sowing in Tears, Reaping in Joy*, 30.

21. Olsson, *By One Spirit*, 444–445.

22. P. Matson, *Sowing in Tears, Reaping in Joy*, 31.

23. Glover, *A Thousand Miles of Miracle in China*, 1. See also Bruce, "Massacre of English Baptist Missionaries and Others in Shansi"; and Yung Cheng, "The Martyrdom

("Righteous and Harmonious Fists"), the latter term giving rise to the name "Boxers." The colloquial name was "Ta Tao Huei," or "The Guild of the Great Sword."[24]

Covenant missionaries had to evacuate Fancheng in the summer of 1900, sailing down the Han to Hankow, which they reached the last week of July.[25] A few weeks were spent in Nagasaki, Japan, and the following winter in Shanghai. When Matson and the others evacuated they said good-bye to 40 members of a young church, "the first fruits of the field." All had made public confession of faith in Christ and been baptized.[26]

Kuling

In the summer of 1901, before the missionaries were able to return to the field, they spent time in Kuling,[27] a retreat center in the Lushan Mountains where missionaries and other Westerners in China went during the summer months to escape the heat. The Covenant Mission bought property there and built houses in which to stay. The Swedish Mission Covenant also built a house at Kuling in 1905. In subsequent years the Covenant Mission had its annual meeting there, as missionaries enjoyed the summer program, which included musical concerts and well-known speakers from abroad, and rested from work at the various mission stations. Kuling, with its expanded summer program, was similar to the famous Chautauque in southwestern New York State and smaller Christian retreat centers across America.

The Kuling retreat center dates back to 1895 when Edward Little succeeded in purchasing property at the top of a mountain above Kiukiang, which at the time was a wasteland where only tigers and wild pigs roamed, and one solitary temple —Hwang lung—survived amidst the ruins of 400 other temples that had been destroyed by the Tai-pings.[28] Little named the place "Kuling," a Chinese form of the English word "cooling."

After some difficult negotiations with Chinese officials during the first year, lots were sold to interested individuals and the London Mission, and bungalows were built. The Scottish Bible Society erected a wooden

at T'ai-yuen-fu on the 9th of July."

24. Ibid., 15 n. 1; on the Boxer Rebellion see further *The Chinese Recorder* 31 (1900), 377–78; and 32 (1901).

25. On the journey down the Han with missionaries of the Hauge Synod Lutheran Mission, see P. Matson, *Our China Mission*, 54–57; "The Siang Fan District, 24.

26. P. Matson, *Our China Mission*, 54–55.

27. P. Matson, "The Siang Fan District," 24.

28. Little, *The Story of Kuling*.

bungalow. A modest road over the wasteland was completed. By the turn of the century, the former wasteland had been transformed by many bungalows, improved and lighted roads, and more than 10,000 trees that had been planted along the roads and in private lots. There were now birds in Kuling, whereas before there were none. Tennis lawns were constructed, and a church was erected at the cost of $4,000.

A missionary conference was held in Kuling from August 22–25, 1898, at which J. Hudson Taylor was present to give an address. A "Declaration of Unity" was adopted at the conference, signed by missionaries who were present. Seven missionaries of the Swedish Missionary Society in Shasi and Wuchang were signatories, including The Rev. Anders and Anna Tjellström and the Rev B. E. and Augusta Rydén from Shasi; Miss Annie Sanders was the only signatory from the "Swedish American Missionary Covenant."[29] In August, 1921 Harry Emerson Fosdick was a featured speaker at Kuling.

MISSION WORK AFTER THE BOXER REBELLION (1901–1911)

Siangfan[30]

When the Matsons returned to Siangfan in September, 1901, they found the mission property pretty much intact, and rejoiced even more to discover that "nearly all the Christians had successfully weathered the storm."[31] With the Matsons were John Sjöquist, now a medical doctor, and his new wife Maria. But tragedy followed. Maria had become sick on the voyage, and after arriving in Fancheng, on November 13, 1901, she died, and was buried in the small Fancheng cemetery. Matson says that with the death of Maria Sjöquist they were left with exactly the same number of missionaries on the field as when they started in 1890—two men and one woman.[32] John remarried in 1904, and went on to make an extraordinary contribution to the medical work of the mission, a story that will be told in the next chapter.

---

29. "Missionary Conference held at Kuling, Central China, August 22nd to 25th, 1898," *The Chinese Recorder* 29 (1898), 493–500, 531–540, 583–592; 30 (1899) 21–24. The "Declaration of Unity" was included as a separate page in this issue of *The Chinese Recorder*. Olsson reports in *By One Spirit* (444) that Annie Sanders left the American Mission Covenant for the Scandinavian Missionary Alliance in the fall of 1897, which would have been a year earlier.

30. "Siangfan" is the name given to the twin cities of Fancheng and Siangyang.

31. P. Matson, "The Siang Fan District," 24.

32. Ibid.

Maria Elisabeth Sjöquist (d. November 13, 1901)

New Missionaries (l. to r.) Hilma Johnson, Isak Jacobson, and Hilda Rodberg
(1901–1902)

**Siangyang Mission Compound in 1903: 1) church; 2) boys' school; 3) station
building; and 4) small storehouse"**

In February, 1902 the small band of missionaries moved into their new
home in Siangyang, across the Han River. It was already under roof at the
time of evacuation. Covenant missionaries were now in residence on both
sides of the Han. Their home in Fancheng had been in rented quarters,[33] but
now they had a place of their own that would become the center of the Covenant Mission during its remaining years in China. After the move Hilda
Rodberg and Hilma Johnson arrived.[34] Hilda was a nurse, the first graduate
of Swedish Covenant Hospital in Chicago, and she began working in the
dispensary even before learning the Chinese language. Later she worked at
Nanchang and Kingmen dividing her time between evangelism and running a school for girls. Hilma was engaged in evangelism and women's work.

In the fall of 1902 Albert and Beda André returned to Fancheng after going home due to Beda's illness.[35] With them came another new ar-

33. P. Matson, *Our China Mission*, 58.

34. *The Chinese Recorder* 33 (1902) 102, although Hilma's name is incorrectly listed
as "Hilda Johnson."

35. Their arrival in Shanghai on October 7, 1902, with two children, is cited in *The*

rival, Isaac W. Jacobson. Albert set about building a station in Fancheng overlooking the Han,[36] and Beda joined Hilma ministering to women.[37] In Siangyang a church building seating 300 people was erected, and a couple years later one of nearly the same size was built in Fancheng.[38] Christian influence in the community was growing and meetings were now crowded.[39] The missionaries opened outstations (schools and preaching places) in more than a half dozen market places 8 to 15 miles from Siangyang. Unsophisticated country folk were receiving the gospel gladly. The Andrés remained at Fancheng until 1907, when they returned home and the next year resigned from the Covenant staff.

Siangfan, the name given to the combined cities of Siangyang and Fancheng, is located in the north of Hupeh Province. The two cities lie on both sides of the Han River. The Han, before turning southeast to meet the Yangtze, here flows nearly due east. Fancheng lies on the north bank of the river, Siangyang on the south. The two cities, which became the northern boundary of the Covenant mission field, were already in Matson's time referred to as Siang Fan.[40] Siangfan was also the name given to the district, which covered an area of ca. 600 square miles, and in 1940 had an estimated population of 300,000. The combined population of Siangyang and Fancheng was over 100,000, Fancheng being the more populous. Fancheng was an old city dating back to 600 B.C.[41] It was on the main road from Western China to Peking, and thus a commercial center, even though Siangyang was the official center of north Hupeh Province. North of Fancheng was a wide plain extending into Honan Province; to the south and west of Siangyang stretched mountain ranges, one of which extended to the lofty Tibetan plateau.[42]

Chinese Recorder 33 (1902) 586.

36. E. V. Nordlund, *The Life and Work of Victor Leonard Nordlund, 1869–1937*, 57.

37. P. Matson, "The Siangfan District," 25; *Our China Mission*, 61.

38. P. Matson, "The Siang Fan District," 25.

39. Ibid.

40. Ibid., 22.

41. E. V. Nordlund, *The Life and Work of Victor Nordlund*, 57.

42. K. M. Nelson, "Glimpses from Our Medical Work in Siangyang," 25.

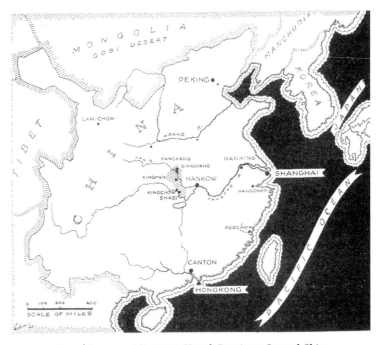

Map of Covenant Mission in Hupeh Province, Central China

Enclosed Mission Compound in Siangyang

When Peter Matson arrived in 1891, Siangyang was reputed to be ultra-conservative and bitterly anti-foreign, while Fancheng, having a somewhat mixed and floating population, was considered liberal and progressive.[43] Matson referred to Siangyang as "that haughty, hidebound mandarin city."[44] The Siangfan district south of the city had mountainous and hilly sections, but most of the wide river valley was fertile and highly cultivated. Staple products were the proverbial "five grains" of China: wheat (i.e., barley), rice, millet, hemp, and beans. Other agricultural products included cotton, sesame, peanut, sweet potatoes, maize, and a great variety of vegetables. Two crops a year was the rule. With rain coming in the summer, the river valley was sometimes exposed to inundations.[45] Dr. K. M. Nelson gives this later account of farmers coming into Siangyang in early morning:

> Early in the morning at daybreak one sees an almost endless stream of farmers bringing in food stuffs, such as rice, wheat, and vegetables; also straw, wood, and charcoal, and articles made in the homes, such as cotton cloth shoes, baskets, and pottery. Most of this is carried, though a good deal is transported by wheelbarrow, oxcart, or donkey. Quite often the farmer will have on one side of his wheelbarrow some member of his family—his wife or child—to be brought to the hospital, and on the other a sack of rice, or a pig, or a bale of cotton.[46]

In 1903 Albert Andre was at work building a mission station in Fancheng overlooking the Han.[47] A few years later a church building was constructed in Fancheng, nearly the same size as a church seating 300 built in Singyang in 1902. Influence in the community was growing and meetings were now crowded.[48] The autumn of 1910 saw a great revival occurring, which was said to touch even the lives of school children. Matson records that the spectacular events of the revival did not last long, but for years afterwards there was "a warming influence in the life and activities of the church."[49]

43. P. Matson, "The Siang Fan District," 22.

44. Ibid., 25.

45. Ibid., 22.

46. K. M. Nelson, "Glimpses from Our Medical Work in Siangyang," 24.

47. E. V. Nordlund, *The Life and Work of Victor Nordlund*, 57.

48. P. Matson, "The Siang Fan District," 25.

49. Ibid., 27.

Participants at Mission Conference in Fancheng (1904)

In February 23–25, 1904, a conference of Scandinavian missionaries convened at Fancheng, at which Peter Matson was elected president.[50] He read a paper entitled, "How to Open a Station in a New Place." The things discussed included what translation of the Bible to use, hymnbooks, catechumens, requirements for baptism, church discipline, women's work, and medical work. At another conference in 1906, held in Siangyang and Fancheng, five Scandinavian missions were represented.[51] Issues here included: how to bring relief to the suffering, orphanages for girls, nursing in missionary hospitals and how to get nurses, and how to improve the condition of the poor. The importance of self-support was also strongly emphasized. Peter Matson may not have been present, for on October 18, 1906 he and his wife arrived in Shanghai with the Rev. and Mrs. C. J. Nelson.[52]

Nanchang

When Isaac Jacobson came to China with the Andrés in 1902, doors were now opening beyond Fancheng and Siangyang, and plans were laid to

50. *The Chinese Recorder* 35 (1904) 375–76.

51. Osnes, "Conference in Siangyang and Fancheng."

52. *The Chinese Recorder* 37 (1906) 652.

expand the Covenant work in territory to the southwest. In the winter of 1902–1903 Isaac and Dr. Sjöquist visited several important centers in the Nanchang district, including the commercial center of Wuanyen. Isaac went on to do the pioneering work in the district, returning to Nanchang in the spring of 1906 to supervise the construction of a missionary home, a church building, and a day school for boys. Nanchang was now a Covenant head station; before it had simply been an outstation of Siangyang. Isaac also opened outstations at centrally located places in the Nanchang district. His wife Anna, whom he married in 1907 and brought over to the Covenant mission from the Norwegian Lutheran Mission, joined him in Nanchang, where she took up women's work and opened a girls' school.

Mission Compound in Nanchang

Mission Station in Nanchang

The Mission Expands

A number of new missionaries arrived in the decade prior to 1911, some preparing to focus on evangelism and women's work. In 1904 Joel Johnson came to do evangelism and schoolwork in Siangyang, after which he went on to open new stations in Icheng and Kingmen.[53] Victoria Sjöquist, who married John Sjöquist in 1904, came the same year for evangelism and women's work at the hospital in Siangyang. She remained until 1918, a year after her husband's death.

In 1906 John Peterson arrived to labor as an evangelist in Fancheng, staying there until 1910 when he relocated to Nanchang (1910–1912). In 1908 he married newly arrived Esther Anderson, who took up women's work at Fancheng and Nanchang. Also in 1908 came Ellen and Amelia Ackerson.[54] Ellen, a nurse, became engaged primarily in medical work at Siangyang, but also served among women. Amelia—after 1915 Mrs. Conradson—was a schoolteacher, but she, too, participated in evangelistic outreach at Siangyang. Oscar Johnson, another arrival in 1908, joined the other evangelists at Fanchang. Oscar remained at Fancheng until 1911, when he married Justine Nilsson and the two relocated to Kingmen.

During this early period missionaries were much aided by Chinese co-workers. The first Chinese man to receive baptism after the missionaries' return to the field in 1901 was Chen Wan-tai. Matson says of their first Chinese evangelist:

> Years ago Chen Wan-tai had heard us preach and had been impressed by the message of salvation through Jesus Christ. At that time he was a corporal in the army and was transferred from place to place, or he would have been baptized much earlier. He had some education and was a gifted man, a born leader. He proved a real godsend to our work and continued till his death to hold the leading position among our Chinese co-workers.[55]

Other Chinese were brought into mission work. At first the most learned Confucian scholars were too proud to associate with the missionaries, although a few Confucian readers or lecturers were successfully recruited. Most recruits were new Christians from different walks of life, e.g., a druggist, a potter, a country schoolteacher, a farmer, and a peddler.

---

53. P. Matson, *Our China Mission*, 62.

54. E. C. Matson, "The Covenant Women's Evangelistic Auxiliary," 87. The arrival of the Ackerson sisters in Shanghai on February 10, 1908, is noted in *The Chinese Recorder* 39 (1908) 174.

55. P. Matson, *Our China Mission*, 59–60; "The Siang Fan District," 26.

Matson says most of them were gifted speakers. A two-year Bible school was opened in 1902 to give these individuals necessary instruction, and some became effective preachers and evangelists in bringing people to a saving knowledge of Jesus Christ.[56] In 1903 the Covenant had eight missionaries in the field, assisted by sixteen Chinese workers.[57]

After the Boxer evacuation, in 1902–1903, more than 60 men and women received baptism in Siangyang and Fancheng.[58] With mission work having expanded to Nanchang, Icheng, Kingmen, and numerous outstations in the districts, records of church membership showed that by 1904 the number of baptisms had increased to 74, and by 1910 to 166.[59] Matson gives this summary of the mission work prior to 1910:

> Year by year the Lord added to the church those that were being saved. There was no revival of the emotional, demonstrative type that we sometimes see at home. Most of the converts were brought in, one by one, through the influence of their friends and relatives. It seemed to be a case of gradual growth, as through instruction and guidance and prayer the light of the new life was borne in upon them.[60]

The autumn of 1910 saw a great revival occurring, in which several school children were affected. It began in Nanchang. John Peterson gives this report:

> The Spirit came over us and there was agony, crying, confession, and prayers through the whole congregation. Nobody seemed to care what those around him heard or thought. The burden of sin had become unbearable, and there was no relief except by full confession.[61]

The revival spread to Siangyang, and Matson said he had never witnessed anything like it in America. Most of those affected were professing Christians or backsliders. Dishonest dealings were brought to light and accounts were settled; old grudges were confessed and reconciliations took place.[62]

---

56. P. Matson, *Our China Mission*, 60; "The Siang Fan District," 26.

57. Olsson, *By One Spirit*, 447.

58. P. Matson, *Our China Mission*, 61.

59. Ibid., 62.

60. Ibid., 63.

61. Ibid.

62. Ibid., 63–64.

Music in the Chinese Church

Mention needs to be made at some point about music, singing, and hymnody introduced by Covenant missionries into the Chinese church. It came first with Emma Nelson, who arrived at Siangyang with her husband Carl J. Nelson in 1906. The two moved later to Kingchow where Carl was on the faculty of the seminary and the middle school. Emma taught music, English, and religious subjects in the middle schools, with her instruction in music and singing considered of particular value.

Later it was Adine Johnson, wife of Joel Johnson, who contributed to music and singing in the Chinese church after coming to Kingmen in the fall of 1913. Adine was a music teacher, and it was not long before the Kingmen station became known as having the best singing in the entire Covenant field. Adine organized a choir that had a reputation for singing exceptionally well. In 1922 she had a piano shipped to Kingmen that required 32 men to transport it from the river port of Shipai. At Kingchow Leonard Larson, offered lessons in organ when he first arrived in 1920, with the result that several boys learned to play easy hymns.[63]

Western hymns were already being translated into Chinese by the mid-nineteenth century, at which time a number of hymnbooks were published.[64] The hymnbook compiled by the Rev. J. Lees in 1891 contained 429 hymns and chants. Some of the hymns in this hymnbook were: "Rock of Ages," "The God of Abraham Praise," "O Worship the King," and "Mighty God, While Angels Bless Thee."[65] "Am I a Soldier of the Cross" was in Chinese translation in 1911,[66] and "I Need Thee Every Hour" was translated and put to a new tune in 1922.[67] At the Christian funeral of Sun Yat-sen, on March 18, 1925, two of the hymns sung were "Abide with Me" and "Jesus Lover of My Soul."[68] Reginald Heber's "Holy, Holy, Holy" was sung in Chinese by 1935.[69] The Covenant published a Chinese hymnbook compiled by

---

63. L. J. Larson, *Son of Prayer*, 80.

64. See *The Chinese Recorder* 40/4 (April, 1909), which is given over to church music, including hymnbooks. Many Ira Sankey hymns were being sung at the time. See also Fitch, "Hymns and Hymn-Books for the Chinese"; and Norris, "Music in the Chinese Church."

65. Candlin, "Chinese Hymnology—(Rev. J. Lees)."

66. *The Chinese Recorder* 42 (1911) 45.

67. *The Chinese Recorder* 53 (1922) 573.

68. Tsu, "At Dr. Sun Yat-sen's Funeral, March 18, 1925," which includes pictures, one of which is the mausoleum in Nanking where his body was finally laid to rest.

69. *The Chinese Recorder* 66 (1935) 769–70.

Joel Johnson and Leonard Larson, which contained a number of Swedish hymn translations by Isaac Jacobson.[70]

My wife Linda and I heard "Thanks to God for My Redeemer" ("Tack, O Gud, för vad du varit") sung in Chinese by the choir at a Sunday worship service in Nanjing in November, 2007. Since it was set to the J. A. Hultman tune,[71] the translation was doubtless the work of Covenant missionaries. Later on May 26, 2008, when Cao Jing and I visited two elderly ladies in the Nanchang church, Qian Xiu-zhen and Yang Chun-hua, before leaving we sang together (in English) the first verse of Reginald Heber's "Holy, Holy, Holy."

Icheng

Early on Matson had passed a number of times through Icheng, which was about 25 miles southeast of Siangyang, but extended work did not begin in the city until about 1905 or 1906, when Joel Johnson came to take charge of the work. Johnson had arrived in China in September, 1904. In 1906, however, Johnson moved to Kingmen, and Icheng reverted to being an outstation of Siangyang. A number of market places in the district were nevertheless opened as outstations, and Chinese evangelists under supervision of the Siangyang missionaries were put in charge. The Icheng area at the time was wide open to the gospel, with people inviting the missionaries to preach and open schools there. The only opposition came from Roman Catholics, who had been in the district for more than 200 years and looked upon Covenant missionaries as intruders.[72]

In 1907 or 1908 Joel Johnson was back in Icheng, and when Peter and Christine Matson visited the city they saw the fruit of an inquirers' class Johnson had been conducting. It was a Sunday, and Matson and Johnson baptized a few people and conducted a communion service, which Matson said was the first ever held in the district. This was the beginning of the church in Icheng.[73] By 1910 the Covenant had a station at Icheng.

In the years following Matson supervised work at Icheng from Siangyang, although because of the distance between the two places, and also

70. Matson, *Our China Mission*, 71–72; Dahlstrom, "The Covenant Missionary Society in China," 159–60.

71. *The (Covenant) Hymnal*, #543.

72. P. Matson, *Our China Mission*, 63; P. Matson and C. O. Anderson, "The Icheng District," 41–42.

73. P. Matson and C. O. Anderson, "The Icheng District," 42. Matson must mean a Protestant communion service and a Protestant church if Roman Catholics had been working there earlier.

Christine Matson's poor health, it was difficult for him to do this. In time Victor Nordlund and Albert Johnson (Dwight) assumed responsibility for the work at Icheng, but were not in residence, coming only on itineration. Eventually these two men built up the Icheng station, and by 1922 it was on a sound basis.[74]

Kingmen

Peter Matson traveled through Kingmen in 1891 on his search for a Covenant field, and in the fall of 1904 Isaac Jacobson visited the city, but actual work did not commence until the spring of 1906, when property was rented and Isaac Jacobson and Joel Johnson opened a chapel.[75] Joel Johnson is credited with opening up Kingmen, making it the center of his labors.[76] He also opened 15 outstations in the district. At first Joel lived with the Chinese evangelist Wang Yung-hsien and his family in crowded quarters connected to the chapel.

Property was purchased in Kingmen and a church building was erected and dedicated with great celebration in June, 1909. Matson was there to preach the first sermon in the new house of worship. His text was Luke 2:10: "Behold, I bring you good tidings of great joy which shall be to all people."

Mission Station in Kingmen

With a mission now established in Kingmen, attention turned to developing outstations. The first was to be in Shipai, a port city on the Han where Joel Johnson and other missionaries had their first look at the Covenant

74. P. Matson, *Our China Mission*, 117.

75. J. S. Johnson, "The Kingmen District," 48.

76. P. Matson, *Our China Mission*, 62.

field. Roman Catholic missionaries had attempted earlier to establish a ministry there, but were driven away. It was assumed that the Covenant missionaries could also be expelled, but that did not happen. God opened a way, and the work prospered, despite one gang leader who was opposed to the missionaries being there and plotted their extermination.[77] A chapel was opened and a Christian school was started. The mission recruited a Chinese evangelist, Yang Kien-tang, who proved over the years to be a faithful worker at Shipai.

In 1909 Oscar E. Johnson joined Joel Johnson at Kingmen, and in the following year came Justine Nilsson, who became Oscar's bride in 1911.[78] Oscar concentrated on evangelism and teaching; Justine, a nurse, opened up a dispensary. The two remained in Kingmen until 1913, when they had to return to the States because of Justine's poor health. On the heels of sickness came tragedy. Oscar, who had taken up study at North Park College, died unexpectedly in his room on October 31, 1913.

Kingchow

Down at the southern border of Hupeh Province Peter Matson came preaching the gospel in Kingchow and Shasi in 1891, and in the next year the Swedish Mission Covenant opened a station at Shasi. In 1900 F. A. Wennborg of the Swedish Mission Covenant began preaching in Kingchow, then an outstation to Shasi,[79] and work was started in the Chinese part of the city. One of the first Christians in Kingchow was an old man by the name of Su, the grandfather of Miss Su, who became a teacher and principal of the girls' school in Kingchow.

Evangelism in Kingchow was carried out under the supervision of the Mission Covenant in Sweden until a few years after the opening of the seminary in 1909, when it became a union endeavor, with the American Mission Covenant. For many years there was only a Chinese evangelist and a Bible woman at Kingchow, both of whom were under the supervision of a missionary teacher at the seminary.[80]

The American Mission Covenant began work in Kingchow in 1907 when it decided to join with the Swedish Mission Covenant in opening a theological seminary. When Peter Matson came to Kingchow two decades earlier, there were no Chinese Christians or Chinese evangelists in the

77. Ibid.
78. J. S. Johnson, "The Kingmen District," 47.
79. John Peterson, "Kingchow and Shasi," 54.
80. Ibid.

province. But after 1900 the Christian community had grown, and there was a need for both pastoral care,[81] and for a school where Chinese preachers could be trained to preach and teach more than the folly of idolatry.[82] Kingchow Theological Seminary opened its doors to students in 1909, the oldest seminary in Hupeh Province.[83] One of its first teachers was the great Chinese evangelist, Marcus Cheng, who came there with his new bride in 1909.[84]

Kingchow Theological Seminary

81. John Peterson, "Kingchow Theological Seminary," 70–71.

82. I have been told by Chinese Christians that this preoccupation with the sin of idolatry probably explains why there is no artwork in the Chinese churches. Our missionaries, coming as they did out of the Lutheran, not the Calvinistic tradition, would have had no aversion to artwork. In modern Chinese churches one sees only a cross, usually red, which might be supplemented by a Bible verse in Chinese.

83. John Peterson, "Kingchow Theological Seminary," 70.

84. Ch'eng, *After Forty Years*, 9.

Students in Seminary Class

MISSIONARY WORK AFTER THE FIRST REVOLUTION
(1911–1921)

In 1911 the Manchu dynasty fell in what came to be known as the First Revolution The Manchus had repressed Christianity, sometimes with fierce persecution,[85] culminating in the Boxer Rebellion, when barbaric acts of the Chinese against foreigners were done under the direction of some high Manchu officials and in accordance with imperial orders. In the 1911 revolution foreigners and foreign property were almost universally protected.[86] The Chinese were glad to be rid of the Manchu dynasty, and the sympathies of the Chinese Church were overwhelmingly with the revolutionary party. It was widely believed that many of the revolutionary leaders were Christian, or if not Christian, were certainly favorable to Christianity and could be expected to lend influence in spreading the Christian religion among the Chinese.[87] Sun Yat-sen (or more correctly Sun Wen),[88] the father of the revolution, was a

85. Editorial in *The Chinese Recorder* 43 (1912) 4.

86. Smith, "The Relation of the Chinese Revolution to Human Progress," 10.

87. Darroch, "Current Events as Seen Through the Medium of the Chinese Newspapers," 32; see also the editorial in *The Chinese Recorder* 43 (1912) 4.

88. [McIntosh], "Sun Wen: Revolutionary and Idealist." He was also affectionately called "Sun Chung-san" by the Chinese; cf. Tsu, "The Christian Service at Dr. Sun Yat-sen's Funeral March 18, 1925," 88.

baptized and professing Christian who desired to be buried as a Christian.[89]

Evacuation and New Arrivals

The revolution of 1911 made necessary another six-month evacuation of missionaries to the coast, but things were not as disruptive in the country as during the Boxer Rebellion, or in the later civil unrest of 1926–27, although Matson said fighting between warlords and bandit chiefs continued until the end of the decade.[90] By June, 1912 it was safe for all missionaries to return.[91] When Matson returned to Siangyang he found things pretty much as he had left them.[92]

New missionaries arrived in this third decade of Covenant mission work, which Matson called "a period of deeper plowing and intensive cultivation."[93] Some came to join in evangelism, women's work, or a combination of the two with other mission activities: Victor and Maria Nordlund (1912); Herman Conradson (1912), joined in 1915 by his wife Amelia—formerly Amelia Ackerson; Mabel Olson (1913); Anna Munson—from the China Inland Mission (1913); Theodore and Hannah Pedersen (1913); and Albert and Elna Johnson—later Albert and Elna Dwight (1915).[94]

---

89. P. Matson, *Our China Mission*, 77; D'Elia, "Dr. Sun Yat-sen and Christianity."

90. P. Matson, *Our China Mission*, 73–74; "The Siang Fan District," 26–27.

91. P. Matson, *Our China Mission*, 74–75.

92. Ibid., 75; P. Matson, "The Siang Fan District," 26.

93. P. Matson, *Our China Mission*, 77.

94. Ibid., 76. Victor and Maria Nordlund were now out under the Covenant Board, having served earlier with the Scandinavian Alliance Mission. Victor was an evangelist and Maria was engaged in women's work. Theodore and Hannah Pederson, after joining the Covenant mission, took up evangelistic work at Siangyang and Nanchang, but their time with the Covenant mission was short. They went home on furlough in 1919, and on July 5 Theodore suddenly took sick and died. Herman and Amelia Conradson did evangelism and educational work in the Siangyang and Kingmen districts (1912–1921). Mabel Olson was engaged in evangelism, education, and women's work in Fancheng and Siangyang. Anna Munson came to Siangyang from the CIM to do evangelism, education, and women's work, but in 1919 she married Rev. John Enoch Gillström from the Swedish Mission Covenant. They worked under the Covenant from 1919–1921, and then moved to Sweden. Albert and Elna Johnson (Dwight) did evangelism at Fancheng, Icheng, and Siangyang from 1915 to 1936.

Siangfan

Meetings in Siangfan were now well attended.[95] Hilma Johnson was at Siangyang and Fancheng where, in 1915–16, she had charge of women's work and was running a girls' school. It was widely anticipated that with the 1911 revolution the liberation of women in China would be far-reaching and permanent.[96] In 1914–15 John Peterson was filling in for Peter Matson at Siangyang, but then he went to Kingchow as the American Mission Covenant's representative at the theological seminary.

In January, 1918 Fancheng experienced general unrest with people fearing an outbreak of war between northern and southern soldiers. In anticipation of soldiers coming to Fancheng, stores and city gates were locked. General Li across the river had declared independence from the Peking government. But he lost the battle, and at his departure the gates of Siangyang were reopened.[97] American flags prominently displayed are said to have saved the mission.

The year 1919 saw the return of Esther Matson, daughter of Peter and Christine Matson, to Siangyang. She was 22, and after schooling in the States wanted now to be a China missionary. But after Christine's death in 1922, she suffered a complete breakdown and had to return home.

Nanchang and Icheng

Mission work at Nanchang was carried out during this time much as elsewhere. The years following 1911 were characterized by extensive building operations. A new church building was erected similar to the one at Siangyang, holding between 500 and 600 people. Emphasis was placed upon preaching and teaching the word of God—in church or chapel, out in the open, or wherever the opportunity presented itself. Sunday Schools were begun, homes were visited, and tracts, booklets, and Scripture portions were distributed. Both men and women were engaged in the work.

In 1915 evangelistic bands were sent out to visit country towns and places where no regular work was being carried on.[98] In the first band were only two workers, Wu Lo-seng and Wu Teng-yung, who visited mountainous areas in the Nanchang district—Maliangping, Tientzeya, Hsiakow,

---

95. For a picture of a mission meeting at Siangyang around 1914 with the mission compound in the background, see *Aurora* (1914) 26.

96. Smith, "The Relation of the Chinese Revolution to Human Progress," 12.

97. E. V. Nordlund, *The Life and Work of Victor Nordlund*, 73–76.

98. Jacobson, "The Nanchang District," 38.

Tungkung, Liuheotsi, and numerous other towns. Some of these eventually became outstations. The evangelists usually stayed a week or two at each place.[99] Isaac Jacobson was the only missionary at the Nanchang station much of the time.[100] Work, in any case, grew substantially in the district. During the decade Matson supervised the work at Icheng from Siangyang.

Kingmen

In 1913–14 Herman and Amelia Conradson were doing evangelism in the Kingmen district, and in Kingmen a new church building was erected, similar to the one at Siangyang, holding between 500 and 600 people.

Kingchow

In 1915, with John Peterson now at the seminary, a 25-year Jubilee was celebrated in Kingchow with President E. G. Hjerpe of the American Mission Covenant present for the occasion.[101] Marcus Cheng, the first Chinese teacher at the seminary, and one of the great Chinese evangelists serving the Covenant mission and elsewhere, gave an address. In November and December of 1917 Victor Nordlund came down to Kingchow from Fancheng at John Peterson's request to hold meetings for students at the seminary, at Shasi, and at various outstations.[102]

Matson said that theological education in the seminary was now beginning to show results. Young men were being graduated and sent to different parts of the field as teachers and preachers. Some old evangelists, improperly trained and lacking in efficiency, were gradually retired. There was measurable growth in missionaries and in the Chinese church. In 1915 25 missionaries were on the Covenant staff,[103] and from 1911–1921 church membership increased from 755 to 2240, and the number of school children rose from 491 to 2131.[104]

99. Ibid.

100. P. Matson, *Our China Mission*, 78.

101. Sköld, "Tankar vid 25-års Jubileet I Kingchow."

102. E. V. Nordlund, *The Life and Work of Victor Nordlund*, 73.

103. Olsson, *By One Spirit*, 450.

104. P. Matson, *Our China Mission*, 79.

Seminary Students with John Peterson

GROWTH, DEVOLUTION, AND EVACUATION (1921–1927)

The decade of the 1920s saw great unrest in China, much but not all of it trace-able to the impact of the Russian Revolution of 1917 beyond its borders. In 1919 the May Fourth Movement in China brought the radical ideas of Marx-ism and anarchism into the country, and in July, 1921 the Communist Party of China (CPC) was organized in Shanghai. By 1924 communists and bandits were roaming the country at will. When Sun Yat Sen, leader of the Kuomin-tang (KMT), the Chinese Nationalist Party, died in 1925, he was succeeded by Chiang Kai-shek, but a struggle ensued within the party as communists wanted more power. In 1926 conditions throughout China were chaotic. Chi-ang massacred tens of thousands of communists, and in 1927 the remaining communists were expelled from the KMT. Fighting between the two groups continued into the 1930s, until the Japanese invasion, when a pause of sorts took effect in an attempt to meet the invader. On December 25, 1936, Chiang pledged to join with the communists in a united front against Japan, but the union was never very successful and the two groups were never reconciled.

The Covenant China mission reached its high point in 1925, when there were 52 missionaries on the staff (up from 25 in 1915), 175 Chinese co-workers, 46 outstations, and 2255 students in the various mission schools. The mission recorded approximately 2500 adult church members.[105] *But when civil war broke out the talk was all about devolution, and in 1926–27 a major evacuation took place. Many Covenant missionaries went home and did not return to China.*

Siangfan

In the early 1920s a new church was built in Siangyang, doubling the capacity of the old one. It seated between 500 and 600 people.[106] Herman Conradson, after returning from furlough in 1922–23, was put in charge of the church. But sadly on September 9, 1926 he was stricken with a severe attack of cholera, and died the next day. Mission work continued apace in the 1920s with a number of new missionaries arriving in Siangfan.[107]

Peter Matson Itinerating on Horseback"

105. Olsson, *By One Spirit*, 450.

106. P. Matson, "The Siang Fan District," 27; *Our China Mission*, 81.

107. In 1920 alone nine new missionaries came, and 1921 saw the arrival of another eleven, some to do evangelism and women's work. The staff at Siangfan now included Edla Carlson; Ivan Lindgren; and Paul and Elin Johnson. Edla Carlson—after 1924 Mrs. Peter Matson—did evangelism and educational work, going on to establish at Siangyang a Bible training school for women. Ivan Lindgren came to do evangelistic work at Siangyang, but stayed only one year before relocating to Kingmen. Paul Johnson became manager of Bethesda Hospital, but also did evangelism. His wife Elin served as a nurse at the hospital.

Nanchang, Icheng, Kingmen, and Kingchow

A number of missionaries were in Nanchang doing evangelism before the mass evacuation of 1927.[108] Others were engaged in evangelistic work in Icheng.[109] Alfred and Ruth Johnson, after a brief stay in Kingmen, arrived at Icheng in September, 1922, and by the end of the year Icheng was established as another Covenant head station.[110] Alfred took charge of the schools and helped with evangelism at the outstations; Ruth did evangelism. But a problem with bandits around Icheng, compounded by Alfred's asthmatic condition, forced their return to the States in 1927.

Oscar and Ruth Anderson came to Icheng in 1924, where Oscar was given responsibility for the Icheng church, eight outstations, and three "preaching places." Icheng, too, had a new church building like those in Siangyang and Nanchang, seating between 500 and 600 people.[111] Expansion of the mission in Icheng had been planned, but was not carried out because of bandits infesting the area. In 1924 they were 10,000 strong, and by 1926 conditions—as elsewhere in China—were chaotic.[112] Ruth Anderson reports:

> This was the fall of 1926, and that winter was rather hectic. At one time in the fall the situation was very tense. Bands of robbers calling themselves Red Spears roamed the countryside. It was feared that they would attack Icheng, and Dad [Oscar] and some others were commissioned to go to the headquarters of the society[113] and try to negotiate peace. The day after Dad had

108. Victor Nordlund and his daughter Esther did evangelism in Nanchang and the surrounding district for two years (1920–1922). Victor's wife Maria was in the States with the children, and in 1922 she died. Isaac and Anna Jacobson returned to carry out evangelism in Nanchang in 1922 after a two-year furlough in the States, and stayed until 1927. Hjalmar and Helen Gravem came in 1922 to be evangelists at Nanchang, remaining until 1927. Alma Mortenson, a nurse, was in the Nanchang district doing work with women.

109. Albert Dwight and Victor Nordlund were engaged in evangelism on itineration at Icheng in 1922–26, and were the ones who built up the Icheng station. Victor Nordlund went home in 1926 and did not return to China. Esther Nordlund remained to do evangelism at Icheng as well as at other Covenant head stations, leaving in the general evacuation of 1927. Elsa Hammerlind was in Icheng doing medical work and evangelism from 1922–1927.

110. P. Matson, *Our China Mission*, 82.

111. Ibid., 81.

112. V. Johnson, *The Momentous Years*, chap. 6.

113. The society called itself the Wanhsien Hui (The Society of Ten Thousand Immortals). By going through superstitious rites they believed they were immune to bullets and swords; cf. C. O. Anderson and R. M. Anderson, *Two Lives of Faith*, 32.

left together with some of the Chinese, the city was attacked and there were dead and wounded outside the city walls. The gates had been shut so the attackers did not get inside. Rumours were flying; one was that the horse Dad was riding had been shot. But in the evening he returned home safely.[114]

In spite of the chaos, Peter Matson spent a week with the missionaries at Icheng in November 1926 conducting Bible studies and experiencing real spiritual refreshment.[115] But by 1927 anti-foreign agitation forced all the missionaries to evacuate.[116] From 1927 to 1933 Icheng had no missionary in residence.[117] During the civil war in 1929 mission buildings were in the hands of rebels,[118] with missionaries from Siangyang making only occasional visits to Icheng.[119] Meetings, nevertheless, continued at Icheng each year, the work otherwise carried on by Chinese preachers.[120]

In Kingmen evangelism was also being carried on,[121] although in 1921 Ivan Lindgren became dissatisfied with the mission work, his comrades, and the Chinese, and in the next year he resigned from the Covenant staff. In Kingchow Alice Larson, wife of Leonard Larson, was working with women from 1920–1926, but otherwise evangelism during these years was carried on by a Chinese evangelist and a Bible woman.

---

114. C. O. Anderson and R. M. Anderson, *Two Lives of Faith*, 31. Oscar gives his own report of serious trouble in the Icheng district in the fall of 1926 (ibid., 32–33).

115. P. Matson and C. O. Anderson, "The Icheng District," 43.

116. Ruth Anderson reports on the evacuation of Icheng in February, 1927 and the trip to Hankow and Shanghai (C. O. Anderson and R. M. Anderson, *Two Lives of Faith*, 34–35). Following is Oscar's report (ibid., 36–38).

117. P. Matson and C. O. Anderson, "The Icheng District," 43.

118. P. Matson, *Our China Mission*, 98.

119. Ibid.

120. P. Matson and C. O. Anderson, "The Icheng District," 42–43. See also E. V. Nordlund, *The Life and Work of Victor Nordlund*, 81–84, where Peter Matson reports in a letter to Victor Nordlund, dated October 28, 1927, destruction seen at the Icheng station when he passed through three weeks ago. The Nordlund home was full of (communist) soldiers and the church had been turned into a stable for horses. Furniture in the Nordlund home had been carried away or left more or less broken. There were hardly any traces of Nordlund's books; a few Chinese books "used for unclean purposes" were found.

121. In 1921 Arvid Carlson arrived to do evangelism in the Kingmen district, and in July, 1923 he married Esther Hanson, who joined him in the work. Esther was a nurse, but also did women's work. In the 1920s Hilma Johnson was also at Kingmen, and Hilda Rodberg, besides work at the dispensary and in a girls' school, was also doing women's work.

Evacuation (1926–27)

In the late 1920s, when missionary work had lost its momentum due to civil unrest, and missionaries were evacuating in large numbers, the talk turned to "devolution," i.e., "the transfer of responsibility and leadership in Christian work from the missionary to the Chinese."[122] It had always been a stated aim of the Covenant Mission to create an indigenous Chinese Church, and Chinese had been brought into mission work from the very beginning, but with large numbers of missionaries evacuating in 1926–27, a transfer was now more urgent.

RETURN TO THE FIELD (1927–1929)

Siangfan

In September of 1927 Peter Matson and John Peterson received permission from the American Consul to return to the field.[123] They took a boat to Shasi, and from there went through the entire field. Matson reports:

> It was a sad sight that met us, as we traveled from one station to another. The mission premises were occupied by robber soldiers who had looted our homes and partly destroyed many of the buildings. In Siangyang the mission station was so filled with these evildoers that we could find no shelter in our own homes, but just had to crowd in on a poor Chinese family.[124]

Nevertheless, Matson and Peterson spent three weeks in Siangyang, where they held a Bible institute for Chinese co-workers. John Peterson said: "This was without gainsaying the best conference we have had in China, considering the atmosphere of mutual understanding and harmony prevailing."[125]

Peter Matson visited Siangyang again in the spring of 1928. It was a difficult time because two warlords were fighting each other, and for three days and four nights the population was in panic from the firing of rifles and machine guns. Finally General Fang Yu-Hsiang, who had become a Christian,[126] managed to oust his rival, Hsu Sheo-chun, and the victorious

---

122. P. Matson, *Our China Mission*, 93–96.

123. The return to the field is reported also in P. Matson, "Shadow and Light in Hupeh."

124. P. Matson, *Our China Mission*, 90.

125. Ibid.

126. [Hedstrand], "The Chinese Cromwell." General Fang was converted to Christianity after witnessing the murder of Mary Morrill in the Boxer uprising, when Miss

troops took possession of the mission station, occupying mission houses and schools.[127] General Fang did not show any opposition to the mission work, so Matson managed to get the troops out of the church building and Sunday services went on uninterrupted. Matson stayed outside the city in the Nurses Home at Bethesda Hospital, where he conducted a Bible study in Acts with the Chinese workers, after which Matson made an adventurous trip down the Han to Hankow, where he joined other missionary comrades. All spent the summer in Kuling.[128]

In September, 1928 women were permitted to return to the field. The following spring Edla Matson organized a Mary Evangelistic Band in Siangyang, the name "Mary" being taken from Mary Magdalene in the New Testament. In this organization 30 women banded together to visit and speak personally with individual women.[129] Ellen Ackerson had returned with Edla in 1928, and resumed nursing at Bethesda Hospital and spent time doing women's work. Later in 1928 Isaac Jacobson and Albert Dwight returned to Siangyang and Fancheng. Anna Jacobson remained at home with the children, while Elna Dwight was with her children at a school for missionary children near Hankow.[130]

Nanchang and Icheng

At Nanchang and Icheng there were no missionaries after the evacuation of 1927. Mission buildings were entirely in the hands of soldiers.[131] Any evangelism or preaching was being done by the Chinese. When Matson and Peterson visited in October, 1927, however, they had the pleasure of opening the church that had been closed since the communist attack in mid-February.[132] Nevertheless, civil war and banditry continued at both Nanchang and Icheng into the 1930s.

Morrill and Miss Gould were beheaded.

127. P. Matson, "Shadow and Light in Hupeh," 802.

128. P. Matson, *Our China Mission*, 92–93.

129. E. C. Matson, "The Covenant Women's Evangelistic Auxiliary," 89.

130. P. Matson, *Our China Mission*, 93.

131. Ibid., 98.

132. P. Matson, "Shadow and Light in Hupeh," 803.

Kingmen

When Peter Matson and John Peterson visited Kingmen in September, 1927 they called together the Chinese evangelists and teachers for a time of Bible study and prayer. It was another unforgettable experience. Matson reports:

> At noon recess, all of a sudden, the city was attacked by a military force. With continual firing and bullets flying everywhere the poor people were scared out of their wits and ran for cover. The hour came for the afternoon meeting and I said to Mr. Peterson: "Let us hunt up our men and get together for prayer." Many of them were panicky, but they all came and we united our hearts in prayer to him who is our refuge and strength. It was pitiful to hear them cry to God to put a stop to the firing as it made them so nervous and they could stand it no longer. While we were yet praying the firing ceased, and when we came out we could see the retreating soldiers running over the hillside.[133]

Matson says the intruders came back demanding occupation of the mission station, and while he and Peterson had great difficulty keeping them out, they did manage to do so. Anxiety prevailed throughout the day and following night, but the next evening they had a blessed meeting when two trusted Chinese evangelists were ordained to the ministry.

John Peterson returned alone to Kingmen in the spring of 1928, and conducted a Bible institute, although nearly the entire time, which was three weeks, the city was in the hands of a robber band.[134] No women were as yet permitted to return to the field, as fighting was going on and the authorities could not guarantee their protection. In December, 1928 when the women were permitted to return, Hilda Rodberg came back to Kingmen, but the following May she became seriously ill and had to seek medical help in Hankow. She died on February 12, 1931, and was buried in Hankow. The Oscar Andersons arrived in Kingman on January 9, 1929.[135] The place had to be cleaned up, but Anderson said mission property had not sustained as much damage as in other places. Most of the furniture was in tact.

Kingchow

In Matson and Peterson's return to the field in 1927 they entered Kingchow to find robber soldiers living in the schools and missionary homes. After

---

133. P. Matson, *Our China Mission*, 91.

134. Ibid., 92.

135. C. O. Anderson and R. M. Anderson, *Two Lives of Faith*, 40.

special pleading, Peterson was allowed to enter his house to retrieve a few books, which he then brought over to the house of Pastor H. C. Wang. An uneasy state of affairs continued for about a year and a half, with soldiers using anything of wood—benches, doors, windows, tables, and floorboards—for firewood. During the winter fires were made in rooms of the school, and Peterson marveled that the entire building was not burned to the ground.

In the spring of 1928 Peterson came again to Kingchow, staying for 3 months. With conditions being slightly better, a cleanup was attempted. They began with the chapel, which for over a year had been used as a stable. Chinese and foreigners, men and women, teachers and servants, all worked together in harmony to carry away rubble and scrub the place clean. When the project was completed, a thanksgiving service was held in the chapel.[136] The school reopened with one class in October 1928. Oscar Anderson came briefly to help before going to Kingmen in January.[137]

CIVIL WAR AND JAPANESE OCCUPATION (1930–1940)

Civil war continued in Hupeh Province into the 1930s, and would be the major hindrance to Covenant missionary work until the end of the decade, when there would be another enemy to contend with: the Japanese. In 1931 General Ho Lung's Red Army made a surprise attack on Kingmen, carrying away three Covenant missionaries along with Dr. Yao and some other Chinese. All returned safely, but not without the Covenant having to ransom Oscar Anderson with a substantial quantity of medicine. Then in 1934–35 was the celebrated but costly Long March of Mao Zedong, which began in Kiangsi Province on October 16, 1934 and ended 370 days later in Shansi Province. It circumvented the Covenant field, going west through Hunan and then circling north to Shansi.

The Japanese invaded Manchuria in 1931 and gradually moved southward,[138] but did not endanger central China until 1937–38 when they came to occupy Shanghai (1937), Nanking (1937), and Hankow (1938). In Shanghai 50,000 Chinese were killed, and the corpses of another 101,000 who died of disease, starvation, or exposure were picked up off the streets.[139] In December, 1937 came the "rape of Nanking," six terrible weeks when an estimated 200,000 (some say 300,000) Chinese were brutally murdered by the

---

136. John Peterson, "Kingchow Theological Seminary," 75–76.

137. C. O. Anderson and R. M. Anderson, *Two Lives of Faith*, 39, 40.

138. On the Japanese invasion of North China in early 1937, see Salters, *Bound with Love*, 91–137.

139. Ibid., 137.

Japanese, and Chiang Kai-shek was forced to move his capital to Chungking in southwest China. On Christmas Day, 1937 the Japanese began bombing Siangyang, and this bombing continued at intervals until May, 1939. The capture of Hankow, capital of Hupeh Province, in 1938 made possible a land invasion of central Hupeh and the Covenant field, which occurred not long afterwards.

Siangfan

In 1930–1932 the Siangfan district was still full of banditry and civil war. Matson says that for months it was impracticable to travel through the district. Nevertheless, ministry in the cities went on, though sometimes mission property was forcibly occupied by undisciplined soldiers. More problems existed in the countryside and at the outstations.[140] Edla Matson opened a Bible school for young women in Siangyang, and Albert Dwight erected a new church building in Fancheng, replacing an old one about to fall down.[141]

More new missionaries arrived, some to do evangelism and work with women in Fancheng and Siangyang.[142] Peter and Edla Matson returned to Siangyang in 1935, bringing with them two new missionaries Mildred Nelson and Viola Larson.[143]

In 1931 a Mother's Society was formed in the Siangyang church where mothers could gather to discuss problems and seek guidance in bringing up their children in the nurture of God. Another aim of this society was to help mothers care for the bodies of their little ones, and assist them with moral problems.[144]

---

140. P. Matson, "The Siang Fan District," 28–29; *Our China Mission,* 97–101.

141. P. Matson, "The Siang Fan District," 28–29.

142. Joel Nordlund (1929); Dora Lindahl (1929)—after 1931 Mrs. Joel Nordlund; Molly Nelson (1930); Carl Branstrom (1933); Mildred Nelson (1935); and Viola Larson (1935). Joel Nordlund did evangelism in the Singfan district, also at Icheng and Nanchang (1929–1934). In 1931 he married Dora Lindahl, a nurse working with women at Siangyang and Fancheng, but Dora took sick, and on July 17, 1933 she died in Kuling, leaving behind a baby boy of two months. Joel went home on furlough the next year, and did not return to China. Molly Nelson came briefly to work with women in Siangyang. Esther Nordlund returned to Fancheng in 1931 to work with women, but then went to Kingmen where, in April, she was kidnapped by the Reds along with Oscar Anderson and Augusta Nelson.

143. Mildred in 1939–41 took over Edla Matson's Bible Training School for Women, which in 1938 had moved to Nanchang. Viola Larson did evangelism, first at Siangyang (1935–1936), then at Nanchang and in the Nanchang district (1936–1940).

144. E. C. Matson, "The Covenant Women's Evangelistic Auxiliary," 89.

In 1933 revival came to Siangfan, which was an extension of a revival on the Lutheran field in Honan Province to the northwest.[145] In the Covenant field it began in Icheng, coming there as an answer to prayer after years of much "sowing in tears."[146] Matson says it occurred during a few years of peaceful conditions in the district. Elsa Hammerlind reported that never in the homeland had she experienced what she heard in Fancheng, when 80 newly converted people gave their testimonies and joined in singing, "At the cross, at the cross, where I first saw the light." Judith Peterson reported the same occurring across the river in Siangyang, where a church comfortably seating 600 was filled to capacity day after day, and on some days people had to remain outside.[147]

In 1935 a disastrous flood in the Han River basin left Fancheng under six to ten feet of water. Mission property was destroyed and flourishing congregations in city and country were scattered. Church members lost their homes and many lost their lives. Matson says it was "a terrible set-back following in the wake of the revival." As a result the mission had to spend considerable money in relief efforts and in rebuilding ruined outstations.[148]

On March 30, 1937 a conference convened in Siangyang to discuss plans for a Chinese Covenant Woman's Auxiliary, modeled on the Covenant Women's Auxiliary in the United States. The "Covenant Women's Evangelistic Auxiliary" was thus formed with 51 charter members. Delegates from all head stations were present. The organization was a success, and survived the bombings that were to come.[149]

In 1937, when the Japanese arrived in Central China, they carried out extensive bombing in Fancheng and Siangyang for the next two years. It all began on Christmas Day, 1937 when Japanese planes made a surprise attack on an airfield near the Fancheng mission station. In November, 1938 the Japanese were again dropping bombs on Fancheng and Siangyang, and this continued until May, 1939.[150] In mid-May, despite panic over the bombings, conditions in Siangfan were relatively peaceful. School in Siangyang was in full swing, with 200 boys and girls in classes.[151] In June, 1939 Peter and

---

145. Dahlstrom, "The Covenant Missionary Society in China," 83.

146. P. Matson, "The Siang Fan District," 29.

147. P. Matson, *Our China Mission*, 120–21.

148. P. Matson, "The Siang Fan District," 29 (for a picture of the flood rushing through Fancheng, see 28).

149. E. C. Matson, "The Covenant Women's Evangelistic Auxiliary," 89–90.

150. P. Matson, "The Siang Fan District," 30.

151. Ibid., 31.

Edla Matson left for the States, concluding a most extraordinary career of bringing the Gospel to people in Central China.

Nanchang

Missionaries were also doing evangelism during the decade at Nanchang.[152] In 1938, when Japanese bombs were falling on Fancheng and Siangyang, evangelism—in conversation and in meetings—was being carried on in the Nanchang district with tangible results.[153] Detachments of the Chinese army were stationed there, and many officers and soldiers accepted the Christian message and were baptized. In good weather open-air meetings were conducted daily in the market place. Outside of the South Gate proved to be another good place for missionaries to meet people.[154] Evangelistic efforts were so successful that the local church decided to rent a suitable hall for preaching purposes. Two church members took on the support of a Bible woman in the East suburb of the city. The missionaries were also given permission to preach to prisoners in the jails twice a week.

---

152. Joel Nordlund came to do evangelism in 1929. Carl Branstrom, after arriving in 1933 and taking language study in Peking, did evangelism for a year at Nanchang. Hjalmar and Helen Gravem returned to Nanchang to do evangelism in 1934, remaining until 1941. Viola Larson, after a brief stay in Siangyang, relocated to Nanchang where she performed extraordinary service at the head station and at outstations in the district, riding horseback into the country to do evangelism. Elsa Hammerlind was also in Nanchang from 1933 to 1945, riding horseback with Viola to do evangelism in the country, and taking charge of the dispensary.

153. Yuen, "Nanchang Items," 171–72.

154. See Jeremiah 7:1; 17:19; 19:1–2.

Viola Larson and Elsa Hammerlind to the Outstations on Horseback

Icheng

There were no missionaries in residence at Icheng from 1927–1933, although Joel Nordlund did some evangelism there after arriving in 1929. In the spring of 1933 came the revival that was said to have "turned a new page in the history of the Icheng mission."[155] It continued into the fall, and spread to Siangfan, Nanchang, and Kingmen. Missionaries from the Lutheran United Mission joined Covenant missionaries in conducting meetings, and many people came under conviction of sin and found peace with God.[156] Students of the Bible School attended the meetings, and "nearly all of them were brought under deep conviction, made open confession of sin, and received forgiveness and newness of life."[157] A new spirit came into the school. Paul and Elin Johnson returned to do evangelism at Icheng in 1934,[158] and remained until April, 1939, when Japanese bombs destroyed the city and the

155. P. Matson and C. O. Anderson, "The Icheng District," 44.

156. P. Matson, *Our China Mission*, 120–23; A. L. Dwight, "Revival Movements."

157. Fu, "Witnessing for Christ."

158. P. Matson and C. O. Anderson, "The Icheng District," 44.

mission station. They then moved up to Siangyang, but in the summer of 1940 Elin was again ill and they had to go home.

Kingmen

There was more than a little drama at the Kingmen station in the early 1930s. In the fall of 1928 troops were still in Kingmen, and it was considered unsafe to live there.[159] But on January 9, 1929 the Oscar Andersons arrived with Augusta Nelson,[160] and Augusta together with Dr. David Yao set about to revive the medical work.

In April, 1931 the Reds made a surprise attack on Kingmen, resulting in the capture of Oscar Anderson, Augusta Nelson, and Esther Nordlund, the only foreign missionaries there at the time. Dr. Yao and some other Chinese were also taken captive.[161] The captives went with the Reds in their march out of the city. Augusta, Esther, and Dr. Yao were soon released, but Oscar remained in captivity for 75 days, gaining his freedom only after the Covenant paid a ransom of 67 boxes of medical supplies. (For more on this, see Chapter 3 and Oscar's account of his trek with Ho Lung's Red Army in Appendix 1.) After the kidnapping the Kingmen station remained vacant, having no missionaries until 1935. Work there was carried on by Pastor Wu and other Chinese.

In the fall of 1931 the Reds were still around Kingmen,[162] but Oscar Anderson after his release was able to make several visits in the district between 1933 and 1936, when an exodus of the Red armies from south and central China brought a few years of relative peace.[163] In the fall of 1934 special meetings were held in Kingmen,[164] with Marcus Cheng as one of the speakers.[165] In the spring of 1935 Oscar Anderson returned to Kingmen for a month of meetings and to conduct Bible courses there and at the outstations. Many decisions were made to follow Christ.[166] Then in the summer came the devastating Han River flood, destroying outstations near the river and much else.

159. C. O. Anderson and R. M. Anderson, *Two Lives of Faith*, 39.
160. Ibid., 40.
161. Ibid., 52.
162. Ibid. 92.
163. Ibid., 92–93.
164. Ibid., 99.
165. Ibid.
166. Ibid.

In the fall of 1935 Joel Johnson took over work at Kingmen after return-ing from furlough, and that fall Mabel Olson also returned. Mabel remained at Kingmen until the early 1940s, when the Japanese came to occupy the city and she, along with Isaac Jacobson and Joel Johnson, were interned to Hankow. Mabel said Chinese women were initially fearful of foreigners, but gradually this was overcome and they came to classes to learn to read and become catechumens. Such was the beginning of direct evangelism among the women at Kingmen. Some Chinese Bible women who had graduated from the Bible School in Siangyang were also employed.[167]

Bible women were used by all mission societies, where a need was felt to visit the Chinese women in their homes. It was said "in the walk between home and home she can tell you more in a few minutes about a family than you could find out in a whole year."[168] At Kingmen women sang together and learned Bible verses, putting the Scripture quotations up on walls of their homes. Tracts with Scripture portions were also distributed to the women. The women also learned to pray. Women's work aimed to make the Chinese homes Christian and to rid them of idols and other marks of heathen worship.[169]

Turmoil continued in the late 1930s at Kingmen, with the Japanese eventually gaining control of the southern portion of the Covenant field. In the spring of 1936 Carl and Lillian Branstrom came, and remained there until going home on furlough in 1939. Isaac Jacobson was also in Kingman at the time; his wife Anna was in the States.

Bombing began in Kingmen in 1938 and 1939 after Hankow fell to the Japanese in October, 1938. In November of that year, 26 bombs fell on mission property, and although buildings were damaged, they nevertheless remained on their foundations.[170] Isaac Jacobson and Joel Johnson had a narrow escape when a bomb exploded in the mission compound in front of one of the houses.[171] There was more bombing in February, 1939,[172] at which time the mission was practically destroyed. Eventually the Japanese came to occupy Kingmen and relocated Isaac Jacobson and Joel Johnson to Hankow,

167. C. O. Anderson, "Chinese Co-Workers," 94; Conradson, "The Young Women's Bible Training School," 120. For pictures of Bible women at Siangyang and Icheng, see Hammarlind, "The Chinese Mother," 111.

168. Evans, "City Evangelistic Work among Women," 35.

169. Olson, "Women's Work."

170. E. C. Matson, "Life under the Shadows of Death," 24 (for a picture of the King-man church, see 25); J. S. Johnson, "The Kingmen District," 49.

171. Reported in a letter from Matson to the American Consul General in Hankow, dated Nov 9, 1938; see also E. C. Matson, "Life under the Shadows of Death," 24.

172. E. C. Matson, "Life under the Shadows of Death," 24.

where they were interned until repatriated to the States in 1942. Work at Kingmen nevertheless bore fruit during these troubled times, for at the end of the decade Kingmen had 524 church members and 604 catechumens.[173]

Kingchow

At the southern end of the Covennt field the years 1932–1936 were peaceful in city and country, allowing schoolwork and evangelism to be carried on normally.[174] Mabel Olson was in Kingchow engaged in evangelism, schoolwork, and women's ministry. Evangelism at Kingchow had been carried on earlier by a Chinese evangelist and a Bible woman, both of whom were under the supervision of a missionary teacher at the seminary. When this became too heavy a load for the seminary teacher, Oscar Anderson came with his family in the fall of 1932[175] to join in evangelism and relief work in Kingchow, Tsienkiang, and the outstations. He also taught at the seminary.

In 1932 work at the two southern locations was divided, with the Swedish Mission Covenant taking charge of evangelism from Shasi, and the American Mission Covenant taking over of evangelism from Kingchow. About this time the American Covenant also assumed responsibility for the Kingchow church, which previously had been a union enterprise.[176]

In the fall of 1934 Oscar Anderson and Pastor Tang made visits to Tsienkiang, a district between Kingchow and Hankow, and found there Christians who were still firm in their faith after visitations by the communists, and more people now who wanted to become Christian. Tang and his family continued to work there and things looked promising, until the Japanese invaded, at which time Christian ministry had to be suspended.[177]

In 1935 Oscar and a Chinese evangelist, Mr. Au, went on another evangelistic tour to market places northwest of Kingchow, but it had to be cut short because of bandits in the area.[178] 1935 was also the year of the great flood, and many came to Kingchow seeking refuge at the seminary because it was located on high ground of the city. The missionaries received them gladly. Oscar and Ruth Anderson remained at Kingchow until May, 1936 when they went home on furlough. Evangelism at Kingchow and the

---

173. J. S. Johnson, "The Kingmen District," 50.

174. C. O. Anderson and R. M. Anderson, *Two Lives of Faith*, 94.

175. John Peterson, "Kingchow and Shasi," 54; C. O. Anderson and R. M. Anderson, *Two Lives of Faith*, 92.

176. Ibid.

177. C. O. Anderson and R. M. Anderson, *Two Lives of Faith*, 93.

178. Ibid., 100.

outstations was then taken over by Albert Dwight. Hilma Johnson was in Kingchow in 1938, until October, 1, when she returned home.

In 1939 Kingchow found itself less than 40 miles from fighting between the Chinese and the Japanese. The Japanese severely bombed the city three times. After the first attack the students scattered for two months, but then returned. Except for a few weeks of interruption, school activity at Kingchow continued to function all during the war.

John Peterson reported one occasion in 1939 when he baptized 162 officers and solders, more than he had ever baptized at one time.[179] It occurred one day in March when a certain Colonel Tang, accompanied by two other military officers, knocked at his door. Peterson had earlier received a letter from Hjalmar Gravem in Nanchang introducing the Colonel, in which Gravem spoke highly of him as a Christian witness within his army. Just now the Colonel had moved from Nanchang to Kingchow, and was coming to Peterson to request baptism for his officers and men.

Not having received such a request before, Peterson consulted his Chinese co-worker, the Rev. H. C. Wang, and the two sought to find out all they could about the Colonel's qualifications and sincerity. Both became convinced that this was the working of God. Air raids were expected at any moment, and Colonel Tang said they could receive orders to go any day. So if the baptisms were to take place, they would have to be done soon. The decision was made to hold a service the following day at 3:00 in the afternoon. Peterson gave Colonel Tang 25 copies of the Covenant catechism and the Colonel promised that every man would read it before the next day.

The following day Japanese bombers were overhead, and air raid warnings were heard most of the forenoon. Shortly after 2 p.m. the men began arriving, and at 3 p.m. sharp the service started. Rev. Wang, then President of the seminary, led the devotional exercises and preached the sermon, speaking for about 40 minutes. Peterson said the spirit of God was very much in evidence. The response of the soldiers, who were all educated and intelligent, was something Peterson had seldom observed in China, or anywhere, for that matter. As Colonel Tang called out their names, one soldier after the other came to the platform to be baptized. Officers came first, according to rank, and the enlisted men followed. Before the ceremony a few questions were put to them and a few promises given. The baptismal ceremony was followed by a communion service, in which the newly baptized men, others in the army who had previously been baptized, and a few Christian leaders in attendance took part. About 240 persons participated. The colonel had

179. John Peterson, "A Solemn Baptismal Act of 162 Officers and Soldiers"; reported also in *The Covenant Weekly* (April 25, 1939) 4.

specifically requested a communion service, since he had never taken communion before. The meeting proceeded without interruption.

Four days later Kingchow was heavily bombed, with the chapel and girls' school suffering considerable damage. A few days later Colonel Tang returned with three of his officers for a visit. Peterson gathered together as many copies of the Scriptures as he could spare and gave them to the Colonel for distribution to the men in his army.

In 1939, a year before the Golden Jubilee of Covenant mission work in China, Peterson was able to report that during the seminary's 30 years of existence, 130 students had been graduated and about 70 were currently serving in the two missions; some had gone to work at other missions. The Kingchow church consisted of 58 Chinese and 36 Manchus, and the two groups were getting along well.[180]

CLOSING YEARS OF THE COVENANT HUPEH MISSION (1940–1948)

After the Japanese entered the Covenant field in the south, Kingchow and Kingmen came under Japanese occupation. The field was cut in two, with the northern stations in Fancheng, Siangyang, Nanching and Icheng under Chinese control. The northern area of Hupeh was called "Free China." This situation remained basically unchanged until 1945, except for a couple brief visits of Japanese troops to Fancheng and Siangyang, after which they departed or were chased out by the Chinese. Then in 1945 Japan surrendered to the Allies, and the Japanese soldiers were rounded up, disarmed, and sent home. In the years that followed, civil war intensified, with the communists gaining the upper hand and Covenant missionaries being forced to abandon the field and relocate to southwest China.

Siangfan

In May, 1940 two squadrons of Japanese planes were again bombing Fancheng and a smaller site five miles to the east. A thousand people were killed or wounded in a crowded marketplace. Then on June 1, 1940 the Japanese crossed the Han and marched into Siangyang. They left the next day, but not before burning nearly the entire city. Mission property was spared after talks between missionaries and the Japanese. This was before

---

180. John Peterson, "Kingchow and Shasi," 55.

Pearl Harbor. After leaving Siangyang the Japanese shelled Fancheng,[181] and then burned two thirds of that city.[182] Esther Nordlund was in Fancheng at the time. The surrounding countryside was devastated, although here, too, the Japanese showed restraint by not destroying any Covenant mission property.

After the Japanese left Siangyang people returned and set about clearing the streets and putting up small houses. Matson says work in the district gradually resumed to normal.[183] People had a new interest in the Gospel, and the mission added to its list a number of new inquirers.[184] At Sunday meetings there was a full house. In October, 1940 the Covenant Mission held its 50 year Jubilee at Siangyang, which was a great time of celebration. Norwegian missionaries came to join in, the weather was good, and there were no disturbances.[185]

In the fall of 1940 Paul Backlund joined Oscar Anderson in the work at Siangyang. Oscar was having a problem with phlebitis, and for a while had to be in bed. When he was up and around in the spring of 1941, he had to walk with crutches. If he went to the hospital or anywhere outside the city, he took a rickshaw.[186] Large crowds attended Easter Sunday meetings. A number of Chinese army officers came and wanted to be baptized. Since they had orders to leave Easter morning, the baptism took place the day before. In the fall Oscar was able to visit outstations, but it was too far to ride a horse, so he engaged a wheelbarrow.[187]

By December, 1941 Fancheng and other stations in the north—Siangyang, Nanchang, and Icheng—were in Chinese hands, and work was being carried on normally. In the fall of 1942 it was decided at a meeting of both missionaries and the Chinese that Chinese co-workers be permitted to engage in other occupations in order to support themselves. The Covenant had increased the allowance for Chinese co-workers, but it was still not enough, for inflation was a major problem.[188] At the meeting self-support of the outstations was also discussed. It was decided that Mr. Chang Hung Hsuin, chairman of the Chinese Council, and Oscar Anderson, represent-

---

181. C. O. Anderson and R. M. Anderson, *Two Lives of Faith*, 122.

182. E. V. Nordlund, *The Life and Work of Victor Nordlund*, 151; C. O. Anderson and R. M. Anderson, *Two Lives of Faith*, 122.

183. P. Matson, "The Siang Fan District," 31.

184. C. O. Anderson and R. M. Anderson, *Two Lives of Faith*, 123.

185. Ibid., 126.

186. Ibid.

187. Ibid.

188. Ibid., 127.

ing the missionary staff, visit all the churches in "Free China," preaching the Gospel and presenting the message of self-support. They went out for a month, traveling by foot, though Oscar was still nursing a bad leg and had to walk with a cane. Oscar stayed well, however, and the response of the churches was gratifying.[189]

At Christmas, 1942 Paul Backlund witnessed an extraordinary baptismal service at Siangyang. He reported:

> At Christmas 1942, I sat with the choir on the platform of our Siangyang church and witnessed a baptismal service that thrills me even yet as I think of it. Three men were baptized. One an old man of about eighty years; the second was an army officer; the third was a young man from the Siangyang prison sentenced to fifteen years imprisonment, escorted to church by an armed guard.[190]

He continues:

> Just at Easter this year a woman was baptized who formerly used to belong to a secret society connected with robber bands in this district. She is a very intelligent woman and seems full of zeal and love for the Master.[191]

Backlund also reported children singing and hearing Bible stories on a Sunday morning in front of a Chinese house facing a side street in Siangyang. He expressed wonderment that this should be going on in war-torn and troubled China of the early 1940s.

In 1943 Oscar celebrated his 50th birthday and went by bicycle to Laohokow to hold meetings with the Norwegian Lutherans. In the fall of 1944 he travelled to Honan Province to help the Norwegians with evangelistic meetings. Stopping at a teahouse, he ate lunch and then paused to help a Chinese man fix his bicycle. As he was working on the bicycle some American officers came by in a jeep. The American Air Force now had a base at Laohokow. The officers were from Fancheng, and Oscar knew them. Would he like a ride home? Of course he would, so his bicycle was tied on the top of their trailer and Oscar climbed into the jeep. The officers had been in Fancheng inspecting Chinese troops.[192]

Oscar spent Thanksgiving with Norwegian missionaries from Norway and the United States. He was asked to preach in one of the Norwegian

---

189. Ibid., 127–28.

190. Backlund, "Glimpses of China Today," 94–95.

191. Ibid., 95.

192. C. O. Anderson and R. M. Anderson, *Two Lives of Faith*, 131.

churches, but several days of snow and rain left the roads in such bad shape that he never got to where he was going. Then Mildred Nordlund called telling him to return to Siangyang, as missionaries were being advised to evacuate to Chungking, as the Japanese were advancing toward Kweiyan in Kweichow Province. This was around Dec. 1.[193] Departure was delayed until after New Years, 1945, when all the missionaries except Oscar Anderson left Siangyang.

On the first Sunday in March, 1945 Oscar preached at the Fancheng church. In the afternoon he spoke at a Bible hour in Siangyang, and in the evening took part in an English service held in Fancheng for American servicemen. A Signal Corps of 15 men was stationed in Fancheng. Then Oscar took sick, and after being in bed for two weeks he heard about movements of Japanese on the ground at night. On March 11 a report came that the Japanese were heading in the direction of Siangyang, and that they were not far away. The Chinese were pulling out, and wanted Oscar to go with them in their truck. Oscar got up at midnight but could hardly stand; nevertheless, he had to pack and arrange for the Chinese to take over. At about 9 a.m. he got an injection and medicine, and said his goodbyes. Oscar heard later at Chungking that when the Japanese approached the mission station in Siangyang the Chinese fled west, barely making it before the Japanese cut off a way of escape. On arrival the Japanese took possession of the buildings, then looted and destroyed them. Nanchang and Ichang suffered the same fate, but the victory was a short one. VJ Day came, September 2, 1945.

After the war was over, missionaries returned to Siangfan.[194] But in 1948 enemies of another sort arrived. A few months after Millie and Ed Nelson left Siangyang in January, 1948, the city was attacked and its gates were beaten down.[195] In May word came to Ed Nelson in Hankow that soldiers were occupying the mission buildings.[196] By then all Covenant missionaries had left.[197] In June the hospital was in the process of being closed. The communists took over in July, 1948, and soon after the mission was destroyed. Work from this point on would have to be carried on by the Chinese Christians.

193. Ibid., 132.

194. When Ann Kulberg visited Siangyang in November, 1947 she was met by Martha Anderson, Joel Johnson, Viola Larson, Judith Peterson, Ruth Edlund, and Millie and Ed Nelson.

195. E. G. Nelson, *China in Your Blood*, 53.

196. Ibid., 85.

197. Carlson, "Mission to China," letter dated June 20, 1948.

Nanchang

At Nanchang an annual conference was planned in June, 1938, but had to be cancelled because the field was overrun with invaders.[198] In 1939–40 work was progressing at the Chuanuantou outstation,[199] and Isaac Jacobson said the future in Nanchang district looked promising.[200] At Chinese New Year 1940 special meetings were held at Nanchang with good results.[201] Norwegian missionaries came down from Laohokow to help. Carl and Lillian Branstrom returned to Nanchang in 1940, and remained until 1945, when they had to flee the Japanese and go to Szechuan Province. Esther Nordlund was head of the Nanchang station from 1940–45. Viola Larson departed Nanchang in February, 1941, sailing out of Shanghai on the last ship to leave China. She remained home a couple years, and then returned to China.

In December, 1941 the Chinese controlled North Hupeh, but the Japanese were still bombing and people were being killed. One casualty was a young girl in Nanchang who had attended the Siangyang Bible School for girls.[202] Another casualty was a Chinese mother in Nanchang carrying a small baby. She was hit while running to a bomb shelter; the baby was uninjured, but the woman died shortly after. Being a former student and friend of Elsa Hammerlind, she had asked Elsa before she died to take care of her baby. Elsa adopted the little girl, who came to be called Minglan Hammerlind.[203]

After war broke out between the United States and Japan the bombing in China tapered off or ceased altogether.[204] In 1941, when many people had to flee into remote areas, Mr. Liu Fangming reported from a place in the southern mountains of the Nanchang district that he had been well received by the residents and was able to preach to them.[205] Paul Backlund wrote, too, that Chinese listened gladly to the gospel at a market place in the little town of Hsia K'o in the mountains southwest of Nanchang, where he had great success also in selling Gospels. This was in about the fall of 1942 when Backlund was in the district with Carl Branstrom and a Chinese evangelist.[206]

198. P. Matson, "The Siang Fan District," 31.

199. Jacobson, "The Nanchang District," 37.

200. Ibid., 37–38, 39–40.

201. C. O. Anderson and R. M. Anderson, *Two Lives of Faith*, 121.

202. Jacobson, "Present Conditions on Our Field in China," 77–78.

203. Personal communication from Minglan Hammerlind Wong, March 6, 2014.

204. Jacobson, "Present Conditions on Our Field in China," 78–79.

205. Ibid., 82.

206. Backlund, "Glimpses of China Today," 94; Branstrom, "From a Missionary's Diary."

Esther Nordlund left Nanchang in the evacuation of January 3, 1945, leaving Elsa Hammerlind alone in early 1945. Elsa wanted to stay, but the Air Force Command warned that if she waited too long there might be no chance to get out. So in late February she agreed to evacuate, and passed through Siangyang on her way to Laohokow. With her was Minglan, the Chinese orphan girl she had adopted. After Oscar Anderson left Siangyang and was on his way home, he heard that when the Japanese came to Nanchang they occupied buildings, looted, and burned one of the mission structures.[207]

In 1947 Esther Nordlund returned to Nanchang, but was there only briefly, for she was one of the missionaries murdered in January, 1948. After this tragedy, people flooded to the mission station at Nanchang to express their grief.[208] Yuen Peh-yung, now President of the Covenant Church in China, reported about the service held in the church sanctuary on January 25, 1948, a cold day with snow on the streets.

Icheng

In early 1940 there were no missionaries at Icheng, which had been largely destroyed by Japanese bombs.[209] In December, 1941, when the Chinese had regained control of Northern Hupeh, work resumed and was being carried on much as in normal times.[210] Then in 1945 the Japanese came again to burn and loot, as they did elsewhere.[211] In January, 1948 the church building was in complete ruin, and in the spring residents were said to be stealing church bricks.[212] A small chapel had been built, and Evangelist Lu and his wife were carrying on the ministry. Many Chinese—including children—were attending meetings, and Joel Johnson said "all the doors are wide open."[213]

When the communists came to Icheng in 1948, they asked the Chinese pastor, "Where is your missionary?" The pastor replied, "Our missionary

---

207. C. O. Anderson and R. M. Anderson, *Two Lives of Faith*, 143.

208. Yuen, "They Did Not Die in Vain."

209. Isaac Jacobson said that by 1942 mission property at Icheng and Kingmen had been almost wiped out of existence; cf. Jacobson, "Present Conditions on our Field in China," 77.

210. Letter of Peter Matson to the First Covenant Church, St. Paul, Minnesota, dated December 23, 1941.

211. C. O. Anderson and R. M. Anderson, *Two Lives of Faith*, 143.

212. E. G. Nelson, *China in Your Blood*, 85.

213. J. S. Johnson, "Gospel-Band Experiences."

left because he was afraid that when you came he would no longer have an opportunity to teach Christianity to the people." The communists said, "There is not a bit of truth in that. You tell your missionary to come back," but the pastor did not carry out the command.[214]

Kingmen

In 1940 Gust E. Johnson reported from the Covenant Office in Chicago that Japanese bombs had destroyed Kingmen, and the entire city was in ruins.[215] Three missionaries were living in Kaoshan, just west of Kingmen: Joel Johnson, Isaac Jacobson, and Mabel Olson.[216] The Japanese had removed the iron roof from the girls' school building, presumably for use as war material.[217]

In the Kingmen district a large percentage of the population had fled their homes to seek safety in the mountainous regions. Several Christians took refuge at outstations some distance from the area occupied by the Japanese. But with food shortages—the only thing one could buy was rice— starvation stared the missionaries in the face as long as they remained at Kaoshan.[218] Kaoshan was a "no man's land": the Japanese occupied Kingmen to the east, and to the west was the Chinese army. Japanese soldiers and officers would come to Kaoshan during the day, foraging, burning, and looting, and then return to the city; Chinese soldiers would come at night. Finally, in June, 1940 the Japanese took the Covenant missionaries in an army transport down to Hankow,[219] where they were interned. In 1942 they were repatriated to the States on the exchange steamers SS Conte Verde (Italian) and Gripsholm (Swedish).[220]

214. E. G. Nelson, *China in Your Blood*, 60.

215. Reported in a letter from Judith Peterson to Rev. Gust Johnson, dated May 21, 1940; cf. Jacobson, "Present Conditions on our Field in China," 77, who says that at several outstations the same was true, but Christians were still carrying on the work.

216. Letter from Judith Peterson to Rev. Gust Johnson, May 21, 1940.

217. Jacobson, "Present Conditions on Our Field in China," 77–78.

218. Ibid., 79–80.

219. Ibid., 80–81.

220. The Conte Verde left Shanghai with 850 missionaries to be repatriated for Japanese prisoners. The ship went to Lourenco Marques Mozambique in Africa, where it met the Swedish ship Gripsholm, and the prisoner exchange was made. Covenant missionaries then sailed on the Gripsholm to New York. The Covenant missionaries repatriated were Isaac Jacobson, Joel Johnson, Albert Dwight, and Mabel Olson. See G. E. Johnson, "Welcome Home." Ragnhild Matson, who was interned in Shanghai, was repatriated in a later exchange in 1943, arriving home on the Gripsholm December 2nd; cf. R. Matson, "Out of Bondage," 1, 9. See also an article about Joel Johnson in *The Seattle Times* (January 18, 1964) 2.

Carl Branstrom returned briefly to Kingmen in 1947–48. In November, 1947 Ann Kulberg visited and reported seeing the ruins of the station. Two large houses inside the compound walls had been riddled with machine gun bullets and shrapnel, and the insides of houses were in very bad condition. The chapel was in absolute ruins, but the foundations were intact. Ralph Hanson, Secretary of Foreign Missions in the Covenant, had been there the week before and laid the cornerstone for a new chapel.[221] Ann saw evidence of bomb craters, and a bomb shelter where one missionary had taken cover. Buildings outside the compound had been totally destroyed, with people living in temporary houses. The Middle School was still standing, however, and 300 students marched in parade for Ann and the others who were with her.[222]

Kingchow

Hilma Johnson was at Kingchow in the early 1940s involved in evangelism and educational work, but in October, 1941 she returned home. In June, 1940 the Japanese came to occupy Kingchow. Albert Dwight and Augusta Nelson were allowed to remain, but were watched closely, with their movements restricted to nearby towns and outstations. John Peterson had gone home in 1940, and Elna Dwight was in the States with her children. A large Vacation Bible School was conducted at the Kingchow Seminary in 1941.[223] Eventually Albert Dwight was interned by the Japanese, and became yet another Covenant missionary repatriated to the States on the Gripsholm in 1942. This left Augusta Nelson as the only foreign worker of the Covenant staff in occupied Hupeh, since she was a Swedish subject.[224]

Times were difficult in Kingchow during the war years of 1942–1945, also in 1945–1948 when revolutionaries of all description and bandits roamed city and country. A number of missionaries returned, nevertheless, some to resume evangelism.[225] Joel reported in a letter to John Peterson that things were actually well preserved after years of Japanese occupation. Missionary houses looked much the same as when Joel last visited in 1939.

221. Hanson, "China's Crisis and Challenges."

222. Carlson, "Mission to China," letter of November, 1947.

223. For a picture, see N. Dwight, "Waldenström Goes to China and the 'Doers of the Word' Seminary."

224. Jacobson, "Present Conditions on Our Field in China," 81.

225. Albert Dwight, after repatriation, returned in 1945; on May 5, 1946 Mabel Olson came; in June, 1946 Viola Larson came; and Joel Johnson after repatriation returned on September 2, 1946.

He said they had Augusta Nelson to thank for taking care of the property and opposing the Japanese. Missionaries were able to hold on to the Shasi hospital, even though Japanese had lived in some of the houses.[226]

By the end of 1946 three evangelistic bands with 12 Chinese workers were functioning at Kingchow. Thirteen churches had resident pastors, although they had to supplement their income with other employment.[227] Then more missionaries returned. In the spring of 1947 Paul Backlund, now married, arrived with his wife Ruth; and in May, 1947 Amelia Conradson came after a furlough in the United States. When Ann Kulberg visited in November, 1947, though the city walls of Kingchow had been ruined during the war, in the mission compound she saw two big houses, a dispensary, and a Bible school.[228]

At Christmas, 1947 disturbances were widespread throughout the Covenant field, causing everyone at Kingchow to be apprehensive. Some expected the communists to arrive at any time. School was dismissed and students returned home. Carl Branstrom came from Hankow to spend the New Year holiday. A missionary council meeting was planned at Kingchow for January 8.[229] Then on January 7 three Covenant missionaries traveling from Siangyang were murdered on their way to the meeting. The looting of bus passengers and deaths of the missionaries took place on a hilly deserted road about 60 miles south of Siangyang, at 2 p.m. in the afternoon. Their bodies were brought to Kingmen, then to Kingchow.[230] Memorial services were conducted at Siangyang, Nanchang, and Kingchow, and another service preceded the burial on January 26, 1948 at the International Cemetery in Hankow, at which Ed Nelson and Earl Dahlstrom officiated.[231] See Viola Larson's account of the tragedy in Appendix 2.

226. Letter from Joel Johnson to John Peterson, dated at Kingchow on September 5, 1946.

227. Dahlstrom, "The Covenant Missionary Society in China," 62.

228. Carlson, "Mission to China," letter dated November, 1947.

229. "China Conference Official Report on the Deaths of Esther Victoria Nordlund, Martha Johanna Anderson, and Dr. Fr. Alexis Berg," page 2, in Covenant Archives.

230. Missionaries in Kingchow at the time were Viola Larson, Carl and Lillian Branstrom, Otelia Hendrickson, Mabel Olson, Paul and Ruth Backlund, Amelia Conradson, and Joel Johnson.

231. Dahlstrom, "The Covenant Missionary Society in China," 246.

EVACUATION, RELOCATION, AND LEAVING THE CHINA MAINLAND (1948–1949)

After the death of the three missionaries came an evacuation that would end finally the Covenant mission work in Hupeh Province. On January 10, 1948 orders came from the American Consul to leave Siangyang, and in three days the Ed Nelsons, Judith Peterson, and Ruth Edlund departed on the St. Paul[232] for Hankow, which was not currently threatened. After a narrow escape from the communists, the missionaries from Kingchow went to Hankow by truck and ambulance.[233] Joel Johnson remained in Shasi with the Swedish missionaries, saying he wanted to be near the Chinese Christians.[234] The Covenant mission in Hupeh was closed in 1948, however, and control was handed over to the Chinese Christians. Covenant missionaries would now seek a new field in southwest China, but they were not destined to remain long on the Chinese mainland. On October 1, 1949 Mao Zedong proclaimed the founding the People's Republic of China.

Changsha

At Hankow it was decided that Carl and Lillian Branstrom, Paul and Ruth Backlund, Mabel Olson, Otelia Hendrickson, Elsa Hammerlind, and Viola Larson should go to Changsha in Hunan Province. Otelia and Elsa would serve as nurses and help out at an orphanage, the others would carry out evangelism, teach English and Bible in the schools,[235] and support mission work in Changsha. Mabel Olson was headed for the Hunan Bible Institute[236] to teach and undertake translation work. By May, 1948 the missionaries had arrived in Changsha, and with the exception of the Backlunds, were living in a dormitory of the Hunan Bible Institute.

Albert and Elna Dwight would remain in Hankow to maintain contact with Chinese in the field. Judith Peterson would also remain there to stay in

232. The *St. Paul* was a DC-3 owned and operated by the Lutheran World Federation that evacuated many missionaries from the China Mainland; cf. Springweiler, *Pioneer Aviator in China*.

233. Kingchow missionaries were the Dwights, the Backlunds, the Branstroms, Amelia Conradson, Mabel Olson, Otelia Hendrickson, and Viola Larson; cf. E. G. Nelson, *China in Your Blood*, 51–61.

234. A. L. Dwight, "Covenant Work in China," 55.

235. Carlson, "Mission to China," letter dated May 23, 1948.

236. For earlier pictures of the Hunan Bible Institute, see *The Chinese Recorder* 55 (1924) opposite p. 345; opposite p. 385 (a dormitory); opposite pp. 592 and 593; and opposite p. 642. These buildings were bombed and burned during the war.

contact with medical people in Siangyang. Amelia Conradson would reside in Hankow to serve as treasurer of the mission. Ruth Edlund would be at nearby Wuchang studying Chinese.[237] Virginia Carlson, Ann Kulberg, and Gertrude Marsh, newly arrived missionaries, were already at the Language School. Earl and Rosalie Dahlstrom would be returning to the American School Kikungshan, now in Hong Kong.[238] They were not there long, however, for by June Earl was in poor health and the two were on their way home to Mayo Clinic.[239]

Chungking, Kweiyang, and Kweiting

The Covenant Mission would now search for a new field, and sights turned quite naturally to Szechuan and Kweichow Provinces in southwest China. Some Covenant missionaries had been there before, and now it was still a relatively safe place in a country otherwise being torn apart by civil war. On March 9, 1948 Ed Nelson and Carl Branstrom left Changsha in a new Chevy pick-up truck owned by the mission on a 2000-mile roundtrip journey to Chungking in Szechuan Province, and Kweiyang and Kweiting in Kweichow Province. It was an adventurous and productive trip.[240] Ed Nelson returned later with Albert Dwight to find a place for the missionaries to live and work.

At the summer conference in Kuling a decision was made that some missionaries would go to Kweichow Province.[241] Amelia Conradson and the Dwights would continue at Hankow for the time being, residing at the Lutheran Missionary Home.[242]

In May, 1948, even before the summer conference had convened, the Ed Nelsons were on a steamer headed for Chungking.[243] Swedish missionaries were still at Shasi, so the Nelsons got off the steamer and had coffee with them.[244] Upon arrival in Chungking they moved into their new house at

237. Carlson, "Mission to China," letter dated February 15, 1948.

238. Hanson, "Current Situation in China."

239. A. L. Dwight, "A Land of Fluctuations."

240. E. G. Nelson, *China in Your Blood*, 63–79; see also Branstrom, "From Temples of Idols to the Temple of God."

241. Carl and Lillian Branstrom, Paul and Ruth Backlund, Hjalmar and Helen Gravem, Judith Peterson, Viola Larson, Ruth Edlund, Gertrude Marsh, and Dr. Signe Berg when she returned.

242. A. L. Dwight, "Where Is the Dispersion?"

243. E. G. Nelson, *China in Your Blood*, 85–93.

244. Ibid., 88.

Red Cliff Villa, a little village near Hua-lung-ch'iao, a suburb of Chungking. They spent the remaining weeks of the summer at Kuling.[245] In November the Nelsons and Ann Kulberg were joined at Chungking by Otelia Hendrickson.[246] Mission work began. Regular preaching services were held, and on Sunday there were worship services, Sunday School, and inquirers classes. At Christmas 17 persons were baptized, joined by a few more later on, and another 10 at Easter. Otelia Hendrickson and a Chinese woman, Mrs. Kao, visited people in their homes. Meetings were also held at Chung Chen Hospital and at the Government tax office.[247]

In September the Carl Branstroms, Viola Larson, and Gertrude Marsh left Wuchang by train for Changsha, and then drove by truck to Kweichow. It took them 9 days. Boxes brought to Changsha in the spring for safekeeping went with them.[248] Upon arrival in Kweichow, the Branstroms took up residence in Tungjen.[249] By the second week of November all the missionaries had reached their destination and begun mission work in their new locations.[250] That month Albert Dwight, chairman of the mission, came to Kweiyang to see how things were going, and stayed over Christmas and New Years.[251]

By July, 1949 there were 12 Covenant missionaries in Kweichow.[252] Living quarters had been secured in both places, and in both places were chapels. A modest hospital had been opened in Kweiting. In both cities preaching services were being held regularly, including worship services and Sunday School held on Sunday. Chinese students were helping in the Sunday School.[253]

Back in Hupeh

On May 12, 1948 Isaac Jacobson received a report that after the communists came into Hupeh Province there were uprisings among peasants in

245. Ibid., 94–103.

246. Ibid., 126.

247. [Hedstrand], "Gist of the China Conference Oral Reports."

248. Marsh, "A Nine-Day Journey in China."

249. A. L. Dwight, "A Land of Fluctuations"

250. A. L. Dwight, "Into the Highways and Hedges."

251. A. L. Dwight, "Gleanings from China," (February 4, 1949).

252. The Carl Branstroms, Viola Larson, Ruth Edlund, and Judith Peterson in Kweiting; the Dwights, the Gravems, Amelia Conradson, Elsa Hammerlind, and Gertrude Marsh in Kweiyang.

253. [Hedstrand], "Gist of the China Conference Oral Reports."

Siangyang, Nanchang, and Icheng because the communists had arbitrarily seized farmers' grain for their troops. The peasants were organizing themselves into resistance bands with headquarters in the countryside, and it remained to be seen what would come of the struggle now taking place.[254]

By October Albert Dwight reported that the communists had invaded the old field in full force, but stations in the north were still in government hands. The Reds controlled area in the country. Damage to mission property had been great, but the amount of human suffering was greater. People were floundering between fear of the communists and dissatisfaction with the present government. Dwight wondered which side would win out.[255]

Things were not as bad in Kingchow, with the communists still 300 miles to the north. Joel Johnson reported in June, 1948 that a Bible School had been conducted in Kingchow and the rebuilt church was now under roof.[256] At Thanksgiving Joel returned from Kuling to find 400 soldier-students in the seminary building preparing to become officers in the Chinese army.[257] About 100 students were living in the missionary houses. Joel offered help by teaching classes in Bible and English. None had ever been connected with a mission, nor did any know much about Christianity, although some had relatives who were Roman Catholic.

Conditions at the Swedish station in Shasi were uncertain, but both high and primary schools were currently over-filled with students. There was a severe problem with inflation, however, and prices were very high.

Joel Johnson said Pastor T'an Kuang-hue had just returned from a few weeks in the Kingmen district and reported that Christians there were carrying on in faith and hope. In one village the chapel had been destroyed by bombs, so the pastor was invited into a Roman Catholic home to hold meetings. The Roman Catholics had started a school in Kingmen where there were now a good number of students, and Joel remarked that "seemingly the Catholics are gaining the field." In the Kingman district 15 American priests were now working, with more expected to arrive.[258]

In the winter of '48 and spring of '49 evangelistic outreach at Kingchow prospered. At Christmas 15 persons were baptized, and not long after another 60 students and officers from the military school were occupying

254. Jacobson, "Peasant Uprising against Communism in China."

255. A. L. Dwight, "Where Is the Dispersion?"

256. J. S. Johnson, "Kingchow Greetings."

257. J. S. Johnson, "Kingchow Tidings and Comments."

258. Kenneth Scott Latourette reported already in 1925 that for the past two decades there had been a development of interest in foreign missions among American Catholics; cf. Latourette, "American Catholic Missions in China."

part of the seminary building.[259] In February, 1949 Joel Johnson and Elsa Hammerlind, who had now joined him, said they intended to stay at Kingchow, which at the time was the only station in the field that had not been overrun by the communists.[260] They did not remain there long, however, for the communists eventually came and they were forced to flee. By February 25 both Joel and Elsa were on their way to Chungking.[261] Joel then returned home, and Elsa went to Kweiyang.

Leaving the China Mainland

Already by Christmas, 1948 Edward Nelson said there were mutterings and grumblings among students in Chungking about new ideas taking hold in China. Pictures of Chiang Kai-shek were being torn down and pictures of Mao pasted up. For three days martial law was declared. Soon after that Ed had tea with the American Consul and his wife, and there was talk about evacuation. By early May it was decided that mssionaries would have to leave Chungking.

The Nelsons and Otelia Hendrickson left on the *St. Paul* for Canton, their destination being Hong Kong. Ed returned to Chungking the middle of June, but just for a brief visit with people in the church. He stayed two weeks, and then returned to Hong Kong on a cargo plane, waving good-bye to China just three years after he first arrived in Shanghai.[262] The Nelsons stayed at the American School Kikungshan in Hong Kong for two weeks during the summer of 1949, and then headed for Japan, where they took up missionary work in a new field being opened there by the Covenant (1949–1952). In 1952 they went as Covenant missionaries to Formosa (Taiwan).[263]

In mid-February, 1949 the Gravems had come to Kweiyang,[264] but by August they made plans to leave and in September evacuated to Hong Kong. The following June they went home, as did the Backlunds and Mabel Olson.[265] By September the Carl Branstroms were in Hong Kong. Some missionaries evacuated on the *St. Paul*.[266] Viola Larson was in Hong Kong in

259. [Hedstrand], "Gist of China Conference Oral Reports."

260. A. L. Dwight, "Gleanings from China." (February 4, 1949).

261. A. L. Dwight, "Gleanings from China," (March 18, 1949).

262. E. G. Nelson, *China in Your Blood*, 146–57.

263. E. G. Nelson, "The Covenant Church in China and Southeast Asia."

264. A. L. Dwight, "Gleanings from China," (March 18, 1949); Ralph Hanson in *The Covenant Weekly* (March 18, 1949) 3.

265. *The Covenant Weekly* (February 18, 1949) 5.

266. Carlson, "Mission to China," letter dated September 10, 1949.

1949 working with Elsa Hammerlind at the Lutheran Mission. In July, 1950 she and Elsa moved to Chuen Wan, a village outside Hong Kong, and Viola began holding services in factories. Viola returned home in 1951, and then went out as a Covenant missionary to Formosa (Taiwan). Amelia Conradson evacuated with other missionaries to Hong Kong, where, in 1950, she was leading women's groups.

Albert and Elna Dwight were the last Covenant missionaries to leave Mainland China, evacuating in November, 1949[267] and arriving in San Francisco on December 12 after a stopover in Japan. On December 10, 1949 communist troops laid siege to Chengtu, the last Nationalist controlled city in Mainland China. The same day Chiang Kai-shek and his son left Chengtu by aircraft for Formosa (Taiwan), and on March 1, 1950 Chiang set up his government in Taipei.

267. Carlson, "Mission to China," letter dated November 7, 1949.

3

Medical and Benevolence Work

BEGINNING OF THE COVENANT HUPEH MISSION (1892–1900)

Fancheng

MEDICAL WORK IN THE first decade of the Covenant Hupeh Mission began right away in 1892 with the opening of a dispensary in Fancheng where Peter Matson took up residence. The Rev. K. P. Wallen, Matson's early co-worker, provided medical help by attending to people's sores and ailments, although he had no medical training.[1] Coming later to the dispensary was Alma Carlson, who graduated from a Minneapolis hospital and went out as a Covenant missionary to China in 1897. Alma also served among women.[2] She stayed only two years, however; in 1899 she married the Rev. T. H. Himle of the Norwegian Lutheran Mission, and severed her connection with the Covenant.

The real pioneer of Covenant medical work in China was John Sjöquist, who came initially to do evangelistic work in Fancheng and was engaged in that for three years (1893–1896).[3] The Covenant Board wanted him to get medical training, so he was called home to enroll in the Rush Medical

---

1. P. Matson, *Our China Mission*, 66.

2. E. C. Matson, "The Covenant Women's Evangelistic Auxiliary," 87; on "women's work" see also Olson, "Women's Work."

3. For earlier medical work in Fancheng by Dr. Hotvedt of the Norwegian Lutheran Mission, see C. B. Nelson, "Heal the Sick," 122; also Fedde, "Bethesda Union Hospital."

College in Chicago, one of the oldest medical schools in Illinois[4] and one of the most prestigious in the country.

MISSION WORK AFTER THE BOXER REBELLION (1901–1911)

Siangfan

When the Boxer Rebellion erupted in the summer of 1900, Covenant missionaries had to evacuate to Hankow, Nagasaki, Japan, and Shanghai.[5] When they returned to Fancheng in September, 1901 John Sjöquist, who was now a doctor, had with him his young wife Maria. After arriving the missionaries moved across the Han River into Siangyang,[6] a twin city to Fancheng on the south bank of the Han. A new house, already under roof before evacuation, was ready for occupancy.[7]

Then tragedy struck. Maria had taken sick on the voyage, and on November 13, 1901 she died, and was buried in the small Fancheng cemetery. Matson says John was heartbroken and for a time lost all zest for life, walking around as if in a daze.[8] He was left with a small baby, Ruth, who lived with him a few years, but then she, too, died. Dr. Sjöquist, nevertheless, returned to the work for which he was now so well prepared, and went on to make an extraordinary contribution to the Covenant medical mission. He is said to have demonstrated for the first time in that area of China the efficacy of western medicine and surgery.[9]

Medical work at Siangyang was given an added boost by the arrival in late 1901[10] of Hilda Rodberg, the first graduate of the Nursing School at Swedish Covenant Hospital in Chicago. Dr. Sjöquist opened a dispensary in an old Chinese house,[11] and the two of them became a fine team.

4. Rush was chartered as a private medical college in 1837, two days before the city of Chicago was chartered, and was opened to students on December 4, 1843.

5. P. Matson, "The Siang Fan District," 24.

6. Ibid., 25.

7. Ibid., 24–25.

8. P. Matson, *Our China Mission*, 57.

9. K. M. Nelson, "Glimpses from Our Medical Work in Siangyang," 26.

10. P. Matson, "Hilda Nathalia Rodberg"; Judith M. Peterson, "Bethesda Training School for Nurses," 134.

11. P. Matson, "The Siang Fan District," 25; Judith M. Peterson, "Bethesda Training School for Nurses," 134.

Working with primitive equipment they were said to have performed many miracles of healing. Hilda was also highly valued for her zeal and efficiency. Peter Matson wanted a hospital in Siangyang, but in 1903 there was only a dispensary-infirmary,[12] yet in that year alone Dr. Sjöquist and Hilda Rodberg treated 1400 patients. This dispensary-infirmary continued until 1914–15, when Bethesda Union Hospital was opened.

In 1904 Dr. John Sjöquist married Victoria Welter, who had been involved in evangelistic and women's work at Siangyang. The two served together at Bethesda Hospital until John's furlough in 1909.[13] Judith Hagstrom, a trained nurse,[14] came to the dispensary in 1906, but was there only two years. The stress of the work and China's severe climate were too much for her, and she became ill and was advised to return home. Judith left Siangyang in the company of Hilda Rodberg, but they got only as far as Shanghai, where, on April 21, 1908, she died.[15] Ellen Ackerson, a trained nurse, came to the Siangyang dispensary in 1908.[16] By 1908 medical activity at the dispensary had increased considerably: 5522 outpatients and 263 inpatients were treated.

With John Sjöquist's leaving on furlough and a lack of staff, medical work in Siangyang leveled off, with only the dispensary treating patients. Then after Hilda Rodberg went on furlough in 1909,[17] for a time there was no Covenant doctor in China and only Ellen Ackerson at the Siangyang dispensary.

Nanchang

Medical work at Siangyang helped prepare the ground for extending the Covenant mission into the Nanchang district, which took place in the winter of 1902–03. Isaac Jacobson, who opened up the Nanchang district, reported:

12. For a picture of the medical facility and staff at Siangyang in about 1903–1904, see *Aurora* (1904) 114.

13. Olsson, *By One Spirit*, 449.

14. Judith received nurses training at Swedish Covenant Hospital in Chicago, from which she graduated in 1905.

15. For a picture of missionaries gathered at her gravesite, see *Aurora* (1913) 101.

16. Ellen Ackerson graduated from the nursing program at Swedish Hospital in Minneapolis in 1906. Augusta Nelson attended North Park College and then entered nurses training at Swedish Covenant Hospital, from which she graduated in 1910.

17. Judith M. Peterson, "Bethesda Training School for Nurses," 135.

Sick and suffering people had been healed through Dr. Sjöquist's skillful treatments, and as they returned with restored health and changed opinions, they had a very interesting and convincing story to tell kindred and friends. Simply and sincerely they related their experiences and observations at the hospital and the mission station, giving special emphasis to the character of the foreigner and the Chinese Christians. This testimony then influenced others to change their opinions and viewpoints.[18]

A delegation was sent to the missionaries from Wuanyen, a populous city in the Nanchang district, urgently requesting that mission work begin there, promising to defray the expense of providing a suitable house if an evangelist could be stationed in that city. Alternate arrangements were eventually made, and in time Wuanyen had a congregation and an evangelist.[19] In 1911 Alma Mortenson, a trained nurse,[20] came and set up a dispensary and began women's work in the Nanchang district. Once again, lacking suitable facilities and medical equipment, Isaac Jacobson marveled at what Alma was able to accomplish:

> Vividly do I remember how one day they had brought a lad who had fallen from a tree. He had a number of deep and ugly cuts. One man that helped to carry him said that one cut in his back was so deep that he breathed through it. In order to stop the bleeding they had smeared dirt into the awful wounds, and it was a problem to make them clean so the gaps could be sewn together. But within a few weeks the boy was well and happy again.[21]

Alma remained at Nanchang until 1926–27, when she and other missionaries evacuated.

Kingmen

As we have seen, in 1906 Joel Johnson opened a Covenant mission station in Kingmen, which lay on the Siangyang-Kingchow road, in the center of Hupeh Province. Justine Nilsson, a trained nurse,[22] came to Kingmen in

18. Jacobson, "The Nanchang District," 33. The direct effect of medical work on evangelism is pointed out by Wu Teng-yung in his article, "The Mustard Seed."

19. Jacobson, "The Nanchang District," 33–34.

20. Alma Mortenson received her nurses training in Seattle, Washington.

21. Jacobson, "The Nanchang District," 36–37.

22. Justine Nilsson graduated from a hospital nursing program in Providence, Rhode Island, where for several years she held the position of head nurse.

1910 and upon arrival immediately opened up a dispensary. The next year she married Oscar E. Johnson, but unfortunately her health failed and in the spring of 1913 she and Oscar had to return home.

MISSION WORK AFTER THE FIRST REVOLUTION (1911–1921)

Siangfan

Augusta Nelson came to China in 1911,[23] the year of the revolution, and upon arrival stayed in Hankow for two years helping the Chinese Red Cross aid the wounded.[24] She worked with the Red Cross again in 1927–28, for which she was accorded special honor and recognition by the Chinese government. Augusta Nelson was another extraordinary individual, living and tending the wounded through two civil wars, being kidnapped by the communists and held captive for five days, and in the late 30s and early 40s giving extraordinary service in Japanese occupied Kingchow. In 1912 she came to the dispensary in Siangyang, and later became superintendent of nurses at Bethesda Union Hospital.

The period following the 1911 revolution was one of significant expansion in all aspects of Covenant missionary work. On the medical front, a great stride forward was taken when Bethesda Union Hospital officially opened in 1915. It stood just outside the West Gate of Siangyang, about three blocks across a moat surrounding the city.[25] The hospital was a 10-minute walk from the mission compound, which was located just inside the west gate. A seven-foot high wall surrounded the five-acre property. Trees were planted, and within the compound lay the main hospital building, a dispensary, homes for nurses, and residences for foreign and Chinese members of staff.[26]

23. Olsson, *By One Spirit*, 449.

24. P. Matson, *Our China Mission*, 75.

25. K. M. Nelson, "Glimpses from Our Medical Work in Siangyang," 23.

26. Ibid., 24; Pedersen, "Bethesda Union Hospital," 261, with a picture opposite p. 261.

Bethesda Union Hospital, Siangyang

Bethesda Union Hospital was built with Covenant funds,[27] so the building became the property of the Covenant Missionary Society,[28] but in the early years the hospital was jointly operated by the Mission Covenant and the Lutheran United Mission,[29] with doctors and nurses from both missions on staff.[30] This union existed until 1933, when it was dissolved[31] and the hospital was taken over completely by the Covenant. When the hospital opened, John and Victoria Sjöquist had returned to the field and were serving there. But John became ill in 1917, and in August of that year he died.[32] Victoria remained at Bethesda Hospital until 1918, when she went home.

27. Dr. John Sjöquist, during his furlough in 1909–10, succeeded in raising funds at home for a new hospital building, but because of the revolution and general political unrest when he returned, the hospital did not finally open until its dedication on February 19, 1915; cf. P. Matson, *Our China Mission*, 67–68; Pedersen, "Bethesda Union Hospital," 261.

28. Olsson, *By One Spirit*, 450.

29. The Lutheran United Mission became heir to the work started by the Hauge Synod Mission; cf. Syrdal, "American Lutheran Mission Work in China," 34.

30. About 1921 Sister Bergitha Nelson of the Lutheran United Mission joined the staff of Bethesda Hospital; see Judith M. Peterson, "Bethesda Training School for Nurses," 137. On the closing of hospital work in Fancheng and the joining with the Lutheran United Mission to run Bethesda Hospital, see P. Matson, *Our China Mission*, 68.

31. C. B. Nelson, "Heal the Sick," 125.

32. His death occurred on August 15, 1917, and besides his wife Victoria he left behind three children; see the obituary by Peter Matson in *The Chinese Recorder* 48 (1917) 731–32.

Early on Dr. Sjöquist saw the need for Chinese physicians to assist him. One outstanding Chinese doctor was Dr. David Ho, whose parents were early converts to Christianity. Dr. Ho took medical training at the Union Medical School of Hankow, which was a mission institution. Another graduate of Union Medical School was Dr. Sung, who for many years served on the staff of Bethesda Hospital.[33] It was said that due to the courageous work of Dr. Ho and Dr. Sung during the troubled years of 1926–27, when the missionaries had to evacuate, Bethesda Hospital was spared the looting many other hospitals experienced. On one occasion, Dr. Ho stood at the hospital gate and told soldiers demanding entrance that they would come in only over his dead body, and they did not enter.[34]

Bethesda Hospital saw patients from Fancheng and Siangyang, as well as towns and villages within a radius of 50 to 200 miles from the two cities. It also served mission and government schools in the Siangfan area, and two or three adjoining missions. In 1915 Ellen Ackerson became the first superintendent of nurses at the hospital.[35]

Nanchang

Hilda Rodberg arrived in 1910 and Alma Mortenson in 1911. Both were trained nurses, so a dispensary was opened. Alma also spent time working with women. Hilda stayed at Nanchang for two years (1910–1912), and Alma remained until the evacuation of 1926–27.

Kingmen

In 1912 Hilda Rodberg went to Kingmen after two years in Nanchang, working in the dispensary there.[36] In no time she became well known for treating the sick. Joel Johnson says: "With her arrival in Kingmen, without any invitation or announcement, sick people came from far and near asking for help and healing."[37] Chinese officials in Kingman urged the missionaries to build a full hospital, but the Covenant had neither money nor doctors for that. What finally happened was that the local people provided the building

33. C. B. Nelson, "Heal the Sick," 125.

34. Ibid. For a picture of Dr. Ho and his family, see *Half a Century of Covenant Foreign Missions*, 85.

35. Judith M. Peterson, "Bethesda Training School for Nurses," 137.

36. Ibid., 135.

37. J. S. Johnson, "The Kingmen District," 51.

and the Covenant supplied Dr. David Yao and a staff of Chinese nurses. At Kingmen Hilda Rodberg also became involved in the education of girls, again achieving remarkable success.

Kingchow and Shasi

At the southern end of the Covenant field a hospital was planned in 1919 at Shasi, five miles east of Kingchow, where the Swedish Mission Covenant had its work. Property was purchased between Shasi and Kingchow, but things moved slowly. Not until 1928 did Dr. Edmund Li, a close friend of the two missions, receive permission to open a private hospital in rented buildings. During these years the Kingchow Theological Seminary ran a dispensary at the school for the use of students.[38]

GROWTH, DEVOLUTION, AND EVACUATION (1921–1927)

Siangfan

Mission work continued apace in the 1920s, reaching a high point in the middle of the decade before the large-scale evacuation of 1926–27. Many of the new missionaries were nurses, including Anna Larson, who came to Bethesda Hospital in 1919.[39] In December, 1920, she married Dr. Karl M. Nelson, who had arrived earlier in the year. The Karl Nelsons were parents of Dr. F. Burton Nelson, Covenant pastor, professor at North Park Theological Seminary, and internationally known scholar of the German theologian and martyr, Dietrich Bonhoeffer.

38. Dahlstrom, "The Covenant Missionary Society in China," 156.

39. Anna Nelson received nurses training at Englewood Training School for Nurses in Chicago, from which she graduated in 1918.

Dr. K. M. Nelson and Staff at Bethesda Hospital

Karl Nelson graduated from North Park College (1912), after which he received an S.B. degree from the University of Chicago and an M.D. degree from Rush Medical College, now affiliated with the University of Chicago. After arrival in Siangyang he became superintendent of Bethesda Hospital. In 1923 the medical facilities in Siangyang were considered first rate. Karl and Anna went home on furlough in 1926, and unfortunately were unable to return to China because of the revolutionary activity in 1927. Karl's leaving was a great loss to the China mission, for both he and Anna had a reputation for excellence. Dr. Nelson gives this description of Bethesda Hospital in 1927:

> This substantial two-story brick building with its light and airy wards, its clean Oregon-pine floors, its 85 white enameled, comfortable iron beds, its recently installed electric light and X-ray, its staff of diligent nurses and doctors, is the only institution of its kind in this great northwest section of the province. About seven hundred patients are treated annually in the hospital, and approximately ten thousand treatments are given in the dispensary.[40]

40. K. M. Nelson, "Glimpses from Our Medical Work in Siangyang," 26.

Having built a hospital in Chicago in 1903, and then a much larger hospital in 1918, the Covenant Church had valuable experience in both medical facilities and medical staff. Swedish Covenant Hospital in Chicago became the model for Bethesda Union Hospital in Siangyang.[41]

Bethesda Hospital treated people from all walks of life. Dr Nelson said:

> We find officials, army officers and their families, teachers, students, merchants, soldiers, farmers, carpenters, masons, blacksmiths—all trades and occupations are represented. The hospital becomes a common meeting place for all these classes. All are given the same service—professionally. Every patient, rich or poor, is given the utmost care and consideration possible.[42]

People seeking treatment would come first to the dispensary, then be charged a small fee, registered, and brought into the waiting room. Most arrived early, and Dr. Nelson says they came in many different conveyances: wheelbarrows, sedan chairs, rickshaws, stretchers, beds, donkeys, oxcarts, and baskets. An hour before the scheduled consultations, an evangelist would conduct a short gospel service, after which he would mingle with the patients, answer questions, and give out tracts and gospel portions. In the consultation room the patient would see the doctor for the first time, and after a period of questioning, the doctor would make a diagnosis of the case and advise treatment.[43]

Once and a while clinics were conducted at outstations, but usually hospital medical staff did not have time for such trips. Doctors, however, did go out to see patients in the community, usually emergency cases, such as opium poisonings or suicidal attempts. They also visited the bedsides of local missionaries and missionaries at other stations and towns. Travel could be difficult, even dangerous, but they went anyway. On such forays doctors would also find plenty of patients at stops along the road.[44]

Paul and Elin Johnson came to China in 1921, serving their first term at Siangyang. Paul was engaged in evangelism and served also as manager of Bethesda Hospital, where Elin worked as a nurse.[45] In 1927 Siangyang had a military contingent of 10,000 Chinese soldiers to whom the hospital gave

---

41. Almquist, "A Brief Review of the Work of the Covenant Hospital and Home of Mercy 1886–1936," 4, 6.

42. K. M. Nelson, "Glimpses from Our Medical Work in Siangyang," 28.

43. Ibid., 28–31.

44. Ibid., 34–35.

45. After taking an English course at the Evening School of Minnehaha Academy, Elin received nurses training at the Swedish Hospital in Minneapolis before going to China with her husband in 1921.

much attention.[46] Bethesda Hospital was always treating sick and wounded soldiers who could not get adequate care in the poor facilities of the Chinese military establishments.[47]

Nanchang

Serving one term as a nurse in the Nanchang district was Esther C. Peterson (not the wife of John Peterson), who came in 1921 and was put in charge of medical work.[48] She is said to have done a splendid job. During this time a suitable dispensary building was erected to meet the needs of the growing number patients coming for medical help.[49] Because medical services were offered at Nanchang, many officers and soldiers stationed there became Christians, and some were baptized in the Nanchang church.[50] Others, too, became Christians after medical treatment and their being healed.

Icheng

In 1921 Ellen Falk came to do nursing and dispensary work at Nanchang and Icheng.[51] In 1922 a dispensary was opened in Icheng with Ellen in charge,[52] but that year she moved to Siangyang and Elsa Hammerlind, who came to China in 1920 to do medical work and evangelism,[53] took her place. Elsa worked at Icheng from 1922 to 1927.

46. K. M. Nelson, "Glimpses from Our Medical Work in Siangyang," 26–27.

47. C. B. Nelson, "Heal the Sick," 126.

48. Peterson got her nurses training at Swedish Covenant Hospital, from which she graduated in 1920.

49. Jacobson, "The Nanchang District," 38.

50. Yuen, "Nanchang Items," 170–72.

51. Ellen Falk took nurses training at Swedish Covenant Hospital, from which she graduated in 1921.

52. P. Matson and C. O. Anderson, "The Icheng District," 43.

53. Elsa attended North Park College from 1912–14, and then took nurses training at Swedish Covenant Hospital in Chicago, from which she graduated in 1917. She also took a post-graduate course at Cook County Hospital in Chicago and spent time at a T. B. Sanatorium.

Kingmen

Hospital work began in Kingmen in 1920 with the arrival of Otelia Hendrickson, who spent her first term there (1920–1925).[54] Otelia was a pioneer in hospital work at this Covenant station, and the first superintendent of nurses at the Kingmen hospital.[55] In May, 1925 she returned home to enroll in a four-month course in theoretic and practical obstetric training at Chicago Lying-In Hospital and Dispensary, receiving a diploma in August, 1926. She could not return to China in 1927 because of conditions there, so from 1927 to 1930 she took a position at the University of Oregon and did public pealth work. Other trained nurses from America came out to help with the medical ministry.[56]

Kingchow and Shasi

In the southern part of the Covenant field, Ida Oström—after 1924 Mrs. Reuben Johnson—arrived in 1921 to do nursing at Kingchow, where she opened a dispensary and worked as school nurse at the theological seminary and middle school.[57] Her husband, Reuben Johnson, was an accountant and bookkeeper, serving also as treasurer for the Covenant China Mission. The American Mission Covenant had no work in Shasi until 1923, when they united with the Swedish Mission Covenant in doing medical work. From 1923 to 1927 Shasi had two Chinese doctors and a foreign nurse.[58]

Evacuation (1926–27)

In 1924–26 the Covenant field was full of banditry and civil war, and unsettled conditions continued until 1932. Matson reported that for months it was not practical to travel through the Siangfan district.[59] Otelia Hendrickson

54. Judith M. Peterson, "Bethesda Training School for Nurses," 135.

55. Ibid., 137.

56. Karen Karlstedt followed Otelia in 1921, doing dispensary work in the Kingmen district. Esther Hanson—after 1923 Esther Carlson—came to Kingmen in 1922 to do nursing and work with women. Judith Peterson, after nurses training and filling various posts in the States, came to China in 1924 and spent her first years in Kingmen.

57. Judith M. Peterson, "Bethesda Training School for Nurses," 137. Ida Oström studied at North Park College and then entered nurses training at Swedish Covenant Hospital, from which she graduated in 1921.

58. John Peterson, "Kingchow and Shasi," 56.

59. P. Matson, "The Siang Fan District," 28.

wrote in a letter that in the winter of 1924 hordes of bandits were roaming the country, and just north of Siangyang a couple of Norwegian missionaries had been shot. One died at Bethesda Hospital. For a couple days 700 bandits were in and around Kingmen. By the summer things had quieted down.[60] Then came the general evacuation in 1926–27.

RETURN TO THE FIELD (1927–1929)

Siangfan

During this unsettled time some missionaries returned after evacuation, and others came for the first time.[61]

Kingmen

Hilda Rodberg evacuated in 1927, but returned to Kingmen in 1929. In May, 1929 however, she became seriously ill and had to seek medical help in Hankow.[62] Hilda died on February 11, 1931, and was buried in Hankow. Her contribution over a period of nearly 30 years to the Covenant missionary enterprise in China was considerable. Augusta Nelson came to Kingmen with the Oscar Andersons on January 9, 1929.[63] She had been superintendent of nurses at the Bethesda Hospital in Siangyang, and now with Dr. Yao set about to revive the medical work in Kingmen.

Kingchow

Not until 1928 was permission given to Dr. Edmund Li to run a private hospital in rented buildings. In 1932 property was sold to Dr. Li where he

---

60. Otelia Hendrickson Correspondence, letter from Kuling dated August 20, 1924.

61. Ellen Ackerson left Siangyang with the Matsons in 1927, but in 1928 returned as instructor and superintendent of nurses at Bethesda Hospital. Judith Peterson evacuated in 1927, but in September, 1928 returned to Siangyang. In 1929 Dora Lindahl—after 1931 Mrs. Joel Nordlund—arrived to do nursing and women's work at Siangyang and Fancheng, but unfortunately she became sick and died at Kuling on July 17, 1933, leaving behind a baby boy of 2 months.

62. C. O. Anderson and R. M. Anderson, *Two Lives of Faith*, 41, 48.

63. Ibid., 40.

began operating his hospital,[64] becoming the doctor in charge.[65] Over the years this hospital worked closely with both missions, and nurses from both missions were on staff.

Edmund Li, together with two brothers and a sister, were from Wuchang where they had grown up in a family converted to Christianity. All attended mission schools of the Swedish Mission Covenant, after which they studied at institutions of higher learning. By 1927 Dr. Li had been doctoring and running the hospital for 11 years; Abel Li was superintendent of the boys' school in Kingmen; and the third son was General Secretary of the Home Mission Board of the Chinese Church. Elizabeth Li had also completed medical studies and was ready now to begin work as a physician at the hospital.[66] The hospital thereafter became known as the hospital of Dr. Edmund and Dr. Elizabeth Li, who were committed to run it on Christian principles. Otelia Hendrickson, who in her first term did medical work with Hilda Rodberg at the Kingmen dispensary,[67] returned now for a second term to work at the Li Hospital, becoming also an instructor of nurses.

CIVIL WAR AND JAPANESE OCCUPATION (1930–1940)

Siangfan

In 1930 Dr. Barton and Muriel Nelson arrived in China, and after a year of language study had moved to Siangyang when Dr. Mildred Nordlund arrived. In 1931 the two doctors began working together at Bethesda Hospital, giving the medical mission a new lease on life and development.[68] During the 1926 and 1927 evacuation Chinese physicians Dr. Ho and Dr. Sung carried on the work, performing their tasks with admirable faithfullness.[69]

Dr. Barton Nelson received his education at the University of Minnesota (B.S. 1927; B.M. 1929; M.D. 1930). Barton became superintendent of the men's hospital (1931–1935). Muriel, a trained nurse,[70] worked with him at Bethesda, but when her health failed, the two went home on furlough in 1935. Muriel's health improved, and they returned to China in the fall of

---

64. Dahlstrom, "The Covenant Missionary Society in China," 154–55.

65. Pronounced and sometimes spelled "Lee."

66. L. J. Larson, "Educational Work in China," 42.

67. J. S. Johnson, "The Kingmen District," 47.

68. P. Matson, *Our China Mission,* 114.

69. Judith M. Peterson, "Bethesda Training School for Nurses," 138.

70. Muriel Nelson graduated from the Nursing School of the University of Minnesota.

1939, working again at Bethesda Hospital, but they stayed only one year, as Muriel again became ill, and she and Barton had to go home.[71]

Dr. Mildred Nordlund, daughter of Victor and Maria Nordlund, received her early education in China, but then went back to the United States for further study. She graduated from North Park College (1922), and then went on to obtain medical training at Rush Medical School (M.D. 1929). Mildred served in China from 1931 to 1936, and from 1937 to 1945, working at Bethesda Hospital where she was resident doctor and then superintendent of the women's hospital.[72]

Nurses in Training at Bethesda Hospital

The women's department of the hospital developed alongside the men's department. Dr. Nordlund was the first woman doctor to serve in the Siangfan district.[73] She told how the Chinese women were more superstitious than the Chinese men. For example, they believed ill luck would befall a home if the woman crossed the threshold within a month after the delivery of her baby, and no amount of persuasion could get her to leave the house, even if the child became sick and needed to go to the hospital.[74] During the Sino-Japanese war, which came to Central China in 1937 and lasted until 1945, Mildred rendered valuable service to the armed forces and civilian population.

71. C. O. Anderson and R. M. Anderson, *Two Lives of Faith*, 120.

72. P. Matson, *Our China Mission*, 119. On the women's department of Bethesda Hospital, see Mildred Nordlund, "Medical Work among Women."

73. C. B. Nelson, "Heal the Sick," 125.

74. Nordlund, "Medical Work among Women," 128–132.

Ragnhild Matson, daughter of Peter and Christine Matson, returned as a trained nurse[75] to Bethesda Hospital in 1931, where she became involved in the training of nurses (1931–1937). In 1934 Judith Peterson was superintendent and instructor of nurses at Bethesda Hospital.[76] Carl and Lillian Branstrom arrived in Fancheng in 1935, but stayed only one year before relocating to Kingmen (1936).

By 1937 the Japanese were at the border of the Siangfan district, and the bombing of Fancheng and Siangyang began on Christmas Day, 1937. Fancheng had an airfield near the mission station,[77] and Chinese military headquarters were located in Siangyang.[78] Mercifully, the Siangyang mission station and Bethesda Hospital were spared destruction in the attack, but some 200 people were killed and many of the wounded were brought to Bethesda Hospital for treatment. Staff at the hospital sometimes worked until after midnight.[79] After the Japanese bombing of Icheng in 1937, Paul and Elin Johnson came to Siangyang, but Elin took sick in the summer of 1940, and the two had to go home. Because of failing health Ellen Ackerson also had to return to the States in 1940, and the next year retired from active missionary service. But in 1940–41 Otelia Hendrickson was back to render service at Bethesda Hospital.

The bombing in Siangfan continued unabated in 1938–39. In March, 1939 Bethesda Hospital was hit,[80] and this time it appeared to be deliberate. Four large bombs destroyed the southwest corner of the hospital, and there was damage to windows and doors in the entire building. No one inside the hospital was hurt. Dr. Barton Nelson's residence, some 200 feet from the hospital, was also partly demolished.[81]

75. Ragnhild Matson got nurses training at Swedish Covenant Hospital, Chicago, from which she graduated in 1927.

76. P. Matson, *Our China Mission*, 119. Judith returned to the States in 1940, and during the war years worked for the American Red Cross in Rockford, training nurses' aides.

77. E. C. Matson, "Life under the Shadows of Death," 21.

78. M. Nordlund, "Flash Pictures of War Time China," 89.

79. Letter from Peter Matson to the American Counsul General in Hankow, dated Nov 9, 1938.

80. E. C. Matson, "Life under the Shadows of Death," 26–27.

81. Letter from Peter Matson to the American Embassy in Chungking, dated March 21, 1939; cf. P. Matson, "Life under the Shadows of Death," 27. For a picture of Dr. Barton Nelson's house after the bombing, see Muriel Nelson, "The Missionaries' Home," 151.

Bethesda Hospital after Japanese Bombing in March, 1939

Dr. Barton Nelson's House after Japanese Bombing in March, 1939

When Oscar Anderson arrived in Siangyang on April 14, 1939, Japanese troops were still east of the Han,[82] but could be expected to cross the river at any time. Judith Peterson was at Bethesda Hospital when Oscar arrived, but by May, 1940 was on her way home via Hong Kong. In

82. C. O. Anderson and R. M. Anderson, *Two Lives of Faith*, 113.

May bombs were again falling on Fancheng and Siangyang, and Bethesda Hospital was taking in the wounded. The next month the Japanese would be crossing the Han and establishing themselves at strategic points west of the river, effectively cutting the Covenant field in half. The Japanese would then occupy Kingmen and Kingchow, while Fancheng, Siangyang, Nanchang, and Icheng would remain under Chinese control, in what came to be called "Free China." During this time mission property at Icheng and Kingmen were nearly "wiped out of existence." At the outstations it was much the same.[83]

On June 1, 1940 the Japanese crossed the Han and entered Siangyang unopposed. The missionaries had put a poster on the front gate of the mission compound saying it was American property and should be respected. An American flag had also been painted outside the gate. As a result the mission property was not destroyed, although the Japanese went on to burn the rest of the city. Some mission buildings up against other burning buildings caught fire, but the missionaries were able to extinguish the flames.

Nanchang

During these years Elsa Hammerlind worked at Nanchang (1933–1945). In her last term she was in charge of the Nanchang dispensary.[84] After the Japanese bombings of 1939 Elsa and a Chinese nurse were particularly helpful to many refugees who came to Nanchang from other districts, also from a military training camp located within the city.[85] During the same period Augusta Nelson was doing dispensary work at Nanchang, Kingmen, and Kingchow (1931–1946).

Kingmen

On April 16, 1931 big trouble came to Kingmen. General Ho Lung and his Third Red Army made a surprise attack on the city, and once inside the soldiers hastened to the mission station to seek out the missionaries, who for a time hid in an attic of the hospital. Later they came out when their continued absence threated the city as a whole. The Reds helped themselves to medicine and medical instruments, the latter they eventually discarded

83. Jacobson, "Present Conditions on Our Field in China," 77.

84. C. B. Nelson, "Our Medical Missionary Work in China," 69.

85. E. C. Matson, "Life under the Shadows of Death," 28; Yuen, "Nanchang Items," 170–71.

because they were of no use to them. They also destroyed the medical facilities, which had just been rebuilt and restored to their former efficiency after a destruction of hospital and medical equipment in 1927.[86]

When leaving the Reds had with them Oscar Anderson, Augusta Nelson, Esther Nordlund, the only foreign missionaries there at the time (Ruth Anderson was in Shanghai with their four children), and Dr. David Yao. They also took a hospital cook to be of service to Dr. Yao, some high school students, and a few other Chinese. When ransacking the home of Augusta Nelson the Reds found the medal of merit she had received from the Chinese Red Cross, and were impressed enough to speak to her about it.[87] But they were not impressed enough to keep from kidnapping her along with the other missionaries.

The Reds wanted ransom for their captives, at first asking $40,000. Later they said they simply wanted guns and ammunition, and a wireless outfit. If these could not be procured, the ransom demand would be upped to $300,000. Should this amount not be forthcoming, Oscar would be shot. The amount was later reduced to $100,000, and finally the Reds said that what they really wanted was medical supplies—in large quantity.[88] General Ho Lung later confided to Oscar in one of their conversations that he did not like resorting to methods they were using, but they were at their wits' end since they needed medicine for their many sick and wounded. The missionaries could therefore "assist them a little." Ho Lung also said he was afraid of Chinese medicine and believed only in foreign medicine, but they were unable to secure the foreign medicine themselves.[89]

Augusta Nelson and Esther Nordlund were released after five days. It was concluded that they would not be able to keep up with the march, and Oscar convinced the Reds that they would get the same ransom for just him as for the three. Later Dr. Yao was also released at Maliangping.[90] He had become so sick that the Reds realized he could no longer be of use to them. They had wanted him to become their army doctor. No ransom was paid; instead, the Reds gave Dr. Yao ten dollars for traveling expenses. Dr. Yao's cook was also released. All reached Kingmen safely.

86. J. S. Johnson, "The Kingmen District," 51.

87. C. O. Anderson and R. M. Anderson, *Two Lives of Faith*, 171.

88. Olsson, *By One Spirit*, 453.

89. C. O. Anderson and R. M. Anderson, *Two Lives of Faith*, 70.

90. Ibid., 63.

Sixty-seven cases of medical supplies, valued at $2000, secured Anderson's release.[91] General Ho Lung had given Oscar a list of what he wanted,[92] which Augusta Nelson carried to Kingmen after her release.[93] The Covenant had a policy of not paying ransom, but made an exception in this case because the ransom would be medicine and could be considered a humanitarian gesture.[94] Peter Matson spent two months in Hankow arranging for the purchase and shipment of medicine.[95] In Hankow was a wholesale drug company that supplied medicine to Bethesda Hospital. A list was sent to the drug company asking it to pack the medicine in boxes, about thirty or thirty-five pounds in each box, and do it as quickly as possible. The medicine would go by steamer to Shasi, and then northward overland to where the Reds were located.

In due time the 67 boxes arrived at Shasi,[96] where the shipment was met by Isaac Jacobson. Custom officials at Shasi at first demanded high duty, but with the help of Isaac and the Swedish Vice Consul, the shipment was allowed to pass duty free. Now the question was how to get the medicine to the Reds. Bandits were still hiding in the mountains, with the Reds pursuing them. The Red Army at the time was in the mountains of northwest Hupeh, close to the border of Shensi Province. Matson would accompany the shipment.

From Shasi the medicine was shipped by truck to Kingmen, which took one day. Pastor Tang of Kingchow went along as an escort. Because of heavy rains the roads were bad and several times the truck had to be unloaded. At Kingmen the medicine was put on another truck to go to Siangyang, this time being escorted by Kingmen pastor, Mr. Wu. But the transit to Siangyang posed difficulties, and Matson had to go back to Hankow to get a pass from military authorities in the province. He was not well, being sick already when he left Hankow. He could hardly walk, and needed help

91. Matson in a letter from Hankow, dated June 29, 1931, says it required a caravan of some 30 men to carry the 67 large boxes.

92. C. O. Anderson and R. M. Anderson, *Two Lives of Faith*, 169.

93. P. Matson, *Our China Mission*, 103.

94. In the Covenant Yearbook for 1930–31 the following is contained in the Foreign Mission Board Report: "Recommended that the ransom for missionary Oscar Anderson in China, which has been reported by Rev. P. Matson, that they have prepared and are ready to pay (about two thousand dollars worth of medicine) be sanctioned by the conference"; cf. *Svenska Ev. Missionsförbundets I Amerika Årsberättelse för Verksamhetsåret 1930–1931, till årsmötet i Chicago, Ill. Den 17–21 Juni 1931* (Chicago: Missionsförbundets Expedition, 1931), 125.

95. Letter from Matson in Hankow, dated June 29, 1931.

96. C. O. Anderson and R. M. Anderson, *Two Lives of Faith*, 169.

getting dressed.[97] With the pass the medicine was able to proceed, but not altogether smoothly. At one point it became necessary to cross a river on a small ferry, and the driver thought he could make it without unloading. But as soon as the truck got on the ferry it sank. Some boxes were soaked clear through. At Siangyang the shipment was taken across the Han to Fancheng, where it was again loaded on a truck to be taken to Laohokow. Now on the last 125 miles of a 700-mile journey it had to be transported over mountainous road. At Laohokow Matson engaged 20 coolies to carry the boxes to Shihuakai, where there was a Norwegian mission station, though now looted and deserted. This was as far as Matson and his companion could go. They left the shipment in the hands of trusted Chinese friends, one of whom was Chang Yuen Fu from Siangyang. With the crates went letters to Anderson and General Ho Lung. Chinese coolies, each of whom balanced the boxes on a shoulder pole, carried the medicine the rest of the way.

Contact was made with the communists in Laohokow, some 50 miles northwest of Siangyang. When the medicines finally arrived at his camp, General Ho Lung came to inspect them, and the next day Oscar was released. Oscar was given twenty dollars for traveling expenses, and another four dollars came from Dr. Chang, the Red army doctor with whom Oscar had become friendly. The coolies who carried the boxes each received five dollars in tips, and Chang Yuen Fu, who accompanied the shipment, got ten dollars. They had walked two weeks with the medicine, avoiding dangers all along the way. Oscar entered the Covenant field safely at Fancheng on July 4, 1931, his captivity having lasted approximately 75 days.[98]

After the kidnapping, the Kingmen station remained vacant, having no missionaries until 1935. Work was carried on by the Chinese, for whom Joel Johnson expressed great appreciation. He said without them "we could never have accomplished what has already been achieved. We need them as well as they need us."[99] Carl and Lillian Branstrom came to Kingmen in 1936, serving there until going home on furlough in 1939.

---

97. Note at the end of Peter Matson's letter from Hankow, dated June 29, 1931, probably written by his wife Edla.

98. For the dramatic story of the kidnapping and release of these three Covenant missionaries, see C. O. Anderson and R. M. Anderson, *Two Lives of Faith*, 52–58, 61–82; also P. Matson, *Our China Mission*, 101–10.

99. J. S. Johnson, "The Kingmen District," 52.

Oscar Anderson after Release by the Communists (1931)

Kingchow

After Augusta Nelson's release by the communists, she went to work at the dispensary in Kingchow. In 1934 Lillian Almquist—after 1935 Mrs. Carl Branstrom—joined Augusta, becoming the nurse in charge.[100] Kingchow had only a dispensary, with no facilities for hospital patients.[101] In 1936, after Lillian Branstrom was married and had moved to Fancheng, Augusta Nelson took charge of the dispensary.[102] Augusta was particularly helpful to

100. Lillian received nurses training at Lord Lester Hospital in Omaha, Nebraska, graduating in 1927. She then took a post-graduate course at Cook County Hospital, Chicago (1929).

101. C. B. Nelson, "Our Medical Missionary Work in China," 69.

102. John Peterson, "Kingchow and Shasi," 55; C. B. Nelson, "Our Medical Missionary Work in China," 69.

the hundreds of refugees that crowded into the seminary in the summer of 1938.[103]

CLOSING YEARS OF THE COVENANT HUPEH MISSION (1940-1948)

Siangfan

In December, 1941 the Chinese were in control of the northern part of the Covenant field, and work there was being carried on more or less normally.[104] The hospital was treating many different kinds of people: Japanese prisoners, Russian engineers and pilots, Chinese from Singapore, Hong Kong, and nearly every province in China. Bethesda continued its policy of accepting anyone needing help. On one occasion the hospital gave free care to a robber, who, when he was nearly well, was taken out and shot by the Chinese.[105]

Disease was rampant during the early 1940s. In the fall of 1943 there was an epidemic of malaria, and people died quickly. Medicine was insufficient. Much relief work was carried on in Siangyang.[106] In the winter of 1943 and spring of 1944 an epidemic of meningitis took many lives. Oscar Anderson contracted the disease while out on an evangelistic trip, and had to walk five miles back to Siangyang, barely making it. He was put to bed and given medicine, which checked the disease, but he could hardly speak. Happily, Oscar recovered.[107]

In the spring of 1944 rumors circulated of a new Japanese advance in the direction of Siangyang, and movements of Chinese troops were passing through the city. Otelia Hendrickson and two Chinese nurses evacuated. Hospital equipment was also moved as a precaution, but nothing came of the rumors, so in the fall the missionaries returned and resumed work.

In the fall of 1944 the missionaries decided to heed the advice of American authorities and evacuate Siangyang, since the Japanese were advancing toward Kweiyang in Kweichow Province. They delayed their departure until after New Year's Day. On January 3, 1945 everyone except Oscar Anderson left Siangyang: Mildred Nordlund, Otelia Hendrickson,

---

103. E. C. Matson, "Life under the Shadows of Death," 28.

104. Letter of Peter Matson to the First Covenant Church, St. Paul, Minnesota, dated December 23, 1941.

105. M. Nordlund, "Flash Pictures of War Time China," 92–93.

106. C. O. Anderson and R. M. Anderson, *Two Lives of Faith*, 128–29.

107. Ibid., 130.

Martha Anderson, and Paul Backlund. Esther Nordlund from Nanchang went along with them. The group traveled by boat to Laohokow, where they were evacuated on an American Air Force plane. Much hospital equipment accompanied them. Chinese doctors and nurses were left to keep the hospital going. Otelia Hendrickson and Dr. Mildred Nordlund went to Anking in Shensi Province.

On March 11, 1945 a report came that the Japanese were heading in the direction of Siangyang, and were not far away. The Chinese were pulling out, and they wanted Oscar to go with them in their truck. Oscar got up at midnight, but could hardly stand. At about 9 a.m., after receiving an injection and medicine, he said his goodbyes. His friend Dr. Ho said there was nothing they could do. Now was the time to leave. Oscar departed Siangyang on a Thursday morning. The following Saturday night the hospital staff and others pulled out. They barely escaped.[108] In March Otelia Hendrickson was also being advised by the American Consul to evacuate to the southwest, and by June she was in Chungking.

Oscar heard later that when the Japanese approached Siangyang the Chinese fled west into the country. Hospital staff journeyed even further to Anking, where Dr. Mildred Nordlund had gone.[109] They just made it before the Japanese cut off a way of escape. When the Japanese came to the mission station they took possession of the buildings, then looted and ruined them.

But the Japanese were not long in Siangyang, and when the war between Japan and America was over, missionaries were able to return. Paul Johnson had been in the United States receiving medical training, and in 1945, after doing medical work briefly in Chengtu in Szechuan Province, he returned to Bethesda Hospital as a doctor.[110] The next year Elin joined him. But in 1947 Elin was again ill, and the two had to go home. In 1946 Judith Peterson was back in Siangyang,[111] and in 1947 was Director of Nursing at Bethesda Hospital. Ruth Edlund, a trained nurse,[112] came to the field in 1946 to serve on the staff of Bethesda Hospital. Mildred Nordlund went home in 1947 due to ill health, and August Nelson also returned to the USA to retire.

Dr. Alik Berg and Dr. Signe Berg joined the Covenant mission at this time, Signe in 1945, and Alik in 1946, both coming from the Norwegian

108. Ibid., 136.

109. Ibid.,143.

110. Ibid., 140, 142.

111. Letter received by [Rev. Ralph Hanson], who was now Covenant Secretary of Foreign Missions, from Judith Peterson, dated July 5, 1946.

112. Ruth Edlund got nurses training at Swedish Covenant Hospital, receiving her R.N. in 1935. After getting a B.S. from Loyola University, Chicago in 1944, she went on to complete a course in public health nursing at Loyola.

Lutheran Mission in Laohokow. The Covenant Annual Meeting of 1946 had called the two doctors to be missionaries for one term. Alik had gone out as a medical missionary to China in 1939 under the auspices of the Norwegian Lutheran Mission, where he served on the staff of Froeyland Memorial Hospital in Laohokow. In 1940–41 he was acting superintendent of Bethesda Hospital for four months. After returning to China in 1947, now under the Covenant Board, Alik became head physician and director of the Bethesda Hospital.[113] When Ann Kulberg visited Siangyang in November, 1947 the hospital was full, for people were coming every day asking and even begging for a bed. Bethesda Hospital was reputed to be one of the best mission hospitals in China.[114]

Alik Berg studied medicine at the University of Dorpat in Estonia (1922–23); at Göttingen University in Germany (1923–1924); and at Helsingfors (Helsinki), Finland (1926–1930). He also took postgraduate work at several hospitals in Finland. A learned man, having published works on ectropic pregnancies and the Friedman pregnancy test, Alik was able to speak eight languages, including Chinese.

Dr. Signe Berg, a member of the Mission Covenant Church of Finland, accompanied her husband to China in 1939, having also gone out under the auspices of the Norwegian Lutheran Mission and serving at the Froeyland Memorial Hospital in Laohokow (1940–45). She took her first medical degree at the University of Helsingfors (Helsinki) in 1931, and a second degree at the same university in 1937. Signe joined the staff of Bethesda Hospital in 1945, serving there until 1947. For a time she was acting superintendent of the hospital.

Nanchang

In late 1940 the Branstroms arrived in Nanchang, but had to flee the Japanese in the mid-1940s and go to Szechuan. In February, 1945 Elsa Hammerlind reluctantly agreed to leave Nanchang, taking with her Minglan, the Chinese girl whom she had adopted. In August, 1945 she was working for the American Red Cross at Kunming in southwest China.[115] When she went home on furlough for a year, she left Minglan at an orphanage in Kunming.

---

113. *Our Covenant* 23 (1948) 156.

114. Carlson, "Mission to China," letter of December 9, 1947, from Huachung University.

115. C. O. Anderson and R. M. Anderson, *Two Lives of Faith*, 144.

Kingchow

In 1940, when other missionaries were forced to leave Kingchow, Augusta was allowed to stay because she was a Swedish subject, but the Japanese kept a close watch on her.[116] It was said that due to her tact and firmness mission property at Kingchow was kept from being completely destroyed.

On her first trip through the Covenant field in November, 1947, Ann Kulberg visited Kingchow and stayed with Otelia Hendrickson, who was there. In the mission compound she reported seeing the dispensary that was still there.[117]

On January 8, 1948 three Covenant missionaries were murdered on the road from Siangyang to Kingchow. They were going to Kingchow to attend a conference. The tragedy occurred about 30 miles north of Kingmen, in a sparsely settled area where bandits were known to operate. The three missionaries were Dr. Alik Berg, Martha Anderson, and Esther Nordlund. Otelia Hendrickson, who returned to Kingchow in May, 1947, was there when the bodies arrived and helped prepare them for burial. Carl and Lillian Branstrom had also come to Kingchow in 1947, and they, too, helped along with others in the burial preparation. The bodies of the missionaries were brought to Hankow, where they were buried in an international cemetery.

Shanghai

Ragnhild Matson returned from furlough in 1940 to find Shanghai under Japanese occupation. She therefore had to remain in the city where she did nursing among refugees, some of whom were Jewish. After war broke out between America and Japan in 1941, Ragnhild was put into a concentration camp. She survived, but suffered malnutrition and saw her weight plummet from 140 to 100 pounds. Ragnhild was repatriated on the *Gripsholm*, which arrived in New York in December, 1943.

EVACUATION, RELOCATION, AND LEAVING THE CHINA MAINLAND (1948–1949)

In early 1948 the communists were rapidly advancing, said to be invading the Covenant field "like grasshoppers."[118] Missionaries were being driven

116. Jacobson, "Present Conditions on Our Field in China," 81.

117. Letter from Ann Kulberg Carlson dated November 7, 1947.

118. A. L. Dwight, "China Missions Suffer."

from their stations. Before the murder of their three comrades, Covenant missionaries had resolved to stay where they were until the communists arrived, regardless of the consequences. After the tragedy, however, the American Consul ordered them to evacuate, which they did. The Edward Nelsons, Judith Peterson, and Ruth Edlund left on the Lutheran Mission plane *St. Paul* from Laohokow. The Carl Branstroms, Otelia Hendrickson, and other missionaries reached Hankow safely after a perilous journey by truck and boat.

Reports in April, 1948 indicated that Siangyang, Fancheng, Nanchang, and Kingmen were still held by Nationalist forces, but Icheng had fallen, and communists were roaming the countryside at will, robbing, looting, and killing.[119] In June Bethesda Hospital was in the process of being closed. Chinese soldiers were living in the mission compound and it was impossible to continue work. The missionaries had all left.[120]

A letter received by Oscar Anderson and Mildred Nordlund from Rev. Chin Tze-show, one of the Chinese pastors,[121] reported what happened when the Red Army came to Fancheng and Siangyang.[122] On July 4, 1948 the soldiers entered Fancheng, and on the 5th attacked the surrounding territory of Siangyang. Fighting continued until July 15, when Siangyang fell and the communists entered through the West Gate. The Chinese General commanding the Nationalist troops committed suicide.

The Covenant mission station and hospital were right in the middle of the fighting. The hospital, houses, school, and church were shelled, but not seriously damaged. On August 4 Siangyang was retaken by Nationalist troops, and roads were again open for traffic. Plans were made to reopen the schools, but it was uncertain whether an opening of the hospital could be managed. The entire staff had scattered; only Dr. Ho remained. Five of the Chinese nurses had been carried off by the communists. The Chinese pastor concluded that the destruction of Mission, for all practical purposes, was complete: the hospital superintendent had been killed; buildings were partially destroyed; equipment and medicine had been taken away; and all doctors and nurses were gone. The communists eventually returned to occupy Fancheng and Siangyang, effectively ending the Covenant Mission in the two cities where it had begun.

119. Ibid.

120. Letter from Ann Kulberg Carlson in her "Mission to China," dated June 20, 1948.

121. Dated August 11, 1948.

122. Chin, "Siangyang Station Destroyed."

After Dr. Signe Berg's departure for Finland and Dr. Alik Berg's death, the Covenant had no doctors in China, although Signe Berg later returned to Kweiting in October, 1948.[123] Nurses Elsa Hammerlind, Otelia Hendrickson, and Lillian Branstrom went first to Changsha, then to cities in southwest China. Judith Peterson remained in Hankow to keep contact with medical people in Siangyang, but later accompanied Ruth Edlund to Kweiting in southwest China.

Changsha

In 1948 Otelia Hendrickson and Elsa Hammerlind took up work at a Changsha orphanage of 150 boys and girls.[124] Elsa wanted to return to Kingchow with Joel Johnson in November, but the two could not get visas. Visas finally came, and they did return. Joel and Elsa remained in Kingchow until the communists took control in February, 1949, when they were forced to leave. Elsa Hammerlind and Joel Johnson were the last Covenant missionaries resident in the Hupeh field. They evacuated to Chungking, after which Elsa went to Kweiyang, and Joel went home.[125]

Chungking

After the 1948 summer conference at Kuling, Otelia Hendrickson was ready to go to Chungking where she would live with the Ed Nelsons. She arrived there in mid-November,[126] and after Christmas began conducting classes for nurses besides teaching and helping in the health program of a war orphan Bible school.[127] Otelia earlier lived in Chungking, when in 1945 the city was being bombed every day by the Japanese.[128]

Kweiting and Kweiyang

At the 1948 summer conference in Kuling it was decided that nurses Lillian Branstrom, Judith Peterson, and Ruth Edlund would transfer to Kweichow

123. Berg, "And God Answered Prayer."

124. A. L. Dwight, "Where Is the Dispersion?"; letter from Ann Kulberg Carlson dated May 23, 1948.

125. A. L. Dwight, "Gleanings from China," (March 18, 1949).

126. E. G. Nelson, *China in Your Blood*, 126.

127. Ralph Hanson, *The Covenant Weekly* (March 18, 1949) 3.

128. E. G. Nelson, *China in Your Blood*, 126.

Province. By early 1949 all were in Kweiting, which had been chosen as the new center for medical work because Kweiyang, the capital of the province, had several good hospitals. Kweiting had none. When Dr. Signe Berg arrived in Kweiting, however, she found the people suspicious and wanting a hospital, but not the gospel. The city was in the grip of the tobacco business.[129]

Judith Peterson said the missionaries were nevertheless ready to open "Bethesda Hospital of the Southwest." In December a building became available when its owner went bankrupt, was forced to give up his tobacco business, and agreed to rent his building to the missionaries for their hospital.[130] This gave them room for a dispensary, wards for 15 patients, operating rooms, storerooms, and nurses' living quarters.[131] After two months the hospital recorded 1633 visits and 22 obstetrical deliveries. Only 6 had been admitted as in-patients. Dr. Li from Shasi and three Chinese head nurses from Bethesda Hospital in Siangyang had joined the team at the hospital.[132]

Leaving the China Mainland

Then the communists came to southwest China, and evacuation became necessary. In May, 1949 Otelia left with the Nelsons on the *St. Paul*, and in September was on her way to Japan. In September the Branstroms, Elsa Hammerlind, and Ruth Edlund were in Hong Kong. A couple years later the Branstroms went home. In July, 1950 Elsa Hammerlind and Viola Larson had moved to Chuen Wan, a village outside of Hong Kong. Judith Peterson evacuated in October, 1949 and later went out as a Covenant missionary to Japan (1950–52), then to Formosa (Taiwan) to help Dr. Signe Berg and Elsa Hammerlind establish a medical clinic. Medical work in this short-lived Covenant field in southwest of China had thus ended.

129. Berg, "And God Answered Prayer," 5.

130. Ralph Hanson, *The Covenant Weekly* (March 18, 1949), 3.

131. Berg, "And God Answered Prayer," 5.

132. [Hedstrand], "Gist of China Conference Oral Reports."

4

Educational Work

BEGINNING OF THE COVENANT HUPEH MISSION (1892–1900)

Siangfan

WHEN PETER MATSON BEGAN the Covenant China mission a decision was made at the very outset to open schools for Chinese boys and girls. In May, 1893 Peter married Christine Svensson from the Swedish Covenant Mission in Wuchang, and Christine, a teacher who had been trained in Sweden,[1] quickly saw the need for a girls' school, and lost no time in opening one in Fancheng. She was helped in this school by Alma Carlson. Thus the beginning of schools for boys and girls in Fancheng. In 1895 two schools had 40 pupils.[2] The Lutheran Mission, too, opened a boys' school and girls' school in Fancheng in June, 1894, and by January, 1895 had another boys' school in Fancheng.[3] When the Matsons returned from furlough in 1896, Christine was happy to find her girls' school growing.[4]

A few years later a boys' school was opened across the river in Siangyang, then another outside the South Gate of Siangyang, and then a third in

---

1. Christine was trained as a teacher at the Normal School in Karlstad, after which she became a school teacher at Stora Kil, a position she held for eight years, until 1890; cf. P. Matson, *Sowing in Tears, Reaping in Joy*, 8.

2. L. J. Larson, "Educational Work in China," 44.

3. Syrdal, "American Lutheran Mission Work in China," 37.

4. P. Matson, *Sowing in Tears, Reaping in Joy*, 30.

a village eight miles out in the country.[5] In Siangyang a house was purchased and the front apartment used as a street chapel where Matson preached several times a week. In the rear of the house Matson opened up his school. The Lutherans made a similar arrangement in the house they purchased in Fancheng.[6] Confucian scholars were brought in as teachers, some of whom later converted to Christianity and became successful preachers of the Gospel.[7]

Country schools met in the homes of Christians. To these Matson went by horseback every week or every other week. He would preach and hear the children recite their lessons. One of the earliest believers in Fancheng was a blind fellow with a very good singing voice, who would go out to the country places and teach the children to sing.[8]

In early 1900 a secondary school was opened in Siangyang. A few high school subjects were added to the curriculum making it a middle (high) school. The first teacher was a graduate of Tengchow College, said by Matson to have been excellent.[9] Because of political unrest, however, this more advanced school got off to a slow start, and it had to be closed when the missionaries evacuated during the Boxer Rebellion. But in the spring of 1902 it reopened.[10]

MISSION WORK AFTER THE BOXER REBELLION (1901–1911)

Siangfan

The secondary school at Siangyang developed into the very successful Siangyang Academy under the direction of Carl J. Nelson, the first full-time Covenant educational missionary in China. Carl and his wife Emma arrived in Shanghai on October 18, 1906 with Peter and Christine Matson.[11] A graduate of Luther Academy in Wahoo, Nebraska (1895), and Carlton College in Northfield, Minnesota (B.A. 1904), Nelson had served briefly as a Covenant pastor before going with his wife to China. Carl had a brilliant,

5. P. Matson, "The Siang Fan District," 23; Wang, "Labors and Results," 167.

6. Syrdal, "American Lutheran Mission Work in China," 37, 108, says the arrangement of a chapel and a school in the same building was made also at the outstations.

7. P. Matson, *Our China Mission*, 48, 51.

8. Ibid, 51–52.

9. Ibid., 52.

10. Ibid., 60.

11. *The Chinese Recorder* 37 (1906) 652.

well-trained mind, coupled with a childlike faith in God. He gave excellent leadership to the Academy until 1911, when he moved to Kingchow to take over the schoolwork there. Emma taught music and singing at Siangyang and Kingchow, contributing significantly to singing in the Chinese church.

One of the fruits of the Matson's school at Siangyang was a young lad by the name of Wang Hwai-chen. Wang recalled his mother taking him to church services in 1900, and then how over the next 15 years he attended schools of the Covenant mission.[12] Wang studied at Siangyang Academy and the Kingchow Theological Seminary, graduating from the latter with high honors. In a personal testimony he said how mission schools contributed in no small way to spreading the Gospel.[13]

Another personal testimony about the influence of Covenant mission schools in his life came from Chin Tze-show, who at 12 entered a school at Siangyang before the First Revolution (1911).[14] He later married in 1916, and then returned to school for another eight years. After graduation Chin began teaching at Siangyang, but had lingering inner turmoil. Not until after the Icheng revival of 1933 did he find real peace.

China had a long history that honored learning. Leonard Larson says:

> For millenniums learning has occupied the pedestal of honor in China, the scholar being placed at the head of the five classes— agriculturalists, artisans, merchants, and soldiers following in the order named. Fortunate indeed was the man who attained to the degree of "Hsiu-tsai," or B. A., and if his learning and persistence won a still higher degree for him, he was considered highly favored by the gods and was feted and honored by the whole district from which he came.[15]

Larson continues:

> No sacrifice was considered too great if it resulted in success, and hope never died in the hearts of those who studied and prepared for the annual examinations. It is related that at the examination halls of Nanking at one examination there were present five men over eighty years and one over ninety, who had come hoping to secure the treasured degree. Year after year they had tried, always hoping the next time success would await them.[16]

12. Wang, "Labors and Results," 166.

13. Ibid., 166–68.

14. Chin, "A Personal Testimony."

15. L. J. Larson, "Educational Work in China," 38; see also Jacobson, "Christian School Work," 63.

16. L. J. Larson, "Educational Work in China," 38–39.

Every family secretly or openly hoped that one of its sons—not daughters, but sons—might become a scholar, and thus bring honor to the clan.

> Often the old father and mother would endure the greatest of hardships and deprive themselves of all the joys of life in order to enable one of the sons to continue his studies. The other children in the family, too, often would help to bring their brother to the coveted goal. It was into such an atmosphere the missionaries were thrown and it is small wonder they found educational work one of the ready avenues of approach to the confidence and good will of the people.[17]

One should add "a ready avenue also to gain a hearing for the Christian gospel."

Learning was particularly honored in Siangyang. Dr. K. M. Nelson writes:

> [Siangyang] was a seat of learning. It was in these famous halls of classical learning that thousands of scholars passed many agonizing hours in writing their thesis or poem on any subject assigned in order to pass the examination which eventually might bring them a civil service position.[18] This system was in vogue for a thousand years, but was abandoned in 1900. . . . After the reorganization of the school system, Siangyang still retained its scholastic standing, and at present several government high schools and normal training schools are located here.[19]

The old educational system was dealt a decisive blow in 1905 when, by imperial edict, competitive examinations were abolished. Isaac Jacobson says:

> The aim of education and training, according to this system, was chiefly to fit the person for official position in a patriarchal social order, making him a leader with power and wisdom to rule, and affording special facility for material gain. Such an aim obviously excluded the female sex from all privileges of government education and training.[20]

Covenant mission schools quite purposely emphasized elementary, secondary, and higher education as being important in the work of evangelization. The aim was to establish an indigenous church with qualified

17. Ibid., 39.

18. For a picture of the examination place seating 2400 persons on benches, see *Missionären* (April 1, 1903), 1.

19. K. M. Nelson, "Glimpses from Our Medical Work in Siangyang," 25.

20. Jacobson, "Christian School Work," 64.

Chinese leaders in all aspects of the work. In Jacobson's view these branches of educational work were not simply supplemental, but indispensible.[21] Covenant mission schools also emphasized social reform, which included the advancement and education of girls. Jacobson said:

> Mission schools have been a tremendous force against social evils and have blazed the trail for reforms of social conditions. Their crusade against foot binding and their emphasis upon the education of girls have resulted in the creation of a new status for women, with greater opportunities and equality with men.[22]

Education of girls had previously been entirely neglected in China. In lower grades of the mission schools there was usually a large enrollment of girls, but only a few continued on to middle school since marriage was considered more important than further study. In the Covenant field Christine Matson was the pioneer of education for girls in Fancheng and Siangyang.

Initially each Covenant head station followed more or less its own program. As outstations were developed, schools were opened there and most students were given a nominal subsidy. In time the country schools served as feeders to the more advanced schools at the head stations where the missionaries were able to devote more time to teaching and supervision. Very few country schools measured up to the primary school at the head station, except when it came to teaching Christian subjects. At the head stations work was carried on in separate schools for boys and girls, as dormitory and boarding arrangements had to be provided for pupils coming from some distance away. The work grew steadily, as pupils came in increasing numbers.[23]

Hilma Johnson arrived in 1902 and labored for four decades as a China educational missionary in Fancheng and Siangyang. Amelia Ackerson—after 1915 Mrs. Herman Conradson—was a teacher and principal of the girls' school in Siangyang after arriving in 1908. She remained in Siangyang until 1914, when she moved to Kingmen to take charge of the girls' school there.

Nanchang

The Covenant expanded its work into the Nanchang district in the winter of 1902–03. Isaac Jacobson built up the Nanchang station and opened up a number of outstations. In the spring of 1906 he came to supervise the

21. Ibid., 65.
22. Ibid., 68–69.
23. Ibid., 66.

construction of a missionary home, a church building, and a day school for boys, starting with one Chinese teacher.[24] Attendance grew to the point where larger quarters became necessary.[25] Isaac's wife Anna arrived a year later, and with a woman now at the station, a girls' school was opened. Isaac and Anna agreed that mission work should consist of both evangelism and education. Enrollment at the girls' school soon grew to 100.[26]

Because of success at the schools the people of Nanchang received the missionary not with suspicion and threats, but with a glad welcome. Leonard Larson said that often the villagers themselves would come to the missionaries asking if a school for their children could be opened. The people would promise to furnish the building and pay part of the salary of the teacher if the mission would take charge of the work and supervise it.[27]

A delegation was sent from the populous city of Wuanyen in the Nanchang district urgently requesting that missionary education be in that city. A day school was opened, and an elderly Mr. Chao was engaged as a teacher in the school. He later served as an evangelist in charge of work at the Nanchang station, and his son-in-law, Mr. Chin, became the schoolteacher.[28]

Icheng

Joel Johnson initiated Covenant work at Icheng in 1905, but when he moved to Kingmen in 1906, Icheng became an outstation under Siangyang. Nevertheless, a number of marketplaces in the district were opened as outstations. The area at the time was wide open to the gospel and teaching, with the people inviting missionaries to come, open schools, and preach the gospel. By 1910 the Covenant had a station at Icheng.

Kingmen

Jacobson and Joel Johnson opened a chapel in Kingmen in the spring of 1906, when property was rented.[29] Joel also opened 15 outstations in the district.[30] In these outstations villagers came asking that a chapel or Chris-

24. L. J. Larson, Educational Work in China," 43.

25. Ibid.

26. Jacobson, "The Nanchang District," 36.

27. L. J. Larson, "Educational Work in China," 43.

28. Jacobson, "The Nanchang District," 33–35.

29. J. S. Johnson, "The Kingmen District," 48.

30. P. Matson, Our China Mission, 62.

tian school be opened. At Kingmen evangelistic work and schoolwork began simultaneously, and Herman Conradson labored together with Joel in evangelism.[31] The first school was opened in a small shanty with Wang Mei-chen, a Chinese evangelist, as teacher. Pupils enrolled in increasing numbers, and soon larger quarters had to be secured.[32]

Kingchow

One of the first Christians in Kingchow was an old man by the name of Su, the grandfather of Miss Su, who later became a teacher and principal of the girls' school there. Kingchow, like Siangyang, had its own tradition as a seat of learning. Leonard Larson writes:

> In the city of Kingchow there still stands an old house in which lived a learned man who won distinction for his city by his success at the examination halls. Outside can still be seen the remains of a tablet which proclaimed to all the world that here lived the possessor of the coveted degree. Still today after hundreds of years the people of the city point out this spot with a great deal of pride.[33]

The American Mission Covenant began educational work in Kingchow in 1907, when it decided to join the Swedish Mission Covenant in establishing a theological seminary in the city. The decision to open a theological seminary was greatly aided by the visit in 1907 of Dr. P. P. Waldenström, well known Bible scholar and President of the Mission Covenant of Sweden.[34] A conference convened in Shasi where the Swedish Mission Covenant had its work, and members of the American Mission Covenant were invited to attend. At this conference the idea of establishing a seminary supported by both missions was discussed. Waldenström expressed much enthusiasm over the idea, providing a great boost to the project. The two missions decided that they would together build and operate a theological seminary at Kingchow, and that the respective parent bodies in Stockholm and Chicago would be asked to allocate the necessary funds for the institution. Property was picked out and later purchased at a reasonable price. Both parent bodies granted the request and appropriated the necessary funds. Joel Johnson of

31. Ibid., 78.

32. J. S. Johnson, "The Kingmen District," 49–50.

33. L. J. Larson, "Educational Work in China," 38.

34. P. Matson, *Our China Mission*, 68–69.

the American Mission and A. P. Tjellström of the Swedish Mission were in charge of erecting the seminary building.[35]

The seminary was dedicated in December, 1909 with nearly all missionaries of the two missions in attendance. Present also were Chinese co-workers, representatives from neighboring missions, and Chinese authorities. Matson recalled how when he first visited Kingchow in 1891 no foreigner was allowed in the city, and how he and CIM missionary Mr. McNair took their lives in their hands by venturing into the city for a single hour. Now, he said, at the dedication of the seminary,

> the Tartar general, in rank above the viceroy, came in person to offer his congratulations, and he honored the school with an inscription in huge golden characters expressing the sentiment that now China and the West were united in their efforts for the welfare of the people.[36]

It was a great crowd.[37] The first teachers at the seminary were S. M. Freden and Marcus Cheng.[38]

MISSION WORK AFTER THE FIRST REVOLUTION (1911–1921)

Siangfan

Mabel Olson came to China in 1913 to do evangelistic and educational work in Siangfan, later becoming principal of Concordia Middle School for Girls in Fancheng, which from 1916 was a united undertaking of the Mission Covenant and Hauge Synod Lutheran Mission.[39] Mabel was the Covenant missionary on staff, Olive Hodnefield the Lutheran missionary. The school developed from an earlier girls' school that had been opened by the Hauge Synod in 1903, which was upgraded to a boarding school with lower and higher primary divisions in 1908 to become the Hauge Girls' Grammar

---

35. John Peterson, "Kingchow Theological Seminary," 72.

36. P. Matson, *Our China Mission*, 69.

37. For a picture of the theological seminary and its dedication, with people standing in front of the new building, see *The Chinese Recorder* 41 (1910), front piece to the February issue, opposite p. 131; also P. Matson, *Our China Mission*, 72, and *Aurora* (1910) 59. Another picture of the seminary with a school in the background appeared in *Aurora* (1913) 100.

38. Cheng, *After Forty Years*, 9.

39. P. Matson, *Our China Mission*, 70.

School.[40] In 1915–16 Hilma Johnson was in Fancheng, where she superintended women's work and ran a girls' school. When President E. G. Hjerpe of the American Mission Covenant visited the field in 1915, Hilma Johnson put on a program for him at her girls' school.[41]

Nanchang

The years following the First Revolution, when extensive construction occurred in the Covenant field, a new church building and schools were erected in Nanchang. Hilda Rodberg relocated to Nanchang (1910–1912), having distinguished herself earlier in medical work at Siangyang.

Kingmen

In 1912 Hilda Rodberg went to Kingmen[42] where she began working in the dispensary, then started a girls' school, while also evangelizing among women. At this school she was again eminently successful, the girls affectionately calling her "Lo Sioo tsie" (Miss Rodberg). Assisting Hilda at the girls' school was Mrs. Abel Li, whose husband, Abel Li, was superintendent of the Kingmen boys' school.[43]

In 1913 Herman Conradson came to do evangelistic work in the Kingmen district, and in 1914 was joined by Amelia Ackerson, whom he married on March 24, 1915. Amelia had been in charge of the girls' school in Siangyang since 1908, and now took over the girls' school in Kingmen. Work at Kingmen—as at every other Covenant station—received a boost by the arrival in 1915 of Mission Covenant President, Rev. E. G. Hjerpe. As a result of President Hjerpe's visit, giving back in the United States increased and new schools could be built at Kingmen.[44]

---

40. Ekeland et al., *White unto Harvest*, 128–30, with picture.

41. E. V. Nordlund, *The Life and Work of Victor Nordlund*, 60.

42. J. S. Johnson, "The Kingmen District," 50–51.

43. Ibid., 50; Abel Li was educated in a mission school run by the Swedish Mission Covenant in Wuchan; cf. L. J. Larson, "Educational Work in China," 42.

44. For pictures of the Kingmen girls' school building and girls attending the school, see L. J. Larson, "Educational Work in China," 41, 49.

Kingmen Girls' School

Kingchow

In Kingchow a preparatory department was added to the seminary in 1911, and Carl J. Nelson came down from Siangyang to be the dean. This developed into a full middle school for boys, said to be one of the best in China.[45] Gradually requirements were raised and students were supposed to take at least two years of middle school before entering seminary. The seminary at first offered a three-year course, which was later changed to four years.[46] Emma Nelson, Carl's wife, taught music, English, and religious subjects at the middle school.

Isaac Jacobson joined the faculty at the seminary and preparatory school in about 1912. His wife Anna served among women and became involved in a girls' school that had just opened. In 1915 John Peterson was elected to be the American Covenant's representative at the Kingchow seminary, where he distinguished himself as a teacher over the next 35 years.[47] With Peterson at the seminary, Carl Nelson could now devote all his time

45. John Peterson, "Kingchow Theological Seminary," 73; P. Matson, *Our China Mission*, 69–70, 78.

46. P. Matson, *Our China Mission*, 69–70.

47. For a picture of the graduation class at the Kingchow seminary in about 1916–17, see *Aurora* (1917) 106.

to developing the middle school.[48] 1915 was the 25th anniversary of the "Sin Tao Huei," the Chinese name for the union of the Swedish Missionary Society and the American Missionary Society, and President E. G. Hjerpe of the American Covenant was present for the celebration. The festivities took place on November 8–15 with 40 missionaries and some 200 evangelists and delegates from the churches in attendance.[49]

In 1915, Wang Hwai-chen, who had attended Matson's school in Fancheng and gone on to study at Siangyang Academy, augmented the faculty, teaching history and allied subjects at the seminary and middle school.

Leonard Larson points out how the growing number of evangelists and teachers in the Covenant mission were products of the mission's educational work. He says:

> More than 50% of the students who pass through our high school department in Kingchow have gone out as teachers in our mission or continued in the Seminary department or higher institutions and later entered the service of the mission. This is a unique record and one of which we are justly proud. As a result our mission is fairly well supplied with native workers with good training, while many other missions are constantly in lack of such men and women.[50]

GROWTH, DEVOLUTION, AND EVACUATION (1921–1927)

Siangfan

The growth of Covenant mission work continued into the 1920s, reaching a climax in mid-decade. Educational work in particular flourished, starting from the modest beginning in boys' and girls' schools in Fancheng to 1925, when, there were 63 schools with 2300 students in the entire Covenant field.

At that time China's adult population was still 85 percent illiterate. Some boys in the family would be sent to school for a few months, maybe even a year or two, but as soon as they were old enough to do the least kind of remunerative labor, like selling candy, vegetables, or other things on the street, or to help with work in the field, they were taken out of school. If they had learned a few of the difficult characters, these were soon forgotten and

---

48. P. Matson, *Our China Mission*, 78.

49. C. J. Nelson, "The Twenty-fifth Anniversary of the 'Sin Tao Huei.'"

50. L. J. Larson, "Educational Work in China," 42–43.

the boy became as illiterate as if he had never attended school. Before the coming of Christian missions "the education of a girl was an exceptional, yes, nearly an unheard of thing."[51]

Mission schools in the mid-1920s were of three types: primary schools (58); high schools (4); and a theological seminary (1).[52] Leonard Larson gives this description:

> The primary schools are of two kinds, lower and higher primary, each consisting of three years of grade work. The lower primary schools are usually co-educational, that is, boys and girls attend the same school and classes. But a division of students is made when they reach the higher primary schools, the boys and girls each attending their own schools; the girls being taught by women and the boys by men teachers. Custom in China makes co-educational work among the older students difficult, though in a few places it is being tried as an experiment. The same division continues through the high school and into the colleges, though some of the latter are being placed on a co-educational basis with good results.[53]

Life in one of the boys' schools typically proceeded as follows:

> The little lad is brought to the school by his parents and is entered in the lowest class. The child will perhaps be rather frightened and awed by his surroundings, but he is extremely polite, bows deeply to the teacher, stands very demurely when being spoken to, and in every way tries to show respect for the scholar who is to become his instructor. He is given a seat and supplied with the necessary books, and is soon busily at work, slowly tracing Chinese characters with a big hand. His class hours are very long compared with the hours at home . . . At present his work, as at home, will consist of reading, writing, arithmetic, geography, and history—usually in the form of stories—, hygiene, and Bible. If he completes the first three years of work, and his parents are able, he is sent to the higher primary school. But for many their studies are completed when they leave the lower primary school. Our higher primary schools are located at the head stations, and the students who are fortunate enough to be able to continue in them must leave their homes and come to the school to live, unless they are fortunate enough to live in the city where the station is located. These schools are boarding

51. Ibid., 39–40.
52. Ibid., 44.
53. Ibid., 44–45.

schools, and as a result the supervision is better, the discipline is stricter, and the subject matter and teaching are on a more modern basis. The students begin to take on the student aspect, wear uniforms, organize football teams and student societies, and carry on various other school activities. The students are now under the direct supervision of the foreign missionary, and attendance at the daily chapel service and Sunday services is required of them all. If at the end of three years he passes the examinations set by the Central China Christian Educational Association, he receives its certificate and is eligible to enter any high school affiliated with the association. Now he has entered the student class and in his little village he is looked up to with a good deal of respect by the other boys less fortunate.[54]

At junior high school, or junior middle school as it is called in China, the fellow will likely change his name. One boy did so three times while at the Covenant school in Kingchow. He will also take on an English name in addition to his Chinese one. The Covenant Mission had two junior middle schools, one in Kingmen and one in Siangyang, and a senior middle school for boys also in Kingchow. Here the boy's general education would be completed, unless he decided to study further at the theological seminary, and after graduation become a mission evangelist or pastor. In the mid-1920s a junior and senior middle school for girls were located in Fancheng, and were a united work with the Norwegian Lutheran United Mission.[55]

The first years of this fourth decade of Covenant mission work saw much building activity in Siangyang:[56] The boys' school was enlarged and a new large girls' school was erected. New missionaries arrived, some to do educational work. Jemima Olson came in 1921, serving one term in Siangyang and Fancheng. At Fancheng she became principal of the Concordia Middle School for Girls, where Mabel Olson had been. Jemima was not in good health, however, and left in the evacuation of 1927. In 1922 Ebba Beckus—after 1928 Mrs. Elmer Fondell—came as an educational missionary to Fancheng and Siangyang, but she, too, evacuated in 1928. Hilda G. Johnson arrived in China in December, 1924 to do children's work in Fancheng and Siangyang, but she evacuated in 1927.

54. Ibid., 45–46.
55. Ibid., 46–48.
56. P. Matson, *Our China Mission*, 81.

Nanchang

In 1920–1927 a number of missionaries were at Nanchang and in the Nanchang district, engaged in evangelism, teaching at the girls' school, and doing medical work. Victor Nordlund and his daughter Esther lived in the district from 1920 to 1922,[57] Victor involved in evangelism and Esther in evangelism and teaching. Nanchang during this time had some well-qualified Chinese teachers. In 1921 Elizabeth Björkgren came to work at the girls' school, and the next year Helen Gravem was in Nanchang helping out at the girls' school and working with women. Her husband, the Rev. Hjalmar Gravem, was doing evangelism. Isaac and Anna Jacobson returned from furlough in 1922, and Anna took up women's work and assisted at the girls' school in Nanchang. A new girls' school had been completed and was going well.[58]

In 1925–26 the area was filled with banditry and civil war. Nevertheless, in the fall of 1926 a revival broke out at Nanchang. Then the communists came, and with them came violence and destruction. In February, 1927 the city suffered extensive damage and all the missionaries had to leave,[59] but Peter Matson received an encouraging letter from Pastor Yü, who said that in the absence of missionaries ministry was nevertheless being carried on.[60]

Icheng

Alfred Johnson arrived in Icheng in 1922 to take charge of the schools and help at the outstations. There were schools for both boys and girls at Icheng. Further expansion was planned, but could not be carried out because in 1927 bandits in the area forced all the missionaries to evacuate.[61] Alfred was also suffering from asthma attacks, and he and Ruth had to go home.

57. Ibid., 78.

58. L. J. Larson, "Educational Work in China," 50.

59. Reported by Oscar Anderson in C. O. Anderson and R. M. Anderson, *Two Lives of Faith*, 36.

60. Ibid.

61. Ruth Anderson reports on the evacuation of Icheng in February, 1927 and on the trip to Hankow and Shanghai (C. O. Anderson and R. M. Anderson, *Two Lives of Faith*, 34–35). This is followed by Oscar's report (ibid., 36–38).

Kingmen

Ministry at Kingmen grew in the 1920s, and in time numerous outstations were opened in the district. Kingmen had a girls' school and a boys' school,[62] which at their zenith in 1924 had a combined enrollment of nearly 300 students.[63] Then came the chaos of 1926–27 when communists, lawless soldiers, and bandits roamed the Covenant field and anti-foreign sentiments forced the schools to be closed and the missionaries to evacuate.

In 1927 the government put a ban on religious education in primary schools,[64] another aspect of the anti-religious movement prevailing at the time, which sought to do away with all religion. All private schools—including mission schools—had to register with the local educational bureau and follow the government educational program. Even though the law was not strictly enforced, the mission had to discontinue a large part of its educational ministry. Middle schools were closed down, and primary schools were turned over to Chinese leaders, leaving the question of registration to their discretion.

Another government requirement was that in the assembly room of every school a picture of Sun Yat-sen was to be hung, and every Monday the whole school was to assemble to make three bows toward the picture, then for a couple of minutes to remain silent. The last will of Sun Yat-sen was usually read or recited. Missionaries had been largely supportive of Sun Yat-sen; he was, after all, a baptized and confessing Christian. Both the missionaries and the Chinese Christians saw this ceremony as coming too close to idolatrous worship, however, and they objected to it.[65] In the 1930s the government rescinded the restrictions, after which religious instruction in classes was allowed to continue as formerly.[66]

---

62. Abel Li, who was educated in a mission school run by the Swedish Mission Covenant in Wuchang, was superintendent of the boys' school; cf. L. J. Larson, "Educational Work in China," 42. Abel later moved to Chungking and was there with Edward Nelson in 1948; cf. E. G. Nelson, *China in Your Blood*, 132.

63. J. S. Johnson, "The Kingmen District," 50. Missionaries involved in education at Kingmen prior to the evacuation of 1927 were, Mabel Olson (evangelism and education); Esther Kjellberg (schoolwork); Hilma Johnson (evangelism and schoolwork); and Esther Nordlund (evangelism, girls' school, and women's work).

64. P. Matson, *Our China Mission*, 85–86; Wang, "Labors and Results," 167.

65. P. Matson, *Our China Mission*, 86–87.

66. Jacobson, "Christian School Work," 66–68.

Kingchow

The beginning of the 1920s saw things going well at the Kingchow seminary, but by 1922 John Peterson said that "the rumbling of an oncoming storm could be heard in the distance."[67] At the end of World War I the German Concession at Tsingtao had been given to Japan instead of being returned to China, its rightful owner, with the result that anti-foreign sentiments began to grow in China. Peterson says:

> Especially the schools were affected. Students ignored their teachers and their classes, going out on strikes and holding demonstrations against foreign invasion, foreign goods, foreign education, and what not. The leaders of this movement became more and more anti-Christian in their attitude.[68]

Carl J. Nelson became ill and had to return to the United States in 1923. His death on August 23, 1923 was a great loss to schoolwork in the Covenant field. The Kingchow middle school stayed open until 1927, when it was forced to close at the approach of the revolutionary army.[69] The Chinese government determined that secular and theological schools were not allowed to function in the same building, or even in the same compound, so the middle school had to go.

After Carl Nelson's death, Leonard Larson took over as principal of the middle school. Leonard and Alice Larson arrived in Kingchow in 1920. Leonard at first studied Chinese and taught upper class men who knew a little English, while Alice offered instruction in English at the Kingchow middle school. Both went home in 1926, and did not return to China.[70]

Marcus Ch'eng taught at the seminary and middle school for 12 years between 1909 and 1925. In 1925 he left Kingchow to join General Feng Yu-hsiang's army as chaplain.[71] Later he became President of the Chungking Theological Seminary in Chungking. Another valued teacher at the Kingchow seminary was Wang Hwai-chen, one of the alumni of Matson's

---

67. John Peterson, "Kingchow Theological Seminary," 73.

68. Ibid., 74.

69. L. J. Larson, "Educational Work in China," 47–48, mentions a senior middle school for boys at Kingchow in 1927, which was a union school with the Swedish Mission Covenant.

70. Teachers at the seminary for longer or shorter periods were S. M. Freden, S. Tonnquist, A. P. Tjellström, and Axel G. Rydberg of the Swedish Mission Covenant, and Carl J. Nelson, John Peterson, Leonard Larson, and Isaac Jacobson of the American Mission Covenant.

71. Ch'eng, *After Forty Years*, 12.

boys' school in Fancheng.[72] After graduating from Kingchow Seminary in 1915 with high honors, Wang took a position teaching history and allied subjects at the seminary and middle school, and on April 25, 1926, he was ordained a pastor. At the time of his ordination the Covenant could say with satisfaction:

> The Christian church of China is coming to its own. Responsibilities that formerly rested on the missionary body entirely are now one by one taken over by Christian Chinese leaders. None rejoices over this fact more than the missionary himself. His labors and his prayers have brought it about.[73]

In 1927 Wang was dean of the middle school, and in 1930 he became president of the seminary.[74]

Evacuation (1926–27)

Political events elsewhere in China during the decade added to unrest in Kingchow. When Sun Yat-sen died in 1926, leadership fell into the hands of Chiang Kai-shek, who began a northward march of his two armies. One was under his command, the other under the command of one of his lieutenants. The latter army, when it reached Hunan, came under the control of the Russians and like-minded communists. The farther north they went, the more violent they became.

Terror reached a peak on December 3, 1926 when the army arrived at Kingchow. Agitators began organizing students and others against work at the mission schools. They sealed bookcases in the library and saw to it that no classes were held. At the request of the students the school was closed. On December 26 all the students left, and in the afternoon army soldiers came demanding to live on the premises. Peterson and others tried to reason with them, but to no avail. They moved in, and destruction followed. Soldiers broke open the doors and stole all the instruments and books. The Joel Johnsons and Isaac Jacobsons went home in 1927. The last of the faculty was gone by March, 1927 when a massacre at Nanking had taken place, after which soldiers broke into the missionaries' living quarters and robbed or destroyed everything the missionaries had left behind.[75] All school records were destroyed.

72. For a testimony, see Wang, "Labors and Results."
73. *Our Covenant* 1 (1927) 72–73.
74. John Peterson, "Kingchow Theological Seminary," 78–79.
75. Ibid., 75.

RETURN TO THE FIELD (1927–1929)

Shanghai and Kuling

After Ebba Fondell evacuated Siangfan in 1928, she and Elmer returned to teach school in Shanghai and Kuling before going home in 1930.

Icheng

From 1927 to 1933 the Icheng station had no missionary in residence.[76] In the spring of 1929 civil war broke out in earnest in northern Hupeh, with rebels swarming over the mission stations in Fancheng, Siangyang, Nanchang, and Icheng. During the civil war mission buildings in Icheng were in the hands of rebels,[77] and missionaries from Siangyang made only occasional visits there.[78] Banditry and civil war continued into the 1930s.

Kingmen

In December, 1928, when women were again permitted to accompany men onto the field, Hilda Rodberg returned to Kingmen, but in May, 1929 became seriously ill and had to seek medical help in Hankow. She died on February 12, 1931, and was buried in Hankow.

Kingchow

In the fall of 1927 Peter Matson and John Peterson returned to Kingchow to find soldiers living in the schools and missionary homes. An uneasy state of affairs continued for about a year and a half. In the spring of 1928 Peterson came again to Kingchow, this time staying for 3 months. With conditions slightly better, a cleanup was attempted.

The school reopened with one class in the fall of 1928. During 1928–29 John Peterson was the only foreign teacher at the seminary. Soldiers were still present in the compound and the situation remained tense. A hasty or impolite word by Peterson to any one of the soldiers could have meant instant death. In the spring of 1929 conditions at Kingchow were still not peaceful. Famine was severe in parts of the district and people were eating

76. P. Matson and. C. O. Anderson, "The Icheng District," 43.

77. P. Matson, *Our China Mission*, 98.

78. Ibid.

a type of white clay and bark off the trees.[79] But in the fall of 1929 the Tjell-ströms returned,[80] and a new class of students was taken in. The last trouble from armed soldiers came in the summer of 1930.

CIVIL WAR AND JAPANESE OCCUPATION (1930–1940)

Siangfan

At the beginning of the 1930s the Siangfan district was full of banditry and civil war, yet Edla Carlson—after 1924 Mrs. Peter Matson—in the winter of 1929–30 opened a Bible training school for young women in Siangyang,[81] which developed from a course of Bible study for girls.[82] When Edla went home on furlough in 1932, Amelia Conradson took her place as head of the school, remaining until 1939, when Millie Nelson relieved her until going home on furlough in 1941. The school had to be closed in November, 1938 because of the Japanese bombings, so it moved then to Nanchang, where it reopened.[83]

To aid in the educational work of the mission, Covenant missionaries translated books, articles, and hymns into Chinese, some of which were published by the Covenant. Two Bible Histories were published, one on the Old Testament and one on the New Testament. These went through many editions and were used by other missions in Central and North China. A catechism in Chinese was also published. John Peterson participated in the translation of Dr. James Orr's *Bible Encyclopedia* (1915), and the Rev. Hjalmar Sundquist's book, *The Credentials of Jesus* (Chicago: Covenant Press, 1930) was translated into Chinese.[84] Joel Johnson and Leonard Larson put together hymn translations into a hymnbook that was published by the Covenant. Included were a number of translations from the Swedish by Isaac Jacobson. In addition, the Covenant published a handbook and several pamphlets in Chinese.[85]

79. C. O. Anderson and R. M. Anderson, *Two Lives of Faith*, 40.

80. For a picture of A. P. Tjellström with S. M. Freden and Joel S. Johnson, see *Aurora* (1910) 63.

81. P. Matson, "The Siang Fan District," 29; Conradson, "The Young Women's Bible Training School," 119.

82. Fu, "Witnessing for Christ," 174.

83. Conradson, "The Young Women's Bible Training School," 120–21.

84. The book was translated in 1931 by Peng Lo-shan under the supervision of Peter Matson, and published by the Religious Tract Society in Hankow; cf. Dahlstrom, "The Covenant Missionary Society in China" 159, 165 n. 75.

85. P. Matson, *Our China Mission*, 71–72.

The most fruitful revival in the history of the Covenant mission brought renewal in the spring of 1932, and for a few years the district was peaceful.[86] Then in 1935 came the great flood in the Han River Valley, and in two years the Japanese would be dropping bombs on Siangyang and Fancheng. But in May, 1939, despite panic over the bombings, things in Siangfan were said to be relatively peaceful. School was in full swing in Siangyang with 200 boys and girls enrolled.[87]

Nanchang

In the spring of 1929 civil war had once again broken out in northern Hupeh,[88] and for a time no missionaries were in residence in either Nanchang or Icheng.[89] Even when General Feng Yu-hsiang, one of the combatants, gave up and went into retirement, peace did not come. An absence of government troops allowed the communists to entrench themselves in wide areas, where they set up their own system (soviet) of government.[90] The winter of 1930–31 was more chaotic than before. By the late 1930s the day school in Nanchang had been closed, though the Sunday School still flourished.[91]

Icheng

From 1927 to 1933 the Icheng head station had no missionary in residence.[92] Soldiers had taken control of the mission, turning the church into a stable and wreaking havoc upon the schools and mission buildings. Before Matson went home on furlough in the spring of 1932, he paid a visit to Icheng and said a spirit of depression pervaded the place. Work at Icheng gradually resumed, until the first Japanese bombings in November, 1938, when mission property sustained extensive damage. More bombings in April, 1939 destroyed the city and the mission station. When the Paul Johnsons left in April, Icheng was again without a resident missionary, and work

86. P. Matson, "The Siang Fan District," 28–29.

87. Ibid., 31.

88. J. S. Johnson, "The Kingmen District," 50; Abel Li, who was educated in a mission school run by the Swedish Mission Covenant in Wuchang, was superintendent of the boys' school; cf. L. J. Larson, "Educational Work in China," 42.

89. P. Matson, *Our China Mission*, 98.

90. Ibid., 99.

91. Yuen, "Nanchang Items" 171.

92. P. Matson and C. O. Anderson, "The Icheng District," 43.

had to be supervised from Siangyang. Seven Chinese workers, two of them women, continued the ministry.

Kingmen

Work at Kingmen was disrupted with the arrival of General Ho Lung and his communist soldiers. Mission property was destroyed and three Covenant missionaries, Oscar Anderson, Augusta Nelson, and Esther Nordlund, together with Dr. Yao, were kidnapped for ransom. The station then remained vacant with no missionaries in residence until 1935. During this time Chinese Christians carried on as before. In 1933–1936 an exodus of Red armies from south and central China made for a few years of relative peace.[93]

In the fall of 1935 Joel Johnson returned from furlough and assumed leadership at Kingmen, and that same fall Mabel Olson arrived from Kingchow to do evangelism, educational work, and women's work. Turmoil returned later in the decade, with the Japanese eventually gaining control of the southern portion of the Covenant field. In 1938 the Japanese dropped 26 bombs on mission property in Kingmen; buildings were damaged, but nevertheless remained on their foundations.[94] There was more bombing in 1938 and 1939, but the missionaries and their Chinese co-workers continued their labors.

Kingchow and Shasi

From 1928 to 1930/31 General Ho Lung and his Third Red Army were active in southern Hupeh,[95] which included Kingchow and Shasi. Isaac Jacobson was teaching at the seminary in April, 1931 when Augusta Nelson and Esther Nordlund were released after their capture by the communists. Isaac went up to Kingmen to escort them down to Kingchow.[96]

About this same time (1931) the American Covenant took over full responsibility for the Kingchow church, which previously had been a union effort with the Swedish Mission Covenant.[97] Since 1912 a school had exist-

93. C. O. Anderson and R. M. Anderson, *Two Lives of Faith*, 92–93.

94. J. S. Johnson, "The Kingmen District," 49. For a picture of the Kingmen church, see E. C. Matson, "Life under the Shadows of Death," 25.

95. C. O. Anderson and R. M. Anderson, *Two Lives of Faith*, 53.

96. Ibid., 168–69.

97. Ibid., 92.

ed in connection with the church, with an average attendance of 45 pupils. It was a fine institution, and continued without interruption until March 26, 1939, when a Japanese bomb hit the building and did major damage.[98] None of the 30 children in the school was killed. One 12 year-old boy, however, had his kneecap blown away by shrapnel, but the bones were unhurt. Nevertheless, he would have to spend the rest of his days on crutches.

The years 1932–1936 were peaceful in Kingchow and in the countryside, allowing schoolwork and evangelism to be carried on normally.[99] Mabel Olson served in evangelism and education in Kingchow before going to Kingmen in the fall of 1935. In July, 1938 between 700 and 800 war refugees were registered at the school, as many as 600 at one time. Most of them came from the Swedish Mission Covenant field near Hankow.[100] Nearly 150 of the refugees became Christian and were baptized, and a number were permitted to attend classes at the seminary.

In 1939 Kingchow found itself less than 40 miles from fighting between the Chinese and the Japanese. The Japanese bombed the city three times, and in one attack the chapel and girls' school suffered considerable damage. After the first air assault students scattered for two months, but then returned. Except for this interruption the school continued to function all during the Sino-Japanese war.

In 1939, a year before the Golden Jubilee of Covenant mission work in China, John Peterson was able to report that during the seminary's 30 years of existence 130 students had been graduated and about 70 were currently serving in the two missions. Some had gone to minister at other missions; others had died or entered vocations of different kinds.[101] John Peterson and H. C. Wang had been teaching at the seminary for 25 years, and Marcus Ch'eng for 12 years.[102]

---

98. John Peterson, "Kingchow and Shasi," 54–55.

99. C. O. Anderson and R. M. Anderson, *Two Lives of Faith*, 94.

100. E. C. Matson, "Life under the Shadows of Death," 24.

101. John Peterson, "Kingchow Theological Seminary," 78.

102. John Peterson has Marcus Ch'eng teaching at the seminary for 16 years ("Kingchow Theological Seminary," 78), but Ch'eng in his autobiography (*After Forty Years*, 10) says it was 12 years. Cheng was the first Chinese teacher at the seminary, beginning there in 1909 when it opened. But he spent considerable time touring America and Europe, preaching, evangelizing, and studying further, graduating from Wheaton College in 1922. Serving as president of the Kingchow Seminary were, S. M. Freden (1910–11); Sven Tonnquist (1911–15; 1923–24); A. P. Tjellström (1915–19); C. J. Nelson (1919–23); F. A. Wennborg (1924–26); John Peterson (1926–30); and H. C. Wang (1930–   ).

CLOSING YEARS OF THE COVENANT HUPEH MISSION (1940–1948)

Siangfan

On June 1, 1940 the Japanese crossed the Han and marched into Siangyang. They left the next day, but not before burning nearly the entire city and neighboring Fancheng. Mission property, however, was spared. People fled to the west but returned soon after and mission work in the district returned to normal.[103] By 1948, with the Japanese gone, communist forces were making rapid advances and Fancheng and Siangyang were said to be "hanging in the balance." Eventually the communists took control of the area, causing the entire Siangfan mission to close down. All mission work from this point on had to be left in the hands of Chinese Christians.

Nanchang

Matson reported in December, 1941 that work was going on in Nanchang much like in normal times.[104] The Covenant field had become divided after the Japanese crossed the Han, and in the northern portion, which included Nanchang, the Chinese were in control. But the Japanese still made periodic raids into the district, inflicting many casualties, including a young girl in Nanchang who attended the Siangyang Bible School for girls.[105]

Later the Japanese came to Nanchang to occupy mission buildings, burn, and loot. When Hjalmar Gravem returned in 1946 after serving as a Marine during the war, mission work at Nanchang was in the hands of the Chinese, but eventually Nanchang was overrun by communist forces.

Icheng

In early 1940 there were no missionaries in Icheng, which had largely been destroyed by Japanese bombs.[106] But in December 1941 Matson reported that at Icheng, as at other stations in northern Hupeh, the Chinese were in

103. P. Matson, "The Siang Fan District," 31.

104. Letter of Peter Matson to the First Covenant Church, St. Paul, Minnesota, dated December 23, 1941.

105. Jacobson, "Present Conditions on Our Field in China," 77–78.

106. Isaac Jacobson said that by 1942 property at Icheng and Kingmen had been almost wiped out of existence; cf. Jacobson, "Present Conditions on our Field in China," 77.

control and work was being carried on almost as before.[107] There, too, however, the Japanese returned to occupy mission buildings, loot, and burn.[108] Eventually communist forces took control of Icheng and the Icheng district.

Kingmen

In 1940 Gust E. Johnson reported from the Covenant Office in Chicago that Japanese bombs had destroyed Kingmen and the city was in ruins.[109] Three missionaries were living in nearby Kaoshan, west of Kingmen: Joel Johnson, Isaac Jacobson, and Mabel Olson.[110] In the spring of 1940 the Japanese began to occupy southern Hupeh, and at Kingmen they removed the iron roof from the girls' school, presumably for use as war material.[111]

In November, 1947 Ann Kulberg visited Kingmen and reported seeing the ruins of the Covenant station. The middle school was still standing, however, and 300 students marched in parade for her and others with her.[112]

Kingchow

By June, 1940 the Japanese occupied Kingchow, forcing the missionaries to evacuate, with only Albert Dwight and Augusta Nelson remaining. Yet in 1941 a large Vacation Bible School was conducted at the seminary.[113] Augusta was still there in 1942, now the only foreign worker of the Covenant staff in the occupied portion of the field.

Conditions were difficult in Kingchow during the war years of 1942–1945, and also after the Japanese defeat in 1945, when revolutionaries of all description and bandits roamed city and countryside. By Christmas, 1947 disturbances were widespread and everyone at Kingchow was apprehensive. Some expected the communists to arrive at any time. School was dismissed and students returned home.

107. Letter of Peter Matson to the First Covenant Church, St. Paul, Minnesota, dated December 23, 1941.

108. C. O. Anderson and R. M. Anderson, *Two Lives of Faith*, 143.

109. Reported in a letter from Judith Peterson to Rev. Gust Johnson, dated May 21, 1940; cf. Jacobson, "Present Conditions on our Field in China," 77, who says that at several of the outstations the same was true, but Christians were still carrying on the work.

110. Letter from Judith Peterson to Rev. Gust Johnson, May 21, 1940.

111. Jacobson, "Present Conditions on Our Field in China," 77–78.

112. Carlson, "Mission to China," Letter of November, 1947.

113. For a picture, see N. Dwight, "Waldenström Goes to China and the 'Doers of the Word' Seminary," 11.

The seminary was closed in 1946 at the suggestion of the Swedish Covenant Mission, and in its place a Bible Training School with an industrial department was opened.[114] By 1948 most all the missionaries had gone, except Joel Johnson and Elsa Hammerlind, who remained until February, 1949 when the communists came and they had to evacuate. With their departure an American missionary presence in Kingchow had ended. The Lutheran Theological Seminary at Shekow closed its doors and relocated to Hong Kong in November, 1948.[115] Eventually it found a home at the Tao Fong Shan retreat center in the New Territories of Shatin,[116] and continues to this day as a leading seminary in the Far East.

EVACUATION, RELOCATION, AND LEAVING THE CHINA MAINLAND (1948-1949)

Changsha

After the murder of the three missionaries in January, 1948 it was decided that the Branstroms, the Backlunds, Mabel Olson, and Viola Larson would go to Changsha for educational and evangelistic work. By May they had arrived at the Hunan Bible Institute, where they began teaching Bible and English in the schools.[117] Mabel Olson was also translating an outline of historical books of the Old Testament.[118] Paul Backlund was teaching at the Hunan Bible Institute and at Hunan University.[119] Mabel Olson and the Backlunds stayed in Changsha until early 1949, when they went home.[120]

Hong Kong

In October, 1948 Virginia Carlson—after 1949 Mrs. William Rigmark—became the Covenant's representative at the American School Kikungshan

---

114. Dahlstrom, "The Covenant Missionary Society in China," 62.

115. Scherer, "The Lutheran Church in China: A Brief History," 392.

116. The Tao Fong Shan Christian Institute carried on a ministry to Buddhist monks; see Sturton, "The Outreach of the Tao Fong Shan Christian Institute"; also "Tao Fong Shan Christian Institute" in *The Chinese Recorder* 70 (1939), 383–84.

117. Letter from Ann Kulberg Carlson dated May 23, 1948.

118. Olson, "Judge Finds Christ."

119. Backlund, "Traveling in China"; letter from Ann Kulberg dated May 23, 1948.

120. *The Covenant Weekly* (February 18, 1949) 5.

in Hong Kong, and would be there the following year.[121] Bill and Virginia Rigmark later went out as Covenant missionaries to Japan.

Chungking, Kweiyang, and Kweiting

Edward and Millie Nelson begin teaching and doing other missionary work in Chungking, Szechuan Province, in June, 1948.[122] Classes taught were largely Bible and English. Marcus Ch'eng at the time was President of the Chungking Theological Seminary, but in December, 1948 he went with his wife on a visit to the United States.[123] Ed Nelson taught at Chungking Provisional Educational College,[124] and Mildred held English Bible classes in various schools, one attended by the entire student body of 800.[125] Ann Kulberg conducted English Bible classes and taught Practical English at the Szechuan Provincial Educational College.[126] In September, 1949, however, Ann evacuated on the *St. Paul*, and in Hong Kong Ann began teaching children at the American school. She was also working at the time on a songbook. In September, 1951 Ann and Viola Larson were on a Swedish freighter sailing for Goteborg, and 18 days later arrived in the United States.

English classes at the time were being taught by missionaries in both Kweiyang and Kweiting.[127] Gertrude Marsh had a Bible class in Kweiyang.[128]

Leaving the China Mainland

Missionaries engaged in educational and evangelistic work at this short-lived Covenant mission in southwest China, along with other Covenant missionaries relocated there, were all gone by December, 1949, when Chiang Kai-shek was forced to leave the China Mainland and flee to Formosa (Taiwan).

121. A. L. Dwight, "Where Is the Dispersion?"

122. [Hedstrand], "Gist of China Conference Oral Reports."

123. G. F. Hedstrand, "An Interview with Marcus Cheng."

124. Letter from Ann Kulberg Carlson dated October 3, 1948.

125. *The Covenant Weekly* (March 18, 1949) 3.

126. E. G. Nelson, *China in Your Blood*, 135; A. L. Dwight, "Into the Highways and Hedges"; *The Covenant Weekly* (March 18, 1949), 3; letter from Ann Kulberg Carlson dated October 3, 1948.

127. [Hedstrand], "Gist of China Conference Oral Reports."

128. Ralph Hanson reporting in *The Covenant Weekly* (March 18, 1949) 3.

5

China in the Twenty-first Century

WITH THE DEATH OF Mao Zedong in 1976 and the end of the Cultural Revolution came an opening up of China to the rest of the world, particularly the West, which had been largely cut off from this ancient nation since the establishment of the People's Republic in 1949. Westerners came to see the Great Wall, the Forbidden City in Beijing, the Three Gorges on the Yangtze, and other sites of interest. Christian missionaries or their children came to visit former mission fields in the country, and they along with other Christians were keen to see Chinese cities important in Christian history; view monuments such as the Nestorian Stele and ruins such as the St. Paul Church in Macau; visit universities, seminaries, and Bible Schools in China; and attend Christian worship services in large and small churches, some of the latter spilling into alleyways and others inconspicuously held in unmarked rooms of apartment buildings. Most important was meeting Chinese people, viewing their ancient and modern ways, strangely juxtaposed, and learning first hand about the rapid growth of Christianity in China in the late twentieth and early twenty-first centuries.

VISITS TO SHANGHAI IN 2008

Shanghai was the first city seen by most all missionaries upon their arrival in China. Ocean liners docked in its harbor, and a few days were spent there arranging travel further into the interior. Covenant missionaries would book passage on a steamer up the Yangtze to Hankow, and from there would either go further to Shasi, which was at the southern end of the Covenant field, or take a small junk up the Han River, which would get them to Fancheng and Siangyang at the northern end of the field. Some would get off at the small port of Shipai, and from there would go overland to Kingmen, which was 25 miles away, or to other mission stations located in the central portion of Hupeh Province. In Shanghai was a fine Missionary Home where missionaries could stay. If it was full, there were other places where the missionaries could get lodging.

Mildred Nordlund, Viola Larson, and Millie Nelson (l. to r.) on Han River Junk

My wife Linda and I visited Shanghai on April 23–26, 2008, and I went again for three days on May 29–31 in connection with a "roots" tour by faculty of the Lutheran Theological Seminary (LTS), where I was currently teaching. Shanghai today is a very large modern city with tall buildings and wide thoroughfares, one of the latter running along the Huangpu River on the other side of the celebrated Bund. Our purpose in going to Shanghai in April was for me to give a lecture at Fudan University, one of China's oldest. My host and translator at Fudan was Dr. Lui Po. While there we toured the university and the city, and walked from People's Square to the Bund, where many of our missionaries had strolled years earlier. When I returned in May, I visited the China Christian Council and Three-Self Patriotic Movement, did some sightseeing, saw an acrobatic show with a student from Fudan, and visited the Water Village outside Shanghai.

VISIT TO NANJING (NANKING) IN 2007

Nanjing (Nanking) is a historic city, in ancient times and before the communist revolution the capital of China. It lies on the Yangtze, 190 miles west-northwest of Shanghai. Covenant missionaries Peter and Edla Matson, together with Millie Nelson and Viola Larson, stopped there in 1935, climbing the stairs to the newly built Sun Yat Sen Memorial, and visiting the nearby tombs of the Ming dynasty. Other missionaries visited the seminary in Nanjing, which since 1952 has become Union Theological Seminary, the national seminary of China's Three-Self Patriotic Movement church.

On Thursday, November 22, 2007 Linda and I left Hong Kong on our first visit to Mainland China. Our destination was Nanjing, where I had been invited to lecture and preach at Nanjing Union Theological Seminary. With us was Meici (Mary) Sun, a student of mine at Lutheran Theological Seminary in Hong Kong who was returning home after a year of study at our seminary. Mary taught and was Dean of Students at Union Seminary, and we were happy to have her accompanying us. She made all the arrangements for our four-day visit to the seminary and the city.

Nanjing Union Theological Seminary traces its origins to an older Protestant Bible School dating back to 1911. The seminary was re-established on November 2, 1952 by the Three-Self Patriotic Movement Committee of the Protestant Church in China. The three-self principles are 1) self-governance; 2) self-support (i.e., financial independence from foreigners); and 3) self-propagation. From the beginning, this seminary has focused on the training of pastoral workers, teachers, and researchers who profess to love both church and country. It also has the stated aim of building unity between believers and non-believers. Faculty and students at the seminary fully respect the authority of the Bible and confess the Apostles' and Nicene Creeds. The seminary offers B.Th. and M.Th. degrees. Every year only about 50 of the 300 students taking the oral and written entrance exams are admitted. To be accepted by the seminary one needs to be a baptized Christian and clear about God's leading into ministry, love both church and country, be of good virtue, be active in church activities for more than one year, and be committed to serve churches in China.

Thirty years earlier, during the Cultural Revolution, it seemed nigh unto impossible that China would ever again have Christian seminaries, much less be given land by the government in a district of the city designated for state universities, yet that is what has happened at Nanjing Union Theological Seminary, which is China's only national seminary. In 2007 China had 18 legal seminaries and Bible Schools located in various provinces throughout the country. Among the educated in this land of 1.3

billion, opposition to Christianity was being replaced by curiosity and interest. Full-time students at Nanjing Seminary pay no tuition, and there is no charge for campus accommodation. The seminary also provides basic health insurance. Needy students can get financial aid by working part-time on campus, or by applying for scholarships. We had read that the library contained 60,000 volumes, roughly half of which were in English, but when we visited in late 2007 we were told that the holdings were now 80,000 volumes. The library also subscribed to more than 100 journals in theology, history, and philosophy.

In 2007 Union Seminary was anticipating its move the next year to a new 33.5 acre campus in University City, which is in the Jiangning district of Nanjing. Here an expansion of facilities and program would enable the seminary to accommodate 500 students. In 2007 the seminary had 210 registered students, 180 of which were full-time and living on campus. There were 96 female students and 84 male students. The average age of the full-time students was 26. Full-time faculty numbered 30, which included three foreign professors and six adjunct professors from other universities. The old campus in the heart of Nanjing was to be retained as a research center. Linda and I visited the site of the new campus on our way in from the airport. Many buildings and elaborate sport facilities had already been completed. Scaffolding surrounded a modern new chapel building, which was nearing completion. Mary Sun pointed out where we could live when I returned one day to teach at the seminary.

I preached at the Friday morning chapel service on Matt 25:1–12, and in the afternoon gave my lecture, "Rhetorical Criticism and the Biblical Book of Jeremiah." The Rev. Manhong Melissa Lin, dean of the seminary and professor of Christian ethics, served as interpreter. We visited the printing offices of the Amity Foundation, adjacent to the seminary. Amity is the largest producer of Bibles in China. In 2012 it celebrated the 100 millionth copy of the Bible to roll off the press, many of which were printed in the various languages of the world.

While in Nanjing we climbed the stairs to the Sun Yat-sen Memorial, now located in the Zhongshan Mountain National Park, and saw the tombs of the Ming dynasty nearby. We also entered a Confucian Temple, connected to which was a cultural center where musicians played for us traditional Chinese songs. After they had finished I was given the opportunity to hit the 2000 year-old bells with a wooden mallet.

On our last day in Nanjing we visited Mochou Lake, which is just outside the city wall in the western part of the city. There we saw the "Winning Chess Pavilion" where the first Ming emperor, Hongwu, also known by his given name Zhu Yuanzhang (1328–1398), played chess with his general, Xu

Da. In a celebrated match, the general used his usual skill to gain the upper hand, but in a deft move he then proceeded to arrange a configuration on the chess board so as to convey the message: "Long life" (*wan sui*). This brought him great acclaim from the emperor. In the park we also heard ancient Chinese music being played and sung, and observed skillful retirees performing with their tops on a string. I took a turn on the tops, but without success. Mary Sun, however, did quite well.

Nanjing has a huge bridge over the Yangtze River where the river narrows. It was begun with Soviet aid, but when the Soviets pulled out in 1960, the Chinese were left to finish the construction on their own. The bridge was completed in 1968, and contains a huge sculpture symbolizing the mid-nineteenth-century workers' revolution. We had a view of the bridge, but a not so good view of the Yangtze River, as the air pollution that day was very bad.

On Sunday we attended worship at St. Paul's Church in Nanjing. We arrived early, which was a good thing, since by the time the service started the church was packed. One very moving moment for me was to hear the choir sing as its anthem the Swedish hymn, "Thanks to God for My Redeemer" ("Tack, O Gud, för vad du varit," August Ludvig Storm, 1891),[1] in Chinese. Since the anthem was sung to the J. A. Hultman tune, it must have been translated by Covenant missionaries. In the service we also sang "What a Wonderful Savior Is Jesus My Lord." After the Chinese worship we attended another worship service at 10:30 a.m. in English. Amy Zhangyan, wife of one of our students at LTS, Xia Yun, preached at this service.

VISITS TO HANKOU (HANKOW) IN 2008 AND 2014

On Thursday, May 22, 2008, I left Hong Kong for the airport in Wuhan,[2] where Cao Jing and her husband, Guo-zhuang, met me. They would accompany me on a five-day visit to places in Hubei (Hupeh) Province of Central China,[3] where Covenant missionaries labored for nearly 60 years. Jing was just the right person to accompany me. Bright, resourceful, and a committed Christian, she lived with her husband in Xiangyang (Siangyang), where she taught at Xiangfan University.[4] I had Jing as a student at LTS in Hong Kong. Already in possession of an earned Ph. D, she was one of my best

1. *The (Covenant) Hymnal*, #543.

2. Wuhan is a modern name for the three-city complex of Hanyang, Wuchang, and Hankow. Earlier missionary documents refer to it simply to Hankow.

3. Hubei is the modern (pinyin) spelling; the older spelling is Hupeh.

4. The name has since been changed to Hubei University of Arts and Science.

students and her enthusiasm and warm smile were contagious. Now she had a prepared itinerary and had begun contacting pastors and church leaders for us to meet. As always in China, some things would have to be worked out along the way.

At Wuhan I hoped to locate the International Cemetery in Hankou (Hankow), where, in January, 1948 three of our Covenant missionaries, Dr. Alik Berg, Martha Anderson, and Esther Nordlund, were laid to rest after being brutally murdered by bandits on the road from Xiangyang to Jingzhou (Kingchow), but I could find no one who knew of the cemetery.

On Tuesday May 27th, after the trip to our former Covenant mission field, I returned by train to Hankou, where I joined the LTS faculty on a "roots" tour in connection with the 95th anniversary of the seminary. Two days were spent visiting Zhong Nan Theological Seminary, the Hubei Church Council, the Lutheran Church Building in Hankou (old Lutheran Missionary Home), and the site of the former Lutheran seminary in Shekow. We were denied entrance into the old seminary as it was now a military installation. This seminary, opened in 1913, had moved to Hong Kong as a result of the civil war in 1948, and there became the Lutheran Theological Seminary of Hong Kong.

My second visit to Hankou took place in October, 2014, when I was again accompanied by Cao Jing on another trip to Hubei Province. With us this time was a young pastor from Inner Mongolia, Zhang Jiang. On Friday, October 17 we left Beijing on a high-speed train (CRH) for Wuhan. The 568-mile journey took just over five hours, compared with seventeen hours by conventional trains. Our purpose on this trip was to try and find the New International Cemetery where our three Covenant missionaries were buried in 1948. I could not locate it in 2008, but now had some new information supplied by Jeannine Nordlund, who had traveled to Hankou some years earlier with her husband Ted and friends. On their visit they were able to locate the Old International Cemetery located at Shing Le (Victory) Street and Eryao Road, which was made into a park in the early 1950s. But they told me that the New International Cemetery, which they did not see, was on Jiefang Road.

In the afternoon Jing, Jiang, and I took a taxi to Jiefang Road, where we were let off at the entrance to a large park. The only evidence of this park being a cemetery was a designated area where "Soviet heroes" had been buried. We walked to this place and saw the monument there. We were told the bodies of the "heroes" had been moved elsewhere. We then walked a considerable distance through the park, with Jing and Jiang talking to old people strolling by or sitting on benches where we stopped to rest, but came up with nothing. The former New International Cemetery may well have been within this park, but if so, we found no evidence of it.

VISITS TO FANCHENG IN 2008 AND 2014

In my visit of 2008, Jing, Guo-zhuang, and I left the Wuhan airport by taxi to go to a bus station some miles away, and there boarded a bus that would take us on a four-hour ride to Xiangfan.[5] With Jing interpreting, we talked to a farmer who sat in the seat ahead of us. The road was a modern toll road running along the eastern border of Hubei Province, with the Han River off some distance to the left. We were in the Han River Valley, and there were no mountains. Virtually no cars were on the road, only a few trucks. People were working in the fields, cutting grain and thinning or harvesting rice in the rice paddies. It was May, the time for the first of two yearly crops to be harvested. I saw no farm machinery to speak of, just people bent over doing the hard work of peasant farmers. Much water made the area lush green. The soil was reddish in color. I also saw a lot of water oxen, as Jing called them, as well as pine and poplar trees, the latter planted in rows. I was on the road to Siangyang.

It was May 22, and we arrived first at Fancheng, one of the two cities I had heard so much about. At Fancheng we left the bus station and went by taxi across the Han River to Xiangyang, where I checked into my hotel. Xiangyang and Fancheng are today large modern cities with buildings 20 to 30 stories in height. Fancheng had a McDonalds, a Kentucky Fried Chicken, and a Wall Mart! Traffic in neither city proceeded in an orderly fashion, so it was a matter of "People (and drivers) beware!" No one stopped for pedestrians in the crosswalk.

On Sunday, May 25 I was outside my hotel at 6:30 a.m. when Jing and Guo-zhuang arrived by taxi to take me across the Han to attend worship at the Fancheng church. After we stopped at a restaurant for breakfast—rice soup, steamed buns, pot stickers, and an egg—we then walked the short distance to the church, which was about a half block from the Han, and which appeared to be the same site as the old mission church. We had to be there by 7:30 a.m., thirty minutes before the worship service would begin.

5. Xiangfan (Siangfan) is the name of the combined cities of Xiangyang and Fancheng.

The Fancheng Church

Cao Jing and Pastor in Front of the Fancheng Church

Sunday Morning Worship in the Fancheng Church

When we arrived at the church a man in full voice was leading worshippers in songs to be sung that morning. A woman was playing the piano at the front of a simple, unadorned sanctuary. Pastor Wang, a woman, greeted us upon arrival. When the service started the main floor was already pretty well filled, and some were sitting in the balcony. Soon after, every seat was occupied, and the pastor later told us that there were about 1000 people in attendance. A chalkboard in the narthex announced the Scripture for the morning, which was Luke 13:1–5; hymns to be sung at the service; and the title of the sermon, which was "Reflections on the Disaster." The Scripture that Sunday was particularly appropriate, being about the Galileans whose blood Pilate mixed with their sacrifices, and the 18 who were killed when the tower of Siloam fell. A few days earlier the Wenchuan earthquake in Chengdu Province had claimed many lives. The sermon would be by Tan Yu-e, the other woman pastor, whose mother had graduated from a missionary middle school in Fancheng.

The temperature was quite warm. An overhead projecture was used at various times—telling people early on to turn off their cell phones and prepare their hearts for worship. Otherwise the front of the church had only a red cross and some Chinese writing. Chinese characters at the top of the arch said "The Lord is Holy." The center pulpit had a red cross on the front. Besides this, there was no artwork at all, only vases with red flowers on the pulpit and a table to the right. Risers behind the pulpit were for the choir, which would sing later. The congregation here—as elsewhere in China—was made up largely of women (I was told later that the ratio was usually about 70% women and 30% men). Also, there were mostly—but not exclusively— older people in attendance, apparently because people in Xiangfan were not as educated as in Beijing or other large cities. In Nanjing and Beijing, where Linda and I have been, lots of young people filled the churches.

The Call to Worship was "The Lord is in his holy temple, let all the earth keep silence before him." The melody was familiar, one I remember singing in the North Park Church Choir. The choir stood singing in the first two rows of the congregation. The hymn was one on keeping watch for Jesus' coming, which I recognized, but could not recall either its title or its words. The hymnbook in use was published in 1983. Looking into the Chinese Bible provided for the worshippers, I noted with satisfaction that the Psalms and portions of the Prophets were formatted as poetry, like in the RSV, NRSV, and other modern English Bibles. The Bible, dated 1998, had been published by the Chinese Christian Council.

The first Scripture lesson, read reponsively with people in the congregation, came from Malachi 3:1–7: "Behold, I send my messenger to prepare the way before me." We sang another hymn, after which Pastor Wang prayed a prayer that seemed to me to be a bit long. We sang another hymn, then Luke 13:1–5 was read, again responsively, and the choir went up on the risers for their anthem, which was the same as the first hymn, focusing on watching for Jesus' coming. The Olympic theme, "Are You Ready?" was invoked. The choir, with robes and stoles, was about evenly divided between men and women. At the end they sang an "Amen."

Pastor Tan Yu-e preached the sermon after another long prayer was offered. Her many Scriptural passages included Luke 21:25–26, about signs of the end times; Job 33:14–17, 29–30, about God giving warnings to people; Luke 13:1–5, the main text, urging repentance; Malachi 3:7, calling for people to repent; Rev 19:7–8, announcing the marriage of the Lamb and his Bride; Amos 4:12, about preparing to meet your God, with the previous verse about Sodom and Gomorrah also being cited; Eph 2:10, about Christians being created in Christ Jesus for good works, a reference here being made to the Titanic disaster; and 1 Peter 4:7–10, about living sane and sober lives when the end is perceived to be near. This last Scripture was read responsively with the congregation.

Early into the sermon there was a disturbance in the balcony, which we later learned was because someone had fainted. Pastor Wang went up to investigate. Then we sang Hymn 121, "When I See my Lord." The song leader was now standing in the front row singing with full voice into the microphone. The congregation recited the Lord's Prayer, followed by the giving of the Benediction. After the service we were invited into Pastor Tan Yu-e's office, and then we all went out to a restaurant for dinner. According to Pastor Tan Yu-e, the Norwegians were first to come to the area in about 1860, which would be 30 years before Peter Matson and his Norwegian comrades came to Siangfan to choose a mission field. The Norwegian Lutheran connection was correct, but her date, I think, was too early.

After lunch, Pastor Tan Yu-e took us to see what was left of the old church and school buildings prior to 1949. In an old part of Fancheng we saw the remains of a building said to be part of the old church. The church had been gone for a long time, and in its place stood another building. Only a one-level structure, where some people were now living, remained. Dr. Mildred Nordlund, who had visited in January, 1981 said the old Fancheng Church she saw was now a carpenter shop.[6] A short distance away Pastor Tan Yu-e showed us what remained of an old primary school. One half of this building, which she estimated to be maybe 100 years old, was still standing. This was on Qian Street in the eastern part of Fancheng. We left to return to the hotel, grateful for this memorable visit to the present-day Fancheng church, and for a look at what may have been the remains of early mission buildings in Fancheng.

My second visit to Fancheng came on Saturday morning, October 18, 2014 when Jing, Jiang, and I boarded a train in Hankou for the two-hour ride to Xiangfan, during which I would get another look at the two cities of Fancheng and Xiangyang. The train went in a northeastly direction, east of the Han River, and then it turned west with the river to enter Fancheng. One station between Hankou and Fancheng was An Lu, which I had read about, because there was a Wesleyan Hospital there. We crossed the river and checked into our hotel in Xiangyang, which was located near the West Gate of the old walled city. The rest of this day and all day Sunday would be spent in Xiangyang and Fancheng.

We were fortunate to get the good help of Brother Ho during these days. Brother Ho worked in a government office dealing with property, and was familiar with old records and could access other records if need be. Jing had made the contact through a friend, and remembered him from when she lived in Xiangyang. I had with me a picture of the facade of the old church in Fancheng, behind which was a new church being built. It was given to me by Vivian Johnson, daughter of Covenant missionaries Oscar and Ruth Anderson, who with her husband Ernie and Norman Dwight, son of Covenant missionaries Albert and Elna Dwight, had visited Xiangfan

6. M. Nordlund, "A China Experience," 11.

some years earlier. Norman Dwight was just a boy when he lived in Xiang-fan, but could remember things and on this visit even met up with a Chinese boy with whom he had once played, now also an old man.

Brother Ho immediately recognized the picture, and said he would return the next morning, which was Sunday, and take us to the church. When we came to the church the next morning we discovered that it was the Fancheng church Jing, Guo, and I visited in 2008. In the picture it was the structure being built behind the façade of the old church. We met the pastor, Cui Shu-ging, who had arrived since my earlier visit.

Pastor Cui said that an old cemetery was nearby, and asked whether I would be interested in seeing it? You bet I would! I knew of the Fancheng cemetery, which is where some of our Covenant missionaries, their small children, and other missionaries (many of them Norwegian Lutherans) were buried. The old cemetery was now inside the Mi Gong Primary School, but Brother Ho knew the principal, so he phoned him and asked if he would come and open the gate. The man was glad to oblige, so we were able to gain entrance. Once inside, we crossed an athletic area, and were then led to the place that used to be the cemetery. It was now named after a famous Chinese calligrapher, and a display of calligraphy surrounded the covered area. As we stepped into the room we were shown five or six gravestones leaning against the wall. The first was said to be the most important, belonging to the mother of someone important to Chou En-lai, who came looking for her grave in 1970 during the Cultural Revolution. After finding it, he made sure the stone was preserved. He is also probably the one responsible for the other stones along the wall being preserved.

Gravestones Surviving from the Old Fancheng Cemetery

Gravestone of Dr. John Sjöquist from the Old Fancheng Cemetery

I was shown this stone, but my eyes skipped two stones away where I saw, to my utter amazement, the gravestone of John Sjöquist, our first Covenant doctor in Xiangyang. I knew his first wife Maria had been buried in this cemetery, and Covenant records indicated that John too was buried there, next to her. His gravestone was artistically inscribed, but some text on the far right was missing. It said he was born in Värmland, which is correct, but I read what I thought was a date of June 30 (the year had been effaced). The date must have been January 30, however, as his date of birth was January 30, 1863. I also saw the gravestone of Gunnar Arnell, the young 21 year old Covenant missionary who was stricken with typhus fever enroute from Hankou to Xiangyang, and was unconscious when he arrived on October 2, 1904. He died five days later on October 7, never seeing the city where he had come to labor. Another gravestone had a Swedish or Norwegian name I did not recognize. So whereas I did not find the cemetery I was looking for in Hankou, here I was able to see the other cemetery where Covenant missionaries buried their dead, and its discovery came to me as an unexpected surprise.

Gunnar Arnell (d. October 7, 1904)

VISITS TO XIANGYANG (SIANGYANG) IN 2008 AND 2014

Xiangyang was the city I was most anxious to see in Hubei Province, for it was the main station of the Covenant mission, and where Bethesda Hospital was located. My first look at Xiangyang was on May 22, 2008 when Jing, Guo-zhuang, and I left the Fancheng bus station after arriving from Hankou, and crossed the Han by taxi to enter the city. The Han was low, as water was being taken from it much like what is happening to other rivers in the world. A new, large island was visible from the bridge. I was taken to the Nanhu Hotel inside the old walled city,[7] and put up there. I was told we were not far from where our old missionary compound was located. Bethesda

7. Located in a beautiful garden complex at 2 Victory Street, Xiangyang, the Nanhu Hotel was reputed to be the best hotel in Xiangyang.

Hospital had been a 10-minute walk outside the wall, but we did not see if the building was still standing.

On the evening of May 26, 2008, after spending the day in Nanzhang, I went to see Jing and Guo's apartment. Jing was teaching at the university in Xiangyang, and their apartment was close by. Jing wanted to serve us some newly made raisin bread, which was very good. We exchanged a few presents. Guo gave me a Chinese brush painting for Linda, and another with Chinese characters for myself. I presented to Jing an olive wood Madonna and Child carved in Bethlehem, which I bought some years earlier from my friend Abrahim in East Jerusalem.

We went to a restaurant on campus for dinner. On the way, Guo met his friend from the Music Department. While at dinner, we talked about my playing the piano in one of the empty rooms of the Music Building after we finished eating, since it was close by. Guo left the table briefly to see whether the Music Building would still be open. He found that it would be, so it was decided that we would go there before I returned to my hotel. Jing wanted me to play "Amazing Grace," a favorite of hers and many other Chinese, even those who are not Christian and have no idea what the words of the song convey. They simply like the song.

On the way to the Music Building we met the head of the Music Department, and he said he would be delighted to let me play one of their pianos. I had in mind a small practice room, but he brought us instead into a central room in the middle of which stood a Yamaha Grand. Some women students in fancy dresses were just getting out of a practice for an upcoming performance, and they, along with a few others, including Jing, Guo, and the music professor, became my unanticipated audience. I played "Amazing Grace," and then "How Great Thou Art," which all of them knew. Then I shifted to some American folk music, playing "Don't Fence Me In" (to which one student began tapping his foot), and "Over the Waves Waltz" ("The Loveliest Night of the Year"). By then my audience had grown to 30 or more, and all gave me appreciative applause when I finished. The music professor asked me what I thought of the piano, and I said the action in the upper register was causing me some problem, but on the whole the piano was a fine one. We left after my 15-minute concert with friendly good-byes, walked to the university gate, and I took a taxi back to my hotel. It had been a fine day, and I had my first opportunity to play the piano in China; it would not be my last.

I visited Xiangyang again, on Sunday, October 19, 2014, after we had spent the morning in Fancheng. Brother Ho took us to see the former Bethesda Hospital, which was right where it was supposed to be, but looked nothing like the old pictures I had seen. The original hospital was larger, and beautifully landscaped. All these former lovely grounds around the old hospital were gone. Another building was now next to it, along with a Buddhist temple. The emergency entrance in Vivian Johnson's picture was now boarded up. We did not go inside, but I was glad just to see the hospital that had been such an important part of our Covenant mission work.

Bethesda Hospital, Xiangyang, in 2014

We left the hospital and went to see the location of the old Covenant Mission compound. Brother Ho knew exactly where it was, just inside the West Gate. Once again, we were glad for his help in locating the place, as otherwise we would never have found it. Two streets bordering the compound were reported to be important commercial streets, indicating that the location was a good one. An old man who was present remembered the church, and said that in 1961 a strong wind blew the roof off. Then in 1970, during the Cultural Revolution, the building was torn down and the land given by the government to charity. Brother Ho showed us where the front of the church was, along one street near the corner, and he said this is where seekers would line up. After the church was razed, or perhaps before, some unsightly apartment buildings were erected on the site.

We went into the courtyard between two of the buildings, where people were happy to talk with us. One old woman remembered the church and the mission compound. We were shown what was said to be remnants of the foundation of one of the old buildings. The portion of a pillar was said to be visible up three or four flights in one of the buildings. Jiang went up to investigate, and said that he saw it.

After a rest, Jing suggested that we take a boat ride across the Han. It was raining slightly, so we brought along umbrellas. The covered boat was small with benches along both sides and in the middle, holding perhaps 40 to 50 people. Today three bridges cross the Han, built at different times, but when the missionaries were there all crossings had to be by boat. The Han is not as deep and wide as the Yangtze, but here at Xiangfan it is wider than at other places, and there was one island in the middle. The current flows from northwest to southeast, with the river emptying into the Yangtze at Hankou.

Little North Gate, Xiangyang

The rain stopped, but the pollution was terrible, so we could barely see across the river. On our way to the boat ride we saw the Little North Gate, which Millie and Ed Nelson, carrying four month-old Mary Beth, passed through when they exited the city for the last time in January, 1948.[8] The day had been full, but since we had seen everything we wanted to see, a decision was made to head south to Jingzhou in the morning. Brother Ho generously offered to drive us the full distance in his Honda van. I requested that we take the old road as I wanted to see the area north of Jingmen where bandits attacked the truck carrying the Covenant missionaries in 1948, robbing its passengers and then killing Dr. Alex Berg, Martha Anderson, and Esther Nordlund.

8. E. G. Nelson, *China in Your Blood*, 7, 52.

DEDICATION OF A NEW CHURCH IN NANZHANG (NANCHANG) IN 2007

After nearly 60 years we are now seeing the fruit of labor by Covenant China missionaries. Congregations and church buildings exist throughout Hubei Province. On November 14, 2007 a newly constructed church building was dedicated in Nanzhang with Covenant representatives present for the occasion: Curt Peterson, Executive Director for Covenant World Mission, Taiwan missionaries David and Judy Dolan, and representatives of the Hillcrest Covenant Church in Prairie Village, Kansas City.[9] One of two elderly women in the church remembered care given her by Dr. Mildred Nordlund and Carl Branstrom, the last two missionaries to serve there. For more on the churches in Nanzhang County, see "A Brief Introduction of Christianity in Nanzhang County" in Appendix 3.

The Nanzhang Church

9. See "Covenant News Service" on Covenant Website for November 17, 2007.

Nanzhang Church Interior

VISIT TO NANZHANG (NANCHANG) IN 2008

On Monday morning, May 26, 2008 Jing, her husband, Guo, and I boarded a bus at the Xiangyang bus station for Nanzhang (Nanchang), about one-hour south. We found the Nanzhang church with the help of a taxi driver, and once there we met the evangelist Leng Jia-quan (he did not call himself a pastor), and his wife, Luo Ling. Later we would meet the two elderly women, Qian Xiu-zhen (87) and Yang Chun-hua (77), who were present for the dedication of the new church building a year ago, and shared memories of the last Covenant missionaries to serve in China. We were given a tour of the church, and then visited briefly with Leng and Luo in one of the rooms on ground level. The two elderly women were called, and they said we could come to the apartment of one of them for a visit. Both would be there.

Evangelist Leng Jia-quan and his wife Luo Ling of the Nanzhang Church

Jack in Pedicab in Nanzhang

It was decided that the trip to the elderly woman's apartment would be made by pedicab, so four pedicabs with drivers were called. I was put in one of them, Jing and Guo in another, Leng and Luo in a third, and a lady from the church in a fourth. My ride to the appointed destination turned out to be an adventure I had not anticipated. We began our caravan through the narrow streets and back alleys of Nanzhang, turning right and left, avoiding people and corners of buildings, and driving at one point over someone's harvested crop drying on the pavement. My vehicle could go a bit faster than the others since it was equipped with a small electric motor, which meant the driver did not have to pedal.

I requested once or twice that my driver pause so I could take a picture. He complied, but I think that because of this we became separated from other pedicabs in the caravan. I was enjoying the ride. We came to a busy street and entered the chaotic flow of traffic. It went without incident, but I watched closely as cars, trucks, and busses whizzed by in both directions as we tried to avoid pedestrians. It all proceeded well, and soon my driver took a sharp turn to the left, and we stopped in front of a building a short distance in from the street. I got out of my pedicab; the others had not yet arrived. I waited, and waited, and waited some more, and still the other pedicabs were not there. My driver remained patiently with me, but since he could not speak English, and I could not speak Chinese, we just looked at each other and smiled. He, too, seemed puzzled that the others had not arrived.

It soon dawned on me that they might not come at all, in which case I was lost. I walked out to the street to see if one might pass by, so I could wave the driver down. But none came. Something had gone awry. My driver was still there, but unable to help. Then a young man came up and asked me in English if I needed assistance. I surely did. I must have looked worried. He told me he had studied English at the University of Beijing, so I proceeded to tell him my story, but he had no more of an idea how to solve my problem than I did. I turned around to see that my driver had now disappeared. The last link to my prior life was cut. Then I remembered having a note in my wallet containing Jing's cell phone number. This fellow had a cell phone, so he could call her. I looked through my wallet and briefcase but could not find the paper. I knew I had it somewhere, but a second time of looking still did not turn it up. Then I looked in the part of my wallet where my money was—where the note should not have been—and there it was! So my newly found friend called Jing's number. No answer.

About this time an older man driving a pedicab came hurriedly toward me, and with him was my cab driver. Was I glad to see the young fellow! The older man motioned for me to get in his cab, which I did, and after saying goodbye to the fellow who tried to help me, we were off, into the busy traffic and back down the narrow alleys and sidewalks, until we came to where my fellow travelers were clustered together. Needless to say, I was very happy to see them, and laughing with relief I began telling my story. But Jing had the look of death on her face, and her tender-hearted husband was near tears. They feared something bad had happened, and had fanned out in all directions asking people if anyone had seen "the foreigner." No one had. Jing had even contacted the police, who happily were not brought into the affair. But me no one could find. I do not know all the details of what actually transpired, but it seems the older man who came to fetch me was the father of my driver. He, too, was a pedicab driver and had become agitated because his son had not come home for lunch. In any case, he was the one who brought us together. It took a while for Jing to calm down, as she was really worried. My driver, it turned out, had taken me to the bus station. They told me later that the young fellow was not too bright. But it all ended well, and after sharing our stories we were back in our pedicabs, on our way to see the elderly women.

Qian Xiu-zhen and Yang Chun-Lua (l. to r.) at Home in Nanzhang

The ladies were waiting for us in a third-floor apartment. The outside of the building was rather shabby, but inside it was cozy and nice. Once we were seated and introductions had been made, I began showing them pictures in the book, *Half a Century of Covenant Foreign Missions*, which I had along with me. Looking at the picture on p. 40 of a group of Chinese individuals, Qian, who had only one eye, immediately recognized Pastor Yu Xing-zai in the first row on the far right. She also recognized Isaac Jacobson on page 24 (far right). We sang together (in English) the first verse of Reginald Heber's hymn, "Holy, Holy, Holy."

Both women recognized the Nanchang Mission Station on page 34, but their memories were different. Apparently there were two buildings looking much the same. One was a residence for two pastors and two women missionaries, used also as a school. The other was an orphanage. Yang, who had lived at the orphanage, said the Japanese bombed that building in 1939, so the pastors gave over their building for use as an orphanage. Qian, however, did not think the orphanage was ever bombed, and remembered both buildings as standing in 1949. She said Yang was not in Nanchang at the time. Both stories may have been credible, or at least partly so. The building could have been bombed in 1939, and then rebuilt so it was standing again in 1949. It is doubtful that Yang, who lived in the orphanage, could have been entirely mistaken about damage being done to the building in which she had been brought up. Oscar Anderson said an orphanage was opened in Nanchang about 1943–44, and that it closed in 1945 because of a Japanese drive through there.[10] In 1949 the ladies told us that the government took over all buildings and property of the Covenant Mission.

I showed them pictures of the Chinese pastor and Chinese evangelist with their families on page 52. They were particularly interested in the photo of Pastor Yuan, whom everyone knew, even the present church evangelist and his wife. They also knew his sons. A granddaughter-in-law was now a worshipper in the Nanzhang Church. Pastor Yuan, pictured here with his first wife, died of TB in 1964. His second wife had introduced Leng and Luo during the Cultural Revolution. Both the second wife and Luo were relocated to the countryside and met in the village where they were living. In 1979 the two families returned to Nanzhang. In 1985 Pastor Yuan's second wife gathered Christians together secretly. The next year Leng and Luo were married. By 1995 Christians could meet publicly in the second wife's home, and in 1996 Leng and Luo joined the church.

We all went to a nearby restaurant for dinner, with the women fully able to walk down the three flights of stairs and the short distance to the restaurant. Contrary to Chinese tradition, where the Chinese host is always expected to treat the guest, I prevailed upon them to let me pay for the dinner. Only after I said it was a gift from their friends in the Covenant Church

---

10. C. O. Anderson and R. M. Anderson, *Two Lives of Faith*, 134.

of America did they agree to let me pay. Yang, a widow, still wanted to pay for the meal, but others said she could ill-afford to do so.

Before leaving Nanzhang we went to a Xerox shop to copy some pages of material I had brought along with me. We then took a taxi to the bus station to return to Xiangyang. As we pulled up in front of the station, I told Jing I recognized the place. Not long ago I had been there.

VISIT TO YICHENG (ICHENG) IN 2008

On Sunday afternoon, May 25, 2008, after we had been to church in Fancheng and gone out for dinner, Jing, Guo, and I took a bus to Yicheng (Icheng), located about 25 miles south of Xiangyang. On the ride we saw people harvesting wheat in the fields, the first of two yearly crops. Large quantities of winnowed grain had been spread in the outer lane of the 4-lane highway, on driveways, and on any available flat surface, to dry. Much had been run over by passing trucks and busses. The terrain was flat, and one could see that this was clearly good farming area.

That day the bus could only take us to the outskirts of the city, as an athletic competition was being held and busses were not allowed inside the city. We were able to get into the city by taxi, however. Having made no advance contacts in Yicheng, we asked the taxi driver if he knew where the church was. He did, and proceeded to drive us there. The name on the outside of the building was Christian Evangelical Church. It was a modest structure, with the sanctuary located on the second floor. Sunday School rooms were on the first floor inside the front entrance.

It was Sunday afternoon when we arrived, between 2:30 and 3:30 p.m., and a worship service was in progress. We quietly took seats on wooden benches in the back row. The man up front was reading the Scripture, after which he offered a prayer. Audible prayers were then spoken by the congregation. A small choir wearing bright orange shirts sang a number, and then a woman, whom we later learned was not the pastor, preached the sermon. When she read a portion of Scripture, all the people read with her in unison. A hymn was also sung.

Sunday Afternoon Worship at the Yicheng Church

The meeting place was simple and unadorned: curtains up front and a small cross above the center pulpit. A television, not being used, was up front to the right. The worship room was not very large, holding perhaps only 100 people. This Sunday it was moderately filled, the ratio of women to men being about 2:1, but people of all ages were in attendance. Men sat to the back on one side.

The sermon this Sunday was on "Why Make Offerings?" A week ago they had collected 3000 yuan (about US $400+) for victims of the earthquake in Chengdu Province, and some people were apparently wondering why the collection was taken. The sermon was meant to answer that question. Four Scriptures were read: Exod 25:1–2 (The Lord telling Moses to take an offering for him); Exod 35:20–22 (Everyone whose heart was stirred brought the Lord's offering to the tent of meeting); Mal 3:10 ("Bring the full tithes into the storehouse"); and Rom 12:1 ("Present your bodies as a living sacrifice"). The preacher had 5 points:

1. Offerings are a present to God, with justice being most important (Mic 6:6–8);

2. Offerings belong to God; they are not ours. God paid a high price to win us back;

3. Attitude of one giving the offering is important: Attitudes are awarded; thus one should not blow a horn before others, and not be a reluctant giver;

4. A citing was made of the widow's mite; and

5. Blessings come from God when we give: God will remember you, and you will have treasure in heaven, with I Tim 6:17–19 given as a reference.

The message took nearly an hour. After a long prayer by the leader we said the Lord's Prayer in unison, and were dismissed. The choir sang again at the end. I noted before the service was over that one of the Chinese Bibles was published in 2002, and a smaller Bible, also present in rack, was published in 1987. The hymnbook—with words and musical numbers above—was published in 1998.

At the end of the service we talked with some people of the church, and were told that this had been an underground church that went public only in 2002. They knew practically nothing about their history, which was now a problem in that they were trying to get official permission to build a church building, and the connection between a prior Christian church had to be established. They seemed to know that the Christian church in Icheng was 100 years old. I confirmed that it was, recalling that in 1905 or 1906 Joel Johnson came to take charge of Covenant missionary work in Icheng. When the people heard this they became very interested in my visit, as they badly needed proof of their history to present to the government officials. I told them about a sister church over in Nanzhang that only recently had dedicated a new building. It turned out that one of the fellows we were talking to had been there for the dedication. I informed him that an early connection existed between churches in Icheng and Nanchang. It was then decided that Jing would translate into Chinese a few pages on Icheng from *Half a Century of Covenant Foreign Missions*, and see that it was given to the people.

VISITS TO JINGMEN (KINGMEN) IN 2008 AND 2014

On Friday morning, May 23, 2008, Jing, her husband Guo, and I took a taxi to the Xiangyang bus station for the 2 ½ hour ride south to Jingmen (Kingmen). I was remembering that at Jingmen Oscar Anderson, Augusta Nelson, and Esther Nordlund were kidnapped by the Red Army in 1931, and that just north of the city three Covenant missionaries were murdered in 1948. These events were uppermost in my mind. We had a fine girls' school in Jingmen, also a small hospital where Otelia Hendrickson worked. What, if anything, remained of Covenant mission work in Jingmen after 60 years?

The journey did not begin well. Our reckless bus driver rear-ended a car, and after a delay of 20 minutes or so, we climbed into another bus to resume the trip. Out of the window I saw fields of spring wheat, rice paddies, and lotus ponds, and stands of poplar trees planted in rows.

When we arrived in Jingmen the rain had stopped. Jing did some inquiring and found out where an older church was located, which was now a primary school. We went to see it on Chant Ning Street in the northern part of the city, across from the railroad station. Then our taxi driver drove us to a new church west of the city center. It was a beautiful tall white building with red trim, on top of which was a large red cross prominently displayed. In gold Chinese characters above the front entrance it said "Christian Evangelical Church." Next to the church building, which had been built in 1999, a large educational unit was currently under construction. A woman at the door invited us to come inside the gate. The interior of the church was simple, with wooden benches that could comfortably seat 400 to 500 people on the main floor. There was also a large balcony. We were told that 1000 people worshiped there on a Sunday. At the front of the sanctuary was a large red cross with Chinese characters above and on both sides. The four characters above said "Immanuel"; characters at the sides said "Jesus Loves You" and "The Lord's Love is Deeper." After a brief visit, we were given a cordial good-bye, and received a wave from the pastor who was busy on the upper floor of the building under construction.

On the second visit to Jingmen, which was on October 20, 2014, we did not actually go into the city. Brother Ho was taking us on the old road to Jingzhou, the purpose of which was to get a look at the deserted, hilly area north of Jingmen where bandits killed the Covenant missionaries. It was raining, and pollution was bad. Leaving Xiangyang we could see small mountains to the west and southwest. To the east the Han River was visible, but soon it disappeared from view as we were driving due south, and the river proceeded southeast to Hankou. The terrain was now flat, although mountains could still be seen to the west. An electric railway ran west of the highway. Soon land to the west became flat. We were entering the center portion of Hubei Province.

We passed through a couple small towns. One, 28 km south of Xiangyang, was called "Small River" and was part of the Yichang District. A sign said the distance to Yichang was 14 km. The road on which we were traveling, called National Road 207, was now going southeast. Rice was growing in the fields. We came to Yichang, where Jing and I had been in 2008, and drove through town. It is 39.2 km from Xiangyang, and now a much larger city than when our missionaries were there. Leaving Yichang we headed south. Brother Ho said the land here was very rich.

Cao Jing in Front of the Jingmen Church

We now began looking for the site of the robbery and murder of the Covenant missionaries, which occurred 60 km (not 60 miles, as reported in Covenant sources) south of Xiangyang. The area here was deserted, but not particularly hilly. We were in the Jingmen District. We learned from some old men sitting alongside the road that an earlier road ran a short distance to the east. So we were in the right area, but not on the same road our missionaries were traveling. I took a picture anyway. We were 60 km south of Xiangyang, near the town of Huang Ni Po. No one we talked to knew of a place called Hoshihp'u, near where the missionaries were killed. It was said to be 5 miles (5 km?) north of Lo Hsiang (Hsien) Kuan. No one knew of this town either.

I took a second picture before we proceeded to a newer high-speed toll road. We were 65 km south of Xiangyang, and 30 km north of Jingmen. It was another 75 km to Jingzhou. From Jingmen a road went east to Wuhan. The distance from Xiangyang to Jingzhou, which was from the northern to the southern end of the Covenant mission field, was calculated to be 207 km. Brother Ho said the old road would have been 204 km. When we arrived in Jingzhou, we wanted Brother Ho to stay and have dinner with us, but he had to get back to Xiangyang as his family was waiting for him. We thanked him for all the help he had given, and he left for home.

VISITS TO JINGZHOU (KINGCHOW) AND SHASI IN 2008 AND 2014

On Saturday, May 24, 2008 I went with Jing and Guo to Jingzhou. I was especially anxious to see Jingzhou, which was an old city with a wall enclosing the Manchu population, and an area outside where the other Chinese lived. In 2005 the population had grown to 1,600,000. Shasi was a port city on the Yangtze, 5 miles from Jingzhou, where the Swedish Mission Covenant had its mission. The two cities were on the southern boundary of the Covenant field. In my mind that morning was the theological seminary operated jointly by the Swedish Mission Covenant and American Mission Covenant, the oldest seminary in Hubei Province.

On that morning we boarded a large bus that took us down a modern road through the Han River Valley. The bus driver was a bit reckless, crossing the double yellow line with abandon and laying on his horn continually, even when it was unnecessary and seemingly to announce only to oncoming traffic that he was coming through. Thankfully there was not much traffic on the road, just a few trucks. The driver was also not averse to spitting and blowing his nose on the bus floor.

We arrived at the large relatively clean city of Jingzhou, and looked first for a place to have lunch. Locating a nice restaurant after inspecting three or four others, we were directed into a private room, and were ready to order when it became obvious that the mosquitoes were more than we could handle. The owner said an adjacent room would be better, so we moved there. Jing and I still put on insect repellent that I had brought along. Guo said he didn't need any. The lunch was good, however.

Jingzhou-Shasi Church

Interior Stairway of Jingzhou-Shasi Church"

A taxi took us to a new church, which turned out to be a large structure with green windows and a red cross at the top. Its name was the Jingzhou Christian Shasi Church. Once inside we found the pastor, the Rev. Ding Jianghua, who with help from others was moving a piano up the stairs. How they would get it up those many flights was anyone's guess. The instrument was for the pastor's daughter. We would have to wait until the moving job was finished before talking with the pastor. So we went upstairs to look at the sanctuary, which was the most beautiful seen thus far. Again, simple benches, but here stained dark. Single yellow flowers at the end of each pew, on the middle aisle, apparently for a special service to be held later, added color to the dark wood. We were told that 500 to 600 people gathered for worship here on a Sunday, most sitting on the main floor, with a few in the balcony. On the back wall of the balcony was Johann Hofmann's famous "Gethsemane" painting. It was unusual to see artwork in a Chinese church.

Jingzhou-Shasi Church Interior

In the front of the church was a large red cross below which appeared "God Be With Us" in English. The church had a divided chancel with small pulpits or lecterns on either side, each having a white cross on the front. A communion table stood in the center. A red banner above a red cross read in Chinese: "(We) offer our prayers for victims of the earthquake in Wenchuan, Sichuan." Yellow banners down the pillars on either side contained words from Luke 2:14: "Glory to God in the highest, and on earth peace among men with whom he is pleased."

We were served tea in a small downstairs room and shown some church pictures, most of which were recent. Some people from Concordia Lutheran Seminary in St. Louis (Missouri Synod) had visited the place earlier, and left a picture of the old Zion Chapel in Shasi, dedicated in 1931 but destroyed by Japanese bombs in 1939. The young pastor had now joined us. He had only a vague knowledge of the old Kingchow Seminary, but said he would be willing to call an 82-year old man in the congregation to see if we could come and visit him. Perhaps he could tell us something. Happily, word came back that we were welcome to come to his house.

Pastor Ding drove us there in a new Buick van. We entered through the East Gate of the old city, and traveled down the main street of Jingzhouan, passing the place where the old seminary was said to have been located, though now it was a military installation. All we could see as we drove past was a tree-lined drive inside the front gate. We were in the middle of old Jingzhou.

We arrived at the apartment of Shing Hua Tang and his wife Kuan Yu Chun, for an encounter that became one of the high points of the visit to Hubei. Hua Tang had attended the Covenant middle school from 1940–1945. He brought out an album and showed me a middle school class pictured in front of the seminary building. It was from 1941. I could not believe what I saw. I had a picture with me of seminary students and teachers in front of the same building.[11] We looked at one another in astonishment. It was an exciting moment! He showed me another picture taken between 1920 and 1922, showing seminary students and teachers at the same place. Hua Tang's father was in that picture. His name was Tang Jin Cheng, and he graduated from our Jingzhou theological seminary.

---

11. *Half a Century of Covenant Foreign Missions*, 71.

Shing Hua Tang and Jack Comparing Old Pictures

Signing Book with Shing Hua Tang and His Wife Kuan Yu Chun

Hua Tang thought he recognized Marcus Ch'eng in a picture I brought along,[12] but named him as Pastor Liu, who appears to have been another Chinese preacher.[13] Hua Tang remembered the murder of the three Covenant missionaries in 1948, and said that his father, Jin Cheng, was the one who met the bodies when they came by truck to Jingzhou. He remembered the day: Friday, January 9, 1948. His father had a part in the service held in

---

12. Ibid., 115.

13. Jacobson, "Present Conditions on Our Field in China," 82.

Jingzhou. I gave him a copy of Viola Larson's account of this tragedy, and showed him pictures of Martha Anderson and Esther Nordlund.[14] He gave me in return a copy of his family history containing a number of pictures, including one of his father and mother.

They wanted us to stay into Sunday, but we told them we could not as we were expected at a service at the Fancheng church. They served us pear slices with toothpicks, and some squares that could easily rival our rice crispy squares. It was a wonderful visit. On the way to the car we paused to look at Hua Tang's small garden, from which he picked two beautiful cucumbers for us to take with us. We said warm good-byes, and were driven off to the bus station.

The three-hour ride back to Xiangyang went without incident. This driver was a good one. But we had to put up with some mindless violence on the overhead TV, until the driver changed to Tom and Jerry cartoons, which were dubbed in Chinese. I learned later that the cartoons were for my benefit. In any case, they were a welcomed change.

My return visit to Jingzhou and Shasi occurred on October 21, 2014, when Jing, Jiang, and I arrived in the good company of Brother Ho. Our hotel was on Jiang Jin Road, which divided Jingzhou from Shasi. We took a taxi southeast to Shasi, where the Jingzhou-Shasi Church was located, and which Jing and I had seen in 2008.

We arrived at the church and found that Ding Jiang-hua was still the pastor. He had been there 15 years, and enjoyed good relations with the government. In fact, he was one of six pastors chosen to carry the torch for the 2005 Olympics. Pastor Ding was busy, so a couple of old ladies sitting at the front door, and the pastor's wife, Peng Jin-wen, welcomed us. We took some pictures outside the church. Peng Jin-wen could not speak English, but as I stood by her I heard her humming "Amazing Grace." I told someone I recognized the tune, and asked if there was a piano in the church that I could play. There was. We walked up the side aisle of the church sanctuary and then onto a stage in front, where, in the corner stood a beautiful grand piano. Jin-wen took the cover off, and I began playing "Amazing Grace." Jin-wen joined in singing the song in Chinese. What a voice she had! I then played "How Great Thou Art," "Thanks to God for my Redeemer," and "What a Friend We Have in Jesus." She sang them all. The latter she began to sing on her own, and I picked it up on the piano. It was great fun. I told her I would be willing to go on tour with her in the United States, which brought great laughter when translated. Later at lunch this was repeated, and it was suggested that her husband should probably go along with her. I said, "Well,

---

14. *Half a Century of Covenant Foreign Missions*, 158, 161.

OK." Just then Pastor Ding came down from upstairs, and we were happy to see each other again.

Jack and Jin-wen in Concert Rehearsal, Jingzhou-Shasi Church

On this trip I wanted to see the old port at Shasi, as this is where our missionaries entered and left the Covenant field from the south. We took a taxi there, and on the way saw a big new bridge that spans the Yangtze. The river here is wide, and we could barely see across because of the pollution. At the old port were many shops, and I asked if this had always been so. They said it had always been a market area. We came to the old stairs descending to the boats. They were "L-shaped," and still in use. It was very moving to think that our missionaries walked these very stairs to and from the water bank, where they got in smaller boats to go further out where the steamers were anchored. We took a number of pictures. Jing went to the bottom of the stairs, and fetched a small round stone from the Yangtze, which she gave to me. Next to the old port was a large Roman Catholic church. The Roman Catholics had already been in Shasi for many years when the Covenant missionaries arrived. We also learned that an American Episcopal Mission had been in Shasi since 1868, reminding me that Covenant missionaries spoke occasionally of having met priests from this mission.

Stairs at Old Shasi Harbor

Old Harbor Stairs

Harbor Stairs and the Yangtze River

After we left the old port of Shasi we returned to the church, where Pastor Ding told us he wanted us to make another visit to Shing Hua Tang and his wife Kuan Yu Chun in their apartment. We had been with them in 2008, and were delighted to be able to see them again. Hua Tang was out in the courtyard to welcome us, and remembered our earlier visit. He said he was now 88 (actually he was 87, adding a year as the Chinese like to do). Pastor Ding said the Chinese do not like to reveal their real age, but another explanation is that a child in the womb is considered one year old as soon as the first Chinese New Year occurs. Yu Chun was now bedridden, suffering from heart trouble and a problem in her legs. On some days people would come to care for her, but today there was no one, so Hua Tang was looking after her. She was said to be 91 (but with the +1 factor, she was probably only 90).

We went up the stairs into the apartment, going first into the bedroom to see Yu Chun. She was frail, but happy to see us. We then went into the living room to sit for a while and visit. Jin-wen remained in the bedroom, talking to Yu Chun and holding her hand. Hua Tang wanted us to have a box of tea, which we accepted with gratitude. He also gave us oranges to eat. We made one last visit to Yu Chun in the bedroom, and then prepared to leave. Hua Tang wanted to walk with us down to the car and bid us good-bye as we drove out. Before we left he went again into his garden plot and this time picked some cabbage to give to Jin-wen.

We then went out for lunch, and we were joined by a woman pastor from another church in Shasi. Her first name was Jiang Hui, and she had also taken the English name of Benita. I tasted some of Jing's fish, which was on the spicy side. My fare was carrots, cabbage, and rice soup, all very tasty.

While we were there Pastor Ding gave me an anniversary booklet of the Jingzhou City Christian Shasi Church, marking the 30th anniversary of the church's renewal in 1983. It was a beautiful book, prepared by the Swedish Mission Church in Sweden. On page 6 was a group picture including Dr. P. P. Waldenström, who visited Shasi in 1907 and gave enthusiastic support to the opening of a seminary. On page 14 was a picture of Tang Jin-cheng, Hua Tang's father, who was a pastor and teacher at the theological seminary. The booklet contained much important historical information and many fine pictures. The next couple days Jing aided me greatly by translating considerable portions of the Chinese text.

After lunch we drove down a small street to the location of the former theological seminary. It is now completely fenced in, and as at the last time we visited, we could not get in because it was an army installation. All we could see this time was an iron fence on the other side of which were two large trees, which Pastor Ding said had likely been planted by the missionaries. Jiang went up another small road to a place where he was able to get a glimpse into the interior. There he reported having seen a large open field.

VISITS TO CHANGSHA IN 2010 AND 2014

On March 25–27, 2010 I visited Changsha to give a lecture at the Hunan Bible Institute. This was not the older more famous school of the same name, but a small Bible school located on 22 Guqu Road North, in the Furong District of Changsha. Time there allowed only visits to the Hunan Provincial Museum, the Hunan Embroidery Institute, and a walk with students in the outdoor mall.

When Jing, Jiang, and I returned to Changsha on October 22, 2014, my hope was to locate, if possible, the former Hunan Bible Institute. This was a well-known Bible school in China before the communist revolution, and I was not sure whether it was still there. All I knew was that the school sustained bombing damage by the Japanese during their occupation of China. Some Covenant missionaries, e.g. Mabel Olson, spent time teaching there, and when our missionaries had to evacuate Hubei Province in 1948 and 1949, she and Paul Backlund were again teaching there before relocating to southwest China.

On October 22, 2014, Jing, Jiang, and I boarded a high-speed train (CRH) from Jingzhou to Changsha. It would go via Hankou, which was east, and then proceed south to Changsha. In Changsha, Jing and Jiang located the old Hunan Bible Institute, which had been taken over by the old Provincial Government. Walking about freely inside the campus, they found an old building and photographed the entrance and a plaque on the wall. The plaque confirmed that this was indeed the former Hunan Biblical Institute, and said it had been connected with the Bible Institute of Los Angeles (Biola) in America. It was built in 1917. This was the place I had hoped to see. Later that day, we were allowed to enter, and I took pictures of the exterior. We then went to the entrance, where I photographed the plaque on the wall. Since no one was around, we decided to go inside.

The interior of the building was beautiful, still looking much like the school I had imagined. I took pictures of the stairway to an upper floor, also of the hallway of doors into the first floor rooms. It was truly amazing to see this old building of the Hunan Bible Institute. We wanted to get a better look at the garden courtyard, so an old lady sitting guard turned on what had to be no more than a 40-watt bulb. It was kind of her, but it made absolutely no difference. The courtyard had to be viewed in near darkness, but we thanked her for her trouble and left.

Interior Stairway, Old Hunan Bible Institute, Changsha

First Floor Hallway, Old Hunan Bible Institute, Changsha

Upon exiting the building we noted a park area a short distance away, beyond which we could see another park with a fountain. There were many beautiful old trees.

VISITS TO BEIJING (PEKING) IN 2008 AND 2014

On March 19–23, 2008 Linda and I, together with our daughter Jeanie who was visiting China, made what was our first visit to Beijing. We went basically as tourists, riding the metro, visiting the Forbidden City, Tian'anmen Square and a stretch of the Great Wall at Mutianyu, 50 miles northeast of Beijing. The high point of the visit was attending the Easter Eve vigil at St. Joseph's Cathedral, located not far from the Forbidden City. The church was packed with worshipers, and we sat for an hour and a half holding lighted candles in semi-darkness. Then, all of a sudden, the great lights in this huge cathedral came on, the choir began singing, and banners went up. We could not understand a word, but we knew what the message was: "Hallelujah, Christ is risen!"

I returned to Beijing in October, 2014, this time preceeding the visit with Jing and Jiang to Hubei, Hunan, and Guling in the Lushan Mountains.

While in Beijing I gave an evening lecture on October 16 to the Logos Forum, a Christian study group meeting in the city.

On the return to Beijing after our trip to central China, on Sunday afternoon, October 26, Jing, her husband Guo, and I attended a small worship service in a rented apartment. At the beginning the leader had everyone practice a song that would be sung. Then we observed a few moments of silence before the service began. After singing a couple songs I did not know, we stood and recited Psalm 103 responsively. Then came more songs.

The man leading the service led in prayers. Someone seated in the back also offered a prayer. The sermon was by a woman visiting from another church, and her title was "Jacob's Wife Rachel Gave Birth to Sons." Texts were Gen 30:14–24; Eph 5:22–33; and Psa 128:1–6. The people all recited Psalm 128 in unison. Then everyone looked up Romans 2:4 and recited it in unison. After that they recited Psa 116:5–14, and sang a song based on Psalm 116.

After more prayers, it was time for me to introduce myself, which I did, as did another woman who was there for the first time. Then on the overhead appeared topics the people were to pray for. I spent the time looking through a songbook that had been given me, and found that many of the songs were translations of old Anglo-American revivalist hymns, e.g., "Follow On" (W. O. Cushing, #737); "Jesus Savior Pilot Me" (Edward Hopper; #736); "Leaning on the Everlasting Arms" (Elisha Hoffman; #734); "All the Way My Savior Leads Me" (Fanny Crosby; #730); "Lead Kindly Light" (John H. Newman; #729); and some William Bradbury song (#728). The service closed with people reciting the Lord's Prayer.

On Monday, October 27, I gave a lecture at Capital Normal University to graduate students in a comparative literature course. The teacher of the class was Professor Yi Xiaoming. I spoke about my work in Jeremiah, the Hebrew Prophets, and a forthcoming book on *Jesus' Sermon on the Mount*. The class consisted of two young men and about 8 or 9 girls. Most understood and could speak some English. After the lecture we had a good time of questions and answers. Before leaving I passed out copies of some of my wife Linda's pencil renderings, which were received with gratitude.

In the evening I attended a Bible study that met in an apartment building. Beforehand we were treated to food brought in from Seven Eleven. I received a container of egg and tomatoes, eggplant, and rice. Jiang opened the study with prayer, after which I spoke to the group about my forthcoming book on *Jesus' Sermon on the Mount*.

VISIT TO GUANGZHOU (CANTON) IN 2007

Guangzhou (formerly called Canton) is located in southern China, a short distance inland from Hong Kong. It is the city that gave sanctuary to Robert Morrison, the first Protestant missionary to China, who arrived there in September, 1807. Covenant missionaries Ed and Millie Nelson, and others, passed through this city in their final evacuation of the Chinese mainland in 1949, on their way to Hong Kong.

I was invited to give a lecture at Sun Yat Sen University, on November 20, 2007, so Linda and I made a day trip on the train from Hong Kong. With us was New Testament Professor Ted Zimmerman of the Lutheran Theological Seminary, Hong Kong.

VISIT TO XIAN (SIAN) IN 2010

Xian (Sian) is another old city in China, the capital of Shaanxi Province. In ancient times it was the terminus of the Silk Road. My purpose in going there on April 7–11, 2010 was to give two lectures at the Shaanxi Bible School. Linda and our daughter Jeanie accompanied me on the trip. On the first day we walked the streets and saw the Bell Tower, which was classic Ming architecture of 1384. I struck the bell for all Xian to hear! We then walked over to the Drum Tower where I gave the drum another mighty hit. Near the Drum Tower was the Muslim Street with little shops, which we visited briefly.

The next day we walked down to the South Gate of the 14th c. city wall. Old Xian was completely walled in, with four city gates. Once up on the wall, Linda and Jeanie were given a rickshaw ride by a friendly driver, after which each had "chops" made by a carver in a shop. He was an incredible craftsman, and it was amazing just to watch him at his work.

On Saturday, April 10, Professor Mark from the Bible School took us to see the museum of terra-cotta warriors and horses of Emperor Qin Shihuang (221–201 B.C.). Three major pits had been excavated. The yield thus far has been 1087 warriors, with many more—perhaps 6000—still underground. Mark also took us to the Xian Beilin Museum to view the famous Nestorian Stele, cut in 781 in Chinese and Syrian. This stele records the history of the first Christians in China—the Nestorians in Chanjan (Xian), 635–638—compiled by a Syriac missionary named Alopen.[15]

On Sunday, April 11, we found an old church about which we had heard, said to be located near the YMCA where we were staying. It was

---

15. Modern scholars now call the Nestorians the "Church of the East."

down an alley that served as an overflow for people who had to remain outside on benches. We arrived while the first service was in progress, and were fortunate to get seats on one of the benches. When the first service was over, we squeezed into the sanctuary of the church amidst the press of worshipers who were leaving, and took seats, intending to stay for at least the first part of the second service. The interior of the church was simple—just a red cross on the front wall. The choir director first went over hymns that would be sung. Since everyone was reading out of Chinese Bibles and hymnbooks, we could understand nothing; still, it was inspiring just to be there.

VISIT TO GULING (KULING) IN 2014

On my China trip of 2014 I especially wanted to visit Guling (Kuling), the retreat center in the Lushan Mountains where Covenant missionaries, along with other missionaries and Westerners resident in China, went during the summer months to escape the heat. It lay above Jiujiang, a city on the southern shore of Yangtze in the north of Jiangxi Province. After the communist takeover in 1949, Guling became a meeting place for the communist party. Mao Zedong and Chou En-lai both had residences there.

On October 23, 2014 Jing, Jiang, and I arrived at the Jiujiang Railway Station, where a man met us who would bring us up to Guling. We would not have to climb the many steps carved out of the mountain, as there was now a north and south road to the top. The road up the mountain was winding all the way, and about all we could see with aid from the car headlights were white painted trunks of unbarked trees, from ground level up about five feet, that lined the roadway. Nevertheless, it was a beautiful drive.

Upon entering Guling we stopped at a small lake in the middle of which were two lit-up pagodas. They were beautiful in the dark, and we took pictures. We learned later this was Lin Lin Lake, adjacent to the villa of Mao Zedong. On Friday, October 24, we woke up to blue sky and morning sun, which we saw for the first time on our trip.

Pagodas in Lin Lin Lake, Guling

Kuling Monument

Guling Street Scene

We hired a taxi driven by a man and his wife who agreed to take us on a search for buildings I wanted to see. I had with me pictures taken by Vivian and Ernie Johnson on their earlier trip, the most important of which were the houses of Peter Matson and Joel Johnson, which had been identified by Norman Dwight, who traveled with the Johnsons. Norman remembered staying with his family in the Matson house when he was young.

First we went to the LuShan Christian Worship Hall, a Protestant church built by the British in 1910, which originally was a medical hall belonging to the British Christian Council. The hall was converted into a place of worship in 1946. Chiang Kai-shek and his wife used to worship there. In 1959 the Communist Central Committee took it over and made it into a meeting hall. Then in 1986 it was returned to Christians for worship.

Old Protestant Church, Guling

Old Protestant Church Interior

We then went to the Anglican Church, where missionaries Carl and Lillian Branstrom were married in July, 1935, and Vivian Anderson was the flower girl. Artwork around the sanctuary depicted biblical scenes from both Old and New Testament. Mao Zedong in his time replaced the floor and used the church as a dance hall. Today the building has been restored as a church, but it was not currently being used for worship.

Anglican Church, Guling

Anglican Church Interior

Next we found Joel Johnson's old house, which could readily be identified from Vivian's picture. It now had bright blue additions. We were then shown a house belonging to the Swedish Mission Covenant, beside which was a sign saying that the SMF was the original owner, and that building began on August 4, 1905. It was a substantial stone building.

Joel Johnson's House, Guling

Upper Portion of Joel Johnson's House

It remained now to locate Peter Matson's house, which proved more difficult. We succeeded finally with the good help of the woman taxi driver, who had a relative working at the Lushan Villas Hotel that was able to provide us with the information we needed. The Matson house and adjacent buildings were now part of the Lushan Villas Hotel, the main building of which was up the hill. The house is well preserved, and serves as a guest house of the hotel. We were told it has three bedrooms upstairs, and with proper credentials one could stay there for 2000 yuan ($333.34) per night. The house is listed as #178 Lin bo-qu Villa, the number being marked at the front door. It is located just inside a (now locked) gate on East River Road. Another well preserved house stood next to it, which could have belonged to the American Mission Covenant, but there was no way to be sure. The houses had nicely kept yards and well-trimmed bushes.

Peter Matson's House, Guling

Peter Matson's House and Front Bushes

Matson's Front Door and Sign for #178 Lin bo-qu Villa

Old British Hospital, Guling

Across River East Road was the former British Hospital where many of our missionaries were cared for. There Vivian Anderson was born in 1932, and Dora Nordlund died in 1933. In recent years the hospital had been made into the LuShan Hotel, but now the building was no longer a hotel. Seeing Peter Matson's old house was for me one of the great moments of my China trip. He was last resident in the house 75 years ago.

The next morning we hired the same taxi driver and his wife to give us an additional tour of Guling. I particularly wanted to see the old mountain walkway that people had to walk or be carried up in sedan chair to Guling, before any car road was built. We could not view the stairs from below as the road was inaccessible, so were taken to the top where the stairway ended and weary travelers entered Guling. We proceeded to an overlook where the upper portion of the walkway was visible.

Upper Portion of Mountain Climb, Guling

At the overlook we could see the walkway carved into the side of the mountain, winding its way downward. An old shirtless man sitting with us on a bench told us that for exercise he goes up and down the walkway every week, all year. While it usually takes people three hours, he makes it in 80 minutes. The man looked to be about 50. Around the overlook were small pine trees.

Small Guling Lake

We then drove to a beautiful lake and sat for a while at a pavilion over-looking the lake. We were told that Mao Zedong and Chou En-lai had their residences there. Later we drove to Lin Lin Lake (Red Grove Lake), which was the lake we had first seen in the darkness on our arrival in Guling. It turned out to be a reservoir, adjacent to the former villa of Mao Zedong. We looked briefly in the villa museum. The taxi driver then drove us down the mountain and left us off at the railway station about 3:00 p.m. We were booked on an overnight sleeper to Beijing.

VISIT TO MACAU IN 2007

Macau is located 37 miles southwest of Hong Kong, and today, like Hong Kong, is a Special Administrative Region in the People's Republic of China (PRC). It was formerly a Portuguese colony—from the mid-sixteenth century until 1999, when it was handed back to China.[16] Linda and I made the short trip by turbojet in September, 2007, staying only one day and returning to Hong Kong in the evening. In Macau are ruins of the St. Paul (São Paulo) Church, built in 1602 by the Jesuits, and said to have been at the time the greatest monument to Christianity in Asia. All that is left of the church is the facade and the foundations. We also visited St. Dominic's Church with its magnificent baroque altar, built in the seventeenth century. Macau is the other city that gave sanctuary to Robert Morrison, the first Protestant missionary to China, in the early nineteenth century.

HONG KONG IN 2007–2008 AND 2010

The American Mission Covenant had no mission station in Hong Kong, which at the time was under British rule. But Covenant missionaries were there, visiting as tourists; teaching, as Earl Dahlstrom and Paul Backlund did at the Kikungshan American School for missionary children, which re-located to Cheung Chau Island after having to leave the Chinese mainland; and early in 1949, when missionaries had to evacuate the Chinese mainland, a number spent time there doing missionary work of various sorts before relocating to Japan, Taiwan, or else going home.

Hong Kong today, which consists of Hong Kong Island, Cheung Chau Island, Kowloon, the New Territories, and some other small islands, is a

16. The treaty between Portugal and China of December 20, 1999 stated that Macau would retain its high degree of autonomy until 2049.

Special Administrative Region in the People's Republic of China (PRC).[17] Linda and I were in Hong Kong during the school year of 2007–2008, and again for all of 2010, when I was Visiting Professor at the Lutheran Theological Seminary, Hong Kong. The seminary, which relocated from Shekow on the mainland before the communist takeover, is now located at Shatin in the New Territories, on the mountain retreat of Tao Fung Shan, which in earlier times carried on a ministry to Buddhist monks.

Each year in the last week of August LTS had its seminary retreat on Cheung Chau Island, a good hike up the mountain to the Salecian Retreat Center. During the year, besides participating in activities and festivities of the seminary, Linda and I visited Chinese and American churches in Hong Kong, which students of the seminary pastored or were members of staff, but on most Sunday mornings we worshiped at St John's Cathedral on Hong Kong Island. Otelia Hendrickson and other Covenant missionaries visited this cathedral when they were in Hong Kong.

CONCLUSION

Visiting sites in China connected with the Covenant Church mission, also other sites important in the larger history of the Christian mission to this land, was informative and inspiring, not simply because it provided a window by which one could better view the past, but because it gave concrete evidence of the growth of Christianity through 30 years of repression into the twenty-first century.

---

17. Hong Kong was returned to China after 150 years of British rule on July 1, 1997. The joint British-China declaration stated that its semi-autonomous status would remain unchanged for 50 years (until 2047).

Appendix 1

Missionaries Kidnapped
by General Ho Lung's Red Army

C. Oscar Anderson

CAPTURED![1]

During the decade of the 1920s foreign missionaries in the interior of China frequently had been carried away by robber bands. Some met death at their hands and others either escaped or paid ransom to receive their freedom. During the period from 1928 to 1931 such outrages were chiefly the work of Communist armies. Life in the interior was thus coupled with danger, especially at smaller places away from large centers.

Kingmen, Hupeh, is sixty miles north of the Yangtze River. The province of Hupeh is in the center of China proper, and Kingmen is right in the center of Hupeh. We were therefore literally at the center of things.

In the twenty-five years before 1927 missionaries were able to work successfully in comparative safety. Then, for two years, no foreign missionaries lived there. In January, 1929 we again took over the work in Kingmen, after which for two years great difficulties were sometimes experienced because of large troop movements. The soldiers were very insistent in their demands to occupy our buildings, since they had been used to such living

1. C. O. Anderson and R. M. Anderson, *Two Lives of Faith*, 52–58.

quarters during the few previous years. This condition greatly encumbered us in our work inside the city. Out in the country large bands of robbers were operating, and when soldiers were absent, they became a menace to the city as well.

During the spring of 1931, although rumors of bandits were rampant, we could move about with more freedom and were quite encouraged in the work. The hospital had just been equipped and the work started in real earnest. Part of the district was peaceful, enabling me to visit some of the outstations. The sun of hope and progress seemed to rise after many difficulties and discouragements. Little did we realize that the storm soon to sweep over our cloudless sky was so close. If we had known, there probably would have been another story. Our foreign staff consisted at the time of two women, Miss Augusta Nelson and Miss Esther Nordlund, and me.

During the previous few years the Communists had gained considerably in central China. In some places they had big armies that were well organized and equipped. Soviet governments were established wherever they were able to abide for any length of time. Their aim was to make China communistic, "thereby making it easier for the common people to get their livelihood." Rich people were stripped of their belongings; when it was found that they had oppressed and defrauded the poor they were killed. In order to get cash the Communists kidnapped rich people and held them for ransom.

Among the Communists were many well-educated men who dedicated their lives to the cause. They positively believed that the application of Communism in the world at large was the only way to lift the poor man and solve many perplexing problems of that day.

The Third Red Army was under the command of General Ho Lung, who had for years been notorious in military circles. For two or three years this army had been active in the southern part of Hupeh. During the summer and fall of 1930 they were operating along the border of Hupeh and Hunan. Gradually they made their way into western Hupeh, where they gained ground very rapidly. We in Kingmen knew nothing about their movements. They were able to move swiftly and could therefore surprise a place, making it impossible for the inhabitants to flee.

Such a surprise attack was made on Kingmen April 16, 1931. A merchant came to see me that morning and said that Communists or robbers—he did not know which—had taken a district west of Kingmen. It was not far from our city, and as we always heard reports about bandits we did not pay much attention to it. About two o'clock in the afternoon, to our great astonishment, they were upon us. I was opening a package I had just received from my family when people came in announcing that the Reds had come.

My birthday was not far off, so besides food the package contained a present, but I never saw what it was. I had only unwrapped the outside covering when the Reds arrived. I went out in the yard and met the women and Dr. Yao. We discussed briefly what to do. The only way to escape was through the north gate, but then someone came in and said that this gate was closed.

The Chinese pastor's wife came with her children (her husband was away) wringing her hands in fright, not knowing what to do. We told her to go to the hospital, which she did. We, too, took refuge in the hospital.

Just then shots were heard outside the city and the local militia fled without firing a single shot. Within a few minutes the Reds were inside the city. They went immediately to our station, searching for us. It did not take long before they found the hospital, also. As a last resort we went up into the attic.

At the foot of the attic stairway was a padlock and the door was locked behind us. It was very warm that day. The sun beating down on the tin roof made the attic seem like an oven. Some of the Reds, among them two young women, came into the hospital. They looked all around the place and questioned the doctor and nurse about many things. Naturally, they asked where we were. The staff answered that they did not know; in this they were correct, because they were not present when we went up into the attic. During their search the Reds took medicine and instruments. Later, during their march through the mountains they abandoned the instruments, which were of no use to them.

After half an hour the Reds left the hospital. Then Dr. Yao and the nurse came and talked with us. A thin wall separated the stairway and the small room where we were, so we could converse easily. They told us that the Reds were searching for us all over the city. A man was beating a gong and shouting that if the foreigners could not be found soon, they would without delay begin to murder and to burn the city. They knew that we were in the city.

When we heard this, we feared that the hospital personnel and the Christians in the city would have to suffer for our sake, so we decided to come out. Miss Shih, the head nurse, ran over to the officer who was leader of the troops and told him that we had come back and were waiting for him. He had gone into our compound and into the missionary women's home. Soon he came, together with some soldiers. All carried pistols and machine guns. A beautiful young woman was also with him. They sat down and began to talk to us. The officer was a young man about 20 years old. His home was in the same part of the country as Miss Shih came from. A sister of his had attended the same school as Miss Shih. This probably was one of the reasons why she was not taken. They also were anxious to have doctors and nurses to help them. The officer had a bullet wound in his arm and asked the doctor to dress it.

After some preliminary conversation he asked us if we would like to accompany them when they left. We expressed the fear that we would be too much bother to them, so it was more convenient for the army not to go to the trouble of taking us along. We were soon made to understand that there was no choice. Later he called me in for a private talk during which he said that they wanted $40,000 from us. Showing me his revolver, he told me that if the money was not forthcoming it could do the work. Toward evening we invited the officer and the young woman, whom he called his lover, to have supper with us.

In the evening I had to go with them to my house and open the safe. Usually I had very little money on hand, but at that time I happened to have several hundred dollars that I had prepared for a special purpose. Most of it belonged to the Mission. While at the house they demanded that I hand over the rifles, which they said I had hidden somewhere. It was almost impossible to convince them that I had no guns. During the afternoon they had found a small revolver that belonged to a missionary who had been there before our time, which strengthened their belief that we had more firearms. The leader said that they would beat me if I did not reveal where the guns were hidden. I told him to beat all he wanted, but there still would be no guns. At last they dropped the matter, foregoing the beating.

When I went back to the hospital I was closely guarded by a fellow with a drawn revolver. Our houses had already been occupied, and the soldiers helped themselves to our clothes and other things. We tried to sleep at the hospital but had difficulty doing so. Soldiers with machine guns and big swords guarded us very closely.

During the night they received orders to leave early the next morning and go back to the place from which they had come. Prior to our leaving we were told to put together some extra clothes to bring along. I went to my room to do so, but there was nothing left, so I had to leave with only the clothes I was wearing at the time. The women were given back some of their belongings and found a few things that had not been taken. Dr Yao, who also was forced to go along, brought with him bedding and clothes carried by a special bearer. Because he was to become their army doctor they treated him better. One of the cooks at the hospital went along to be of service to him.

It was sad indeed to have to leave our previous environment. On our march down the street we saw many of the Christians and other friends. Miss Shih went with us half way through the city. She was broken-hearted when she left. It was impossible to hold back the tears. Everything seemed hopeless. What would become of us? I was especially thinking about my family down in Shanghai. How would my dear wife be able to endure the blow? Nevertheless, the Lord comforted us and gave us grace to lean on Him. We were able, calmly, to face uncertainties.

Outside the city the whole contingent of troops had assembled, about seven or eight hundred in all. There were some prisoners, persons taken for ransom. Among them was one of the Christians, a druggist. He was released a few days afterward upon paying a small sum of money. There were also about eighty students taken at the government high school. Some of them were later released, others escaped, and one or two were executed for spreading anti-Red propaganda. During a rest period outside the city one of the Reds, who could speak a little English, came up to Miss Nelson and said: "God bless you." That he did not mean what he said we knew afterward when we learned to know him personally. When everything was ready, the whole company moved on. The women were carried on stretchers, such as were used for carrying sick and wounded. Dr. Yao and I were given horses to ride.

The first day we went through well-known territory. About a month earlier I had traveled that road, spending a week at two of the outstations. In the woods the birds were singing so joyfully. I said to myself, "You happy creature that you are able to sing your song of freedom." I was tempted to wish that I had been one of those little birds. Then I, too, could have sung a song. Now I was unable to sing. We were just like the Israelites at the rivers of Babylon. Our harps were hung up.[2] In spite of these feelings the Lord was very near to us. We were not deprived of our freedom in Christ. No one could take that precious freedom away from us.

At noon we rested at a place called Hwangkiatsi. We had an outstation there with a resident evangelist. Where he and his family had gone I did not know, but they were all safe somewhere.

The first night out we spent at Kwanyinsi. We had an outstation there too, but, of course, we were unable to get in touch with any of the Christians. Dr. Yao and I shared one bed and the women were in another house. They spent a sleepless night because the soldiers on guard came in repeatedly and looked at them to make certain they were still there. It certainly was not easy for them in such a plight. Afterward, other arrangements were made causing them to feel more secure.

The second evening a delegation came to present their demands for ransom. They were very definite and made us feel the seriousness of the situation. There were three points in their demands. What they desired

2. Ps 137:1–4.

above all was ammunition and guns. They also were talking about a wireless outfit. If we could not procure these things we would have to pay a sum of $300,000. Failing to comply with any of these demands, I was to be shot.

We tried to reason with them and they seemed to soften somewhat. They found out, they said, that Miss Nordlund was the poorest of us three. Next came Miss Nelson, who had a little money, and I was the big capitalist. The reason for this was that I handled most of the money at the station. Miss Nelson had the hospital account, while Miss Nordlund had no responsibility for any mission money. Dr. Yao helped us to great advantage in explaining to them that the money which we handled was not our own. If they believed it or not, I cannot say. However, nothing was decided at that place.

The following day we reached the headquarters of the army, where our case was turned over to that body. In the evening we were brought to the quarters of the medical corps for the eighth division. A regiment of this division had captured Kingmen. After supper General Ho Lung came with some of his officers to have a look at us. The General put some questions to us, but he seemed to be in a mood for joking, so one did not know if he was to be taken seriously. With one accord they ridiculed Christianity and us for being followers of Christ.

The young woman with whom we became acquainted in Kingmen made coffee for the party, and we were included. The coffee belonged to Miss Nelson, but of course she was not given credit for the treat. While the coffee was being prepared and consumed, the general entertained us all by telling stories about his own experiences before he came into the ranks of the Communists. While he was in the national army he had more than one wife, but now he limited himself to one. The Communists had abolished polygamy in their ranks, as well as many other old customs. They were very free; nothing of the old conventional stiffness. Ho Lung was a very good-looking man with a splendid physique, about forty years of age at that time.

After we went to bed a conference was held where our fate was decided. I was told a long time afterward that our lives hung in the balance that night. It was to be decided which section of the army should take the responsibility for us. All declined. Then the officer in command of the troops that came to Kingmen said, "If it is this way, then I will take them out and shoot them immediately." Hearing this, the others became concerned, and Dr. Chang, the head of the central medical corps, promised to take us into his group. He had previously refused. The situation was indeed very critical, but the Lord would not let anything happen that was contrary to His will.

The previous demands for ransom were not repeated. Now they wanted only medicine. It was also decided that Miss Nelson should be released in order to secure it. But through the influence of Dr. Chang and, we think, also of Mr. Liu, the head of the central police department, Miss Nordlund also was released. They realized that it would be very hard for the women to keep up with the movements of the army. Thus, after five days of captivity, they were permitted to go back, and they reached Kingmen safely. We surely were thankful to God for His wonderful leading. Dr. Yao had very little hope of ever gaining his freedom, and I did not know what the future would have in store for me, but we were glad to see the two women leave for home.

After they left we stayed at a place called Liangkiatai for a week. A messenger from Kingmen came there with a letter from Mr. Jacobson of Kingchow. I was extremely happy over receiving this word from my comrade. I wrote a letter for the messenger to take back, but on his way home he was taken for a spy and killed by the fanatical Red Spears, bands of resistance fighters drawn from the country people who, made desperate by marauding soldiers, had organized the Red Spear Society to prey on whatever small groups of soldiers they could handle. They were bitter enemies of the Communists.

While we still were at Liangkiatai I had my birthday. Did I receive any congratulations? Dr. Yao knew it somehow, and in the morning he put his arm around me and wished me happy birthday. Was it happy? Not exactly so, but I thank God that circumstances were not any worse. We even had a cup of coffee together. Miss Nelson brought along a can of coffee that had been overlooked by our captors; through her generosity it became our property when she left, but we could never finish it. Extra things had to be left behind when constant marching became the order of the day.

That week seemed as long as a month. We had nothing special to do and could not spend our time walking in the hills. We were allowed to go outside, but had to confine ourselves to the immediate vicinity of the house. It is natural that our physical wellbeing suffered somewhat because of food we were not used to, and because of our lack of exercise. We were well treated, however.

In the meantime the news of our capture was flashed around the world. My family was notified by wire from Kingchow. Anyone can imagine the shock felt by my dear wife. A few days afterward the papers reported that I had been killed, but fortunately this was refuted the next day. My aged father in Sweden got the news over the radio late one evening. The day the women came back to Kingmen, the Swedish Vice Consul from Hankow arrived there together with Mr. Jacobson of Kingchow and Mr. Sommarstrom of the Swedish Mission at Shasi. They had made the trip to try to effect our release. One can realize their joy when they saw the the two women come back. After a day or two at the station they all took a car and left for Shasi.[3]

THE CHASE BEGINS[4]

One day orders came to leave Liangkiatai because troops were converging from different points to fight the Reds. We went a day's journey to a small place where an outstation to Nanchang is located. I talked to some people there who told me that the evangelist had left and his family was in the country. They knew Mr. Jacobson, who had been there several times.

Our destination was Kuohoping, where the Reds intended to locate their base hospital for about a month to treat their many sick and wounded. That plan was frustrated. The government troops drew closer and the chase began. Because it was hard for Dr. Yao to travel, they sometimes had to carry him on a stretcher. He had a weak stomach for years and could not get the right kind of food. He suffered considerably and grew very thin. In spite of it all, we had very sweet fellowship together. The Lord blessed us as we often united in prayer. God was our comfort and strength. Dr. Chang and all those connected with the hospital work were very kind to us. We were not guarded, but were free to go in and out at will.

The next stage of the journey was from Kuohoping to Pantsiao. The first day out they encountered opposition from the local Red Spears, who had already killed a few men of the Red army and were now prepared to make attacks as the Reds came along. The Red Spears believed that no bullets could hurt them after going through their superstitious practices, but the Reds did not believe in any kind of superstition, so were not afraid of them. A small body of troops advanced and soon the local braves were on the run. In the meantime the rest of us stayed behind in a wheat field. Finally, the road was clear and everybody moved on.

They had a hard time keeping order, especially among the hundreds of sick people. The order was given to walk fast, and no was allowed to fall behind; if he did it meant death. A few minutes' walk brought us to the scene of battle. Here dead and wounded were lying on the road with heads split open—a gruesome sight indeed. Out in the fields others had fallen. Some were still living and we could plainly hear their moaning. In order to make a strong impression on the local people, four or five big houses were put to

---

3. Cars were now being used in China. This was still the "Model A era," and Ford had a dealership in Shanghai.

4. C. O. Anderson and R. M. Anderson, *Two Lives of Faith*, 61–73.

torch. These belonged to the leaders of the Red Spears. Only at this place did I see homes burned.

It was already late in the afternoon, and we had a long way to walk. We marched in the moonlight quite a distance and then stayed at a farmhouse for the night. The house was rather small for the hospital crowd, but we had to make the best of it. All the doors were taken down and used for beds. This was a common practice wherever they came. That night I could get no sleep. I was constantly thinking about the experiences of the day, and the moon was shining brightly on my bed.

The following day we came to Pantsiao, where the scenery was very beautiful. A big house, belonging to a rich and prominent family that had fled, was invaded by the hospital staff. There was a great deal of food and everybody feasted. Homemade wine was found in great quantities, and most of them liked to visit those big jars. No doubt the owners would have taken more things with them when they fled, but evidences showed that they had made a hasty exit. Many very large trays of silkworms were left in the kitchen, but no one was there to feed them, so they shriveled up and died.

We were hoping for a prolonged stay, but were disappointed. Troops closed upon the Reds again and one day, about noon, an urgent order came to leave. It rained almost all day. Dr. Yao and I had no umbrellas, so we were drenched. One of the men among the Reds saw that I was without an umbrella and tried to persuade another fellow who had one to give it to me. Although he would not give in, this showed that some were sympathetic toward us and tried to do their best to help us.

The roads were terrible in places and we had to climb very high mountains. My horse gave in and was left behind. I walked the rest of the day, and as we had about twenty-five miles to go that afternoon, we were compelled to walk about seven miles in the dark. The last few miles of the road went along a river. I got hold of a cane during the day, with which I felt my way in the thick darkness. Sometimes the road went very high above the river and the banks were very steep. One unfortunate fellow slid down into a deep hole by the roadside, and we could hear his moaning deep down there somewhere. I fail to know how many times we crossed that river. We were unable to see to jump across on the stones, so there was nothing else to do but plunge in. I still had my leather oxfords at that time, but holes were worn in them so the water could easily run out.

Finally we came to the place where we should stay overnight. There a soviet regime had been established by the local people, and they invited us to their headquarters. They had charcoal fires going, which made it possible for us to dry our clothes and get warm. My bedding did not come that night, so I slept together with Dr. Liu, the physician for the eighth division.

The following day, early in the morning, we started off again, and after an eight-mile march came to a large market town called Maliangping. There the Nanchang Mission had an outstation where good work was being carried on, but because of disturbances it had to be temporarily given up (The work was later resumed.)

After we arrived, Dr. Yao and I were invited to a place where we were given hot biscuits and boiled water. It tasted very good and we had our fill. It was not very often that we could get bread, so we considered this a special treat. Our appearance caught the eye of onlookers. How did we look? My face had not felt a razor for over two weeks. Our clothes were spattered with mud. My shoes, old and worn as they were when I left Kingmen, were special objects of attraction. I am sure that we would have been arrested if we had appeared on a street of an American city.

Some good fellows among the Reds thought very kindly about my shoes. The next day they presented me with a pair of Chinese cloth shoes and a pair of stockings. After a week I was compelled to discard my leather shoes and the Chinese shoes were very much appreciated. I had never worn such shoes before except as bedroom slippers, but for almost two months I wore them every day. The peculiar thing was that they did not wear out even though I walked hundreds of miles in the mountains; neither did my feet blister. I liked them because they were light and did not easily slip.

We remained two days at Maliangping. There they decided to let Dr. Yao return home. He was so sick that they realized he could be of no service to them. Dr. Chang helped in effecting his release. No ransom was paid; instead they gave him ten dollars for traveling expenses. The man who went along from Kingmen to be of service to Dr. Yao also was permitted to return. Both reached Kingmen safely. In all we could see God's wonderful leading. It was rather hard to see him go as now I was left alone, but I thanked God for His mercy in delivering our brother.

I had more reason to thank the Lord because of what we experienced the very day Dr. Yao went. That morning the entire army left Maliangping. Medical corps, sick and wounded, and other sections of the army were ordered about eight miles out in the country. About two hundred soldiers were dispatched to give protection. The rest of the soldiers withdrew to the mountains around Maliangping. They prepared to confront the government troops that had come from three directions to fight them. I have been told that close to ten thousand troops were there to give battle to the Reds.

Our hospital crowd was given a big farmhouse to live in. The owner treated us very kindly. Toward evening a sudden order came for us to rush off. A band of Red Spears had made a surprise attack on the soldiers assigned to protect us. I was sitting by a charcoal fire trying to get warm because malaria bothered me at the time. I felt pain in my abdomen also, and certainly was not fit for a strenuous march. I had a little bottle of brandy in my pocket that I had gotten from Miss Nelson when she left. I had not used it before, but just a few minutes prior to our leaving, I drank a little and it seemed to relieve the pain somewhat.

Horses and mules were not ready for the sudden departure, and we did not see them until late the following day. Thus, we had to walk—or, rather, run. A battle took place a short distance from our dwelling and being outnumbered, the soldiers had to retreat gradually. The farmer at the place where we stayed was asked to lead the way. The road took us back to Maliangping.

At first we were by ourselves, but after a while we joined other groups that came from different directions. The sick and wounded moved very slowly. Some rode horseback, and there were many mules carrying rifles and other things. They would block the paths, causing a general commotion.

Everybody was afraid of falling into the hands of the Red Spears. Many of the sick people did fall behind, and were killed outright. One of the hospital nurses had a very narrow escape. Those who were able tried to get past, and ran through the fields most of the time. Dr. Chang and I ran hand in hand, trying to keep together, but soon were separated. In the scramble we sometimes fell into ditches and stumbled on uneven ground. Our legs and arms were bruised. My glasses were knocked off and never to be seen again. At times I thought of trying to escape, but did not dare.

For a long distance I saw none of the hospital staff. At last some of us got together again and managed to keep in company the rest of the way. They sympathized with me and thought it too bad that I should have to endure such hardships. I told them that I ought to be able to stand it as well as they did. They replied, "We are used to it, but you are not."

As we neared Maliangping a great commotion appeared ahead of us. Those in front came rushing back up the road, nearly trampling the rest of us. We knew nothing of what had happened, so we also turned around and followed. After running a short distance, we decided to stop and find out the reason for all the excitement. Soon orders came to proceed. There was no special danger. Those ahead had been halted by someone below the mountain, and they thought enemies were hiding down there.

When we came near the street, orders were given to ascend a high mountain nearby. General Ho Lung with his staff, as well as the soldiers, were already there. There was no one to lead the way, so we took the wrong road and nearly came into the very nest of the dreaded enemy. So we had to return and start all over again. This time we got on the right road and the ascent began.

It must have been close to midnight when we started our climb. Fortunately we had moonlight and clear sky—a beautiful night. The mountain was very steep and we were already tired, so it was difficult to go upward. I carried a bundle of clothes on my back, which hindered my movements. I thought of throwing it, especially while running, but those few pieces of clothing were precious, so I hung on to them.

I am sure that the ascent was close to five or six miles. Coming half way, we lay down on the ground and rested. The hospital men had thin blankets, which they shared with me. We slept awhile, then started on the last stage of our march. Finally we got to the top, where General Ho Lung had his quarters. I was exhausted when we arrived, and felt unable to take another step. The house was very big, with a good second story. We went up there and slept on the floor the remaining two hours of the early morning.

I never really knew the correct time because my good Elgin watch was taken away from me before we left Kingmen. But it seemed to be about five o'clock when we were called on to continue the journey. Food was prepared, and we ate a little. As I went out, ready to stand in line, I met General Ho Lung. I told him that it would be very difficult for me to walk that day because of the strenuous march during the night. He told me to ride his big mule. This I thought was too generous of him, so I protested and did not want to accept the offer. But I was assured that, besides the mule, he had a good horse, which he would use. I certainly did appreciate this special kindness. I realized many times that if they had wished they could have treated me altogether unsympathetically; but as a rule they did not.

After we left, the Red soldiers fought the government troops, but were outnumbered and had to retreat. A whole regiment was cut off from the rest and considered lost, but a month later they managed to join the others. In the meantime their number had increased. This showed their ability to keep together. Unity of purpose was their strength. They were also able to make the right maneuvers and to move very fast. For that reason they were not easy to surround.

The government troops reported after they got back that the Reds were scattered and almost exterminated. Afterward I saw a Chinese newspaper stating that Ho Lung had only about a thousand poorly equipped men left. This sounded good to the reading public, but it was far from the truth. After that flight it was reported that I had been killed. Some students who were taken at Kingmen and later released said they had seen my grave. No authentic news could get through, so this report was believed for some time.

For a week or more after this experience we had to march every day, except once, when we rested for two days. On account of my previous exertion, malaria got the best of me again. Sometimes I had chills and fever.

I also suffered pain because of a digestive condition. These pains would increase in severity if I had to walk too much. At times I was unable to eat anything except a little rice soup. In spite of all this, I was able to keep pace with them, whether I had to walk or ride horseback.

At times it would rain all day, but still we had to travel. At first I used to pray and pray again that it would cease raining, but I realized that such prayer was not justified and seemed selfish. In whatever difficulty and discouragement I would be, I always prayed for strength to endure. The Lord heard my prayer.

One day it was raining very hard. About two o'clock in the afternoon we came to a stream that was difficult to cross because of the large boulders in its bed. My mule stumbled and fell in the middle of the stream, and I was thrown into the water. The weather was chilly, and when I got up on dry land again I was shivering. Feeling cold, I did not dare to ride any more that day. Thousands had preceded us so the road was in a terrible condition. We were descending a mountain, and I thought we never would come to the foot of it. It required all afternoon. About dusk we took refuge in a farmer's home. Here a bonfire was lit and we tried to dry our clothes. I had to wrap a quilt around me while mine were drying. It required half of the night to finish the job. That day I caught a severe cold, which stayed with me for over a month.

We had left the Nanchang district and come into Paokang. The mountains were just as high and the roads, if anything, more difficult. Grand scenery often met the eye. It would have been a treat to make that trip under ordinary circumstances, but as it was I had grown extremely tired of seeing nothing but mountains. In those mountains, however, were many interesting things. In the most impossible places one could see farmhouses on the hillside, around which patches of wheat and corn were growing. The ground was stony and most of the crops were on the side of the mountain. In some places terraces were built to utilize every bit of ground. The crops were very meager, mostly corn. A great deal of opium poppies was being cultivated. The poppies were in bloom at that time, creating a very beautiful sight. But what a curse all that opium was to the people of China!

Where we stopped overnight almost everything edible was finished off. Where the stay was prolonged to several days everything seemed to be cleaned out; sometimes they had to go to some other locality to get rice and vegetables. Sometimes when we left a place the only living thing that could be seen was a lonely cat or a rooster.

The people usually left before the Reds came, but sometimes they stayed at home. The Reds, as a rule, did not take anything from the poor. They paid for what they got. The Red discipline was very strict. If a soldier extracted money from some poor person he was likely to be shot. I recall an instance when this happened. A soldier took three dollars from a farmer and was executed. The rich, however, lost what they had. Some were captured and held for ransom.

At a place near Maliangping a young girl, seventeen years old, was taken and held for ten thousand dollars ransom. I saw her many times and felt sorry for her. She was compelled to walk from place to place. Her feet had not been bound, which was fortunate for her. The money was not forthcoming, so she was sent to the army hospital to receive training. She seemed to be satisfied with this arrangement. More than a week before I was released she was sent home without paying a cent. It had been decided to establish a Soviet regime at her home place. One of her near relatives was the leader of this undertaking; therefore she was released. It was a pity to see some of the prisoners. If they could not follow along but dropped by the roadside, they were shot on the spot. Once I was a close witness when an old, gray-bearded man was shot.

Day by day we traveled. Gradually we left the big mountains. I was glad when I could see those lofty mountains behind me, and those ahead gradually growing smaller. The roads were somewhat better. The weather, which had been rainy and cool, began to get warmer. I remember the first time that I heard the wild cuckoo bird. It was May 15, our son Edward's birthday. I especially thought of my family that day. Although there was a birthday in the home, they could not rejoice in a full measure because they did not know how Daddy fared. I could get no news and was unable to send any message to them.

On May 16 we came to a marketplace called Kwanyintang, where the Norwegian Mission of Laohokow had an outstation. We were then forty miles from Laohokow. The evangelist had left the outstation, and two old women were in charge of the houses. The hospital corps made the mission station its living quarters. They thought that I could feel at home as I had come into the atmosphere of mission work. Those two old women were very good to me. One of them was a Christian. They helped me wash and mend my clothes, and we talked together, which brought relief to my soul.

While we were at that place I was asked to write a letter to the mission in Siangyang. The Reds wanted them to send the medicine, bought for my release, to Siangyang, and then to await further instruction. Although I knew nothing about what had been done to effect my release, I wrote the letter. Mr Liu of the Political Department took the letter with the intention to have it mailed. I learned afterwards that it was not mailed before a week had passed. After I got out, Mr. Matson told me that he never received the letter. Thus I made no contact at that time.

About five miles from Kwanyintang, out in the country, was a Catholic Mission. They had worked there one or two hundred years and established great institutions. In order to get income to carry on the work they had bought great tracts of land. A detachment of Red soldiers went there, captured the three Italian priests, killed two Chinese priests, and carried away a good portion of loot. They also found several Italian rifles with long bayonets, a number of pistols, two shotguns, and some ammunition. Surely they got a big haul at that place. A pair of high shoes were taken and offered to me. But I declined on the ground that I did not deem it honorable to wear their things; then, too, the shoes were several pounds too heavy. I would rather step around in my cloth shoes.

At that time a Catholic bishop and a priest were on their way to the station. They met a contingent of Red troops on the road and were captured. Thus the Reds had five more foreigners in their hands. They were not kept with the crowd where I was, but had to be together with other prisoners. Sometimes I saw them tied with ropes. A ransom of fifty thousand dollars was set for their release.

The reason for the difference in treatment meted out to them and to me was explained to me once by the secretary in the general's headquarters. He had been a church member and a teacher for several years in a mission at a large center in central China. He said: "as God is a righteous God so are we also on our treatment of you and the priests." "They are big landowners," he said, "and besides they had guns and ammunition at their station. Therefore, we treat them as we treat the Chinese great landowners." He said further: "you are no property holder and for that reason we give you better treatment." I appreciated that they learned the difference between the working methods of the Catholic and the Protestant Church; however, I felt sorry for the priests. It was not that they personally owned anything; they suffered more because of the policy of their organization.

One of the doctors told me that they treated the priests as if they had been "toys," always making disrespectful remarks to them. To begin with we also were targets for such talk. I was glad that the women did not have to be exposed to it more than they were. They ridiculed us because we trusted and believed in God. "What kind of a God is that who permitted us to take you?" they asked. Sometimes accusations were brought against us because we were foreign missionaries. We led people astray and "drugged" them with our preaching. "What is the use to preach the Gospel or believe in God? There is no God but Communism." There was no use to try to refute what was said. Many a time I had to listen to such talk, and much more. Sometimes I argued with them, but usually I kept quiet. These experiences gave me a better understanding of why Christ was silent before his accusers.

Because I was with the army hospital I had a good opportunity to meet many of the officers and leading men. General Ho Lung himself used to come and visit. I had long conversations with many of them. They used to ask me what I thought concerning communism, and then we got to world problems. Russia, of course, was their ideal. Some of the leaders had studied in Russia, and a few had visited other European countries.

One told me that the United States was the foremost imperialistic country in the world. "Its capitalistic system must be broken down," he said. "The world revolution," which is the dream of communists all over the globe, "will bring about its downfall . . . the working man can never come to realize his rights unless individual capitalism is crushed." They asked me about social conditions in the United States and whether we had any beggars. I told them that people were not allowed to beg, and that we have institutions for the aged and hospitals for the sick. They said that this was included in their plans if they would have a chance to govern.

Sometimes we got to religious questions. One said that in a way those who preach the Gospel are working with the same goal as they were. "But this method of preaching does not work in our present age," he said. "Religion has no place in this age of science. A revolution by force is inevitable and the only way to transform society." One told me that when he was younger he thought Christianity possessed the qualities that were necessary for the salvation of China. But then he became acquainted with communism and realized that its doctrine was the only hope of a new China. To transform society by converting individuals was too slow. It had to be done by external force and by putting the theories of communism into practice.

Once I asked two of the leaders what attitude the communist movement would take toward Christianity and other religions in China. Would they forbid the preaching of the Gospel? They replied that they believed in religious liberty. They had that clause in their constitution. "If foreign missionaries or Chinese preachers tend only to their business and do not meddle in politics or in any way hinder the Red revolution, they will suffer no persecution but can go on with their work," one said. Why did they capture us then? "They wanted medicine, that was all." General Ho Lung himself told Dr. Yao and me that they did not like to resort to those methods, but they were at their wits' end and needed medicine for their many sick and wounded. They wanted us to "assist them a little." He said also that he was afraid of Chinese medicines and believed only in the foreign, but they were not able to secure foreign medicines themselves.

At the same time he told us that they had killed a foreign Catholic priest a few weeks before they came to Kingmen. They had found large quantities of ammunition—shells for small guns—stored at his station and thought that he was dealing in ammunition, so they shot him. After I arrived in Kingchow, the real story about the ammunition was told me by a Catholic father at Shasi: government soldiers had lived at the station before the Reds came and had left the material when they departed. A life was cut short because of the soldiers' negligence and because they forcibly occupied the Catholic station. But that is not saying that the Reds were without blame. They should have investigated actual conditions, but did not bother to do this.

Several of the officers with whom I conversed occasionally became my good friends. One I became acquainted with towards the last. He was very sympathetic and promised to do what he could for me after I explained to him my circumstances. To begin with I feared that, even if they received the ransom wanted, they would not let me go, but as I became acquainted with many of the officers I knew there were those who would take my part even if others harbored different opinions.

Leaving Kwanyintang we traveled towards Kunhsien, a big city on the Han River about 60 miles above Laohokow. There the Norwegian Mission had a head station where a Bible school was conducted before the Reds took the place. Several missionaries were stationed there, and as we marched in that direction I prayed constantly that the Lord would lead them out of the approaching danger. They got away just in time. During their first night out their boats were anchored only a mile or two above the city and the shooting was plainly heard.

While they were still at Kwanyintang one division of the army went to Sihuakai, a large town on the south side of the river opposite Laohokow. There the Norwegian Mission had two women stationed. One of them had gone to another place to hold meetings. The one remaining at home did not know that the Reds were coming until it was too late. They came in and began to talk to her, but she answered nothing. Then she was brought to the commander, who could not get a word out of her either. I suppose they thought she was deaf and dumb or else that she did not understand Chinese. He then gave orders to release her. She was caught three different times, but released each time. Many of the missionaries on that side of the river were in great danger, but none was taken.

Kunhsien was taken after a hot engagement, but not before they burned down one of the gates. About five hundred soldiers guarded the city, and when they saw that they were unable to hold it any longer they made good their escape. During the siege we stayed in the country about eight miles out. The day after it was taken everybody was ordered to town. All were happy and in high spirits. Many good things were in store for them. I was among the hopeful as I thought that possibly my release could become a reality while we were in that area. But in that I was disappointed.

The hospital was given a spacious house inside the city. Here were comforts compared to life in the mountains. But I had never been so uncomfortable at night as I was in that house. They gave me a bed of straw. It looked very luxurious, and I would have been at ease if the bed had not contained other living things. I endured it for two nights. The third night, the last, I slept on two chairs.

Our bill of fare was much improved. In the mountains very little food could be secured. I usually ate rice gruel and vegetables, and at times even vegetables were scarce. When pork or chicken could be obtained we were very fortunate. At Kunhsien we really feasted. I had not seen any mirror for weeks, but this city even had such luxuries. I thought it would be interesting to take a look at myself. I was startled at what I beheld. My face, with a beard several weeks old, was very thin and carried a dismal expression. I am afraid that my own people would not have recognized me if we had met.

When the Reds first arrived they went over to the mission station and hauled out all the groceries they could find. They came and handed me a few cans of milk, a big can of cocoa, a bottle of ketchup, some Kraft cheese, and a can of rolled oats. This was my part of the loot. I did feel badly that the station should be robbed of all these good things and was reluctant to use any of it, but thought that I might as well, rather than see it destroyed. The day we arrived I went over to the mission station with Dr. Liu. It was sad, beyond words, to see the wanton destruction going on. After the Reds had taken what they wanted, the local people went in and carried away everything that remained. Even doors and windows were taken out. Books were strewn all over. Only a skeleton of the house was left after they had satisfied their greed. I thought to myself that they certainly do not know what they are doing. An organ was carried over to where I stayed, and someone was playing on that all the time. Dr. Liu, who was a Christian, knew how to play. After he had found a hymnbook with notes, he and I played and sang some hymns together.

Big shops inside and outside the city were thrown open to the poor people. There they could come and receive things for nothing. The day they made their entrance into the city I saw ever so many country people loaded down with different commodities hurrying to their homes. Of course they had to suffer afterwards, when the government troops came and some of the stolen goods were found in their homes. But they were foolish not to think of this at the time. They only thought of the golden opportunity that suddenly came to them. The small storekeeper was protected and could go on with his business. More than ten people were executed. It was said that they were all bad characters and oppressors of the poor. I saw four, stripped to the waist, being led out. Among them were a woman and her husband.

After three days in the city, orders came to cross the Han River. The troops went to Yuinyang, another big city about forty miles above Kunchow. The remainder of the army, together with some soldiers as guards, lived in the country across the river for about two days.

While there I had a very precious experience showing that God was with me and that he knew what I needed just then. One of the men at the hospital had gotten hold of a preacher's long coat. While he was searching the pockets a slip of paper fell out. I was standing close by and noticed the paper fall. Picking it up I found a Norwegian song written on it. The topic of the song was "Wait on the Lord." The general thought of the four stanzas was as follows: "God will surely plan your daily experiences so that everything will be for the best. And if you take everything to Jesus you will be able to carry the heaviest load. Truly and firmly God will establish your way throughout life, and as you rest in Him you are guided from sorrow and calamity. When the hour of departure has come, everything being prepared, then, you who have complained will feel ashamed because before you know it you will be at home. Amen, amen, in thy name, My Jesus, I am still. Thou, Lord, will surely plan my days as thou dost see fit."

I cannot explain my feelings as I tried to read that song. It contained a message which strengthened my faith and gave me new courage. I put it in my New Testament and read it time and again during the remaining weeks of my captivity. The friends at Laohokow sang the song for my benefit when I passed through there a month later.

At Yuinyang the Reds were not successful, and had to retreat, bringing with them many wounded. How many were killed I do not know. During the siege of Yuinyang about twenty foreigners were in the city, all of them Norwegian missionaries and their children. They had congregated there from two other places because the way down to Laohokow was blocked. The danger was very great, but the troops fought valiantly. This was significant, as almost all of the government soldiers were former bandits who had been taken into the National army.

After the Red troops came back, we crossed the river again and stayed in the city one night. Government troops were sent against them and the Reds had to return the same way they came for about fifteen miles. At this juncture my mule was lost, and I had to walk. The troops attacked and the Reds had to retreat to the north. There was very little rest, as we sometimes had to keep going during part of the night. We were now about ten miles from the foot of a mountain called Wutangshan. This whole mountainous area, having a circumference of more than two hundred miles, is owned by

Taoists who have a number of noted temples there and gods of all description. Every year a vast number of people make their pilgrimage to this place.

A MESSAGE AT LAST[5]

Very early one morning we received orders to ascend the mountain. It was
a beautiful morning. The full moon lit our path as we very quietly went on.
They seemed to be nervous, possibly fearing an enveloping movement by
the troops. A little way up the mountain some of the Red soldiers stood
ready for battle if necessary; however, nothing happened. That day we
marched about twenty-five miles, climbing upwards almost continually.
Together with the medical corps I landed in the temple of the god of wealth.
An old vegetarian was our host.

About ten miles from there was the highest point, the Chin Ting
(golden top), where the most prominent temple is located. It was a disap-
pointment not to have a chance to see that wonderful top. They say that the
temple there is of gold, but it is not altogether true. Pillars and walls were
made of brass, the images are covered with gold, and there may have been
other things also made of gold.

Below the top are many large buildings and temples. Here the Red
army located their base hospital, with hundreds of sick and wounded on
their hands. An agreement was made with the priests that if they guaran-
teed the safety of the sick ones the Reds would not in any way molest them
or destroy their temples. This promise was kept as far as I could observe.
The hospital crowd that I followed still went with the troops, and after two
days we had to descend the mountain and go back to a place where we had
walked through before. From there we again went up the mountain, a distance of about five miles. I am at a loss to know why we had to walk back and
forth like that, but there must have been some kind of strategic scheme to it.

We stayed in the mountains a week, and enjoyed a few days of rest.
During that time the hospital doctor took sick with a fever. His condition
was very serious. I prayed for him, and once I noted a marked improve-
ment. But then a doctor was called who practiced Chinese medicine. He
prescribed a preparation that almost killed the poor man. He was sick for
more than a month after that and was carried from place to place.

While we were down on the plains I hoped that I could, in some way,
make connections with my comrades, but no messenger came through.
Realizing that we would again have to climb mountains, where communi-
cations were more difficult, I addressed a letter to the headquarters asking

---

5. C. O. Anderson and R. M. Anderson, *Two Lives of Faith*, 74–82.

them, kindly, to set me free since the medicine could not get through. Summer was upon us, and I told them that I would not be able to endure constant marching in the intense heat. I was not well, either. I was not thinking so much about my own welfare as that of my family. What would happen to them if I were taken away? They could not promise to release me but told me to write another letter for the medicine and to try to find a man who would take it to Siangyang. Now they wanted the medicine brought to the base hospital at Wutangshan.

I then wrote to Mr. Matson and tried several times to get a man to go, but without success. They were all too busy in the fields and, I think, afraid to venture out. At last I got a man among the hospital crew to escort me down to a market town five miles away. We had been through that place twice, and I knew a man whom I thought would go. He worked at oil pressing but had nothing to do then as business was at a standstill and his employer was not at home. He was afraid of the Reds and had made good his escape. I found this man, a great big Honanese, at home. To look at him you would think that he was afraid of nothing. This was, however, not the case. Still, after much talking and explaining, he promised to go. I had five dollars in my pocket, which I had carried since Dr. Yao left. I gave him four dollars, the rest he was to collect at Siangyang.

The same day he took a burden of oil and started out for Laohokow. He thought that he would get through easier if he carried something. I learned later that he arrived at Laohokow without meeting any trouble. I had also written a letter to friends there asking them to help the man to get down to Siangyang by auto. But he went no further. They wrote a letter to me and sent it back with him. They also thought kindly of my physical needs and gave him some groceries to bring to me. I neither saw the letter nor the food.

At Laohokow they thought Mr. Matson had already gone down to Hankow. But the next day one of their men came back from Fanchang, and the letter was immediately sent down to Mr. Matson, who was still at Siangyang. He then got the shipment of medicine sent up from Kingmen and brought it to Laohokow himself, and then further on to Shihuakai, which was nearer to the territory occupied by the Red army.

At the place where I engaged my messenger I had a haircut and a shave. My beard was a month old, so I felt that it was no luxurious demonstration to have it shaved off. I had a dollar in my possession and I gave it to the barber with the thought that he should give me back some change. But because I was a foreigner he tried to take advantage of me. I told him this was all the money I had and asked him, please, to give me a few coppers back. He grumbled, but handed over a few. He knew my plight but still had the gumption to rob me. The Chinese would not have paid half of what I had to give.

Others whom I had occasion to meet were not that unkind. A farmer's wife at Wutangshan told me to visit them if I happened to come back that way. She said she wanted to treat me to a good meal. Both she and her husband had heard the Gospel, but were not professing Christians. Another person, a shopkeeper, in whose house we lived a few days, also was very kind to me. He gave me a pair of chopsticks. I appreciated that gift very much because I felt that it was more sanitary to have my own sticks to eat with, and at some places it was difficult to find enough of those implements to go around. When I left I gave him my coat, which I wanted to leave behind because it was too warm and heavy to carry.

Every day I expected my messenger to come back but he never showed up, since the Nationalist troops came again and forced the Reds away from Wutangshan. We had to cross the mountains and march toward Fanghsien, a walled city that was quite large. The Norwegian Mission had a station there with several resident missionaries who had escaped two or three weeks before the Reds got in. After leaving Wutangshan, we went through very beautiful territory. The mountains were just gorgeous.

At one little place in the mountains we stayed several days. We had our quarters on a farm and I had a chance to be by myself a great part of the time, so I sat in a grove reading my New Testament, praying and meditating. I was still looking for the messenger, but at last gave up hope. We had gone too far and many dangers were lurking on the way. I was always praying for my liberty, and knew that many were praying for me. Liberty would come, but how? Possibly I would never get back, but be liberated through death. Such thoughts sometimes went through my mind. Whichever way I turned the road seemed to be closed, but, thank God, the upward way was always open for communication. Sometimes I felt assured that the Lord would bring me out in some way.

While I was sitting in that grove meditating, the thought came to me that I ought to believe that I had received what I already had prayed for. This thought brought greater peace to my soul. I figured out afterward that just at that time the messenger who finally brought me a letter from Mr. Matson was on his way.

While we were at a place fifteen miles from Fanghsien city, Mr. Matson's messenger together with two other men came with a letter. I was out by the road washing my clothes when they came. The messenger was from Siangyang and I knew him personally. I cannot express what I felt when I sighted him. I just seized him by his arms and praised God for answered prayers. He was very much moved, too, so that tears came to his eyes.

For two months I had not heard a word from the outside world. Messengers had been sent, but none got through. Now, when it seemed almost impossible, a letter came with the message that the medicine was on its way. They only wished to know where to send it. To ship all that medicine was no small matter. Mr. Matson and others as well had a difficult task in getting it through. Fortunately they were able to get passes from high military authorities. The Swedish Vice Consul at Hankow also gave valuable assistance.

The medicine had to be bought at Hankow and then shipped by steamer to Shasi. At Shasi a high duty was demanded by the customs, but through the efforts of the Reverend I. W. Jacobson and the Swedish Vice Consul it finally went through duty-free. From Shasi it was shipped by truck to Kingmen under the care of Pastor Tang of Kingchow. Because of previous heavy rainfall, which made the road very bad in places, they had to unload the truck several times.

When my letter was received asking that the medicine be sent to Wutangshan, it was again put on a truck and escorted to Siangyang by the Kingmen pastor, Mr. Wu. He also had difficulties. At one place a river had to be crossed on a small ferry. The driver thought he could make it without unloading the boxes, but as soon as the car got on the boat it sank. Some of the boxes were soaked through. Much of the cotton was still wet when it arrived at Fanghsien, and some of the instruments were rusty, but nothing was said about it. At Siangyang the shipment had to be brought across the Han River to Fancheng, and again loaded onto a truck that went as far as Laohokow. In all, the medicine had to be shipped about seven hundred miles. The last hundred and twenty-five miles it had to be carried over a mountainous road.

The day after the messengers came with the letter, they returned with instructions as to where to send the medicine. The same day—a Sunday— we also entered the city of Fanghsien. On the following Sunday the bearers came, twenty-four in all, carrying the medicine boxes. During that week I had waited and wondered how it would turn out. At times I feared that troops would come again and drive the Reds away. If so, they probably would have retreated toward the province of Shensi. But they were now left in peace.

Those who brought the medicine did have difficulties, especially because of the Red Spears; however, owing to the tact and ability of Chang Yuen Fu, the Siangyang man who brought me the letter and came back with the medicine, they managed to penetrate the danger line. The bearers also made trouble at one place, but Fu said that he demonstrated his ability at boxing and they were subdued. We surely owe much to Chang Yuen Fu. He performed his task splendidly: for two weeks or more he walked every day, not knowing what minute his life might be in danger. But the Lord also cared for him.

The day after the ransom came I was permitted to leave. They wanted to keep me a few more days; then, they said, the whole army would escort me, as they intended to advance in that direction. But I told them I was not afraid of the Red Spears and had not heard of any bandits operating in that part of the country. I mentioned also that I had friends waiting for me at Laohokow, so wanted to leave as soon as possible. Finally they gave me a pass, and I started off.

It was even a little touching as I bade farewell to the hospital staff. We had learned to know one another through dangers and hardships. Several said that they were sorry to see me go—especially Dr. Chang, with whom I had formed a close friendship through many intimate talks. An officer who was confined to the hospital because of a gunshot wound almost broke out in tears as I said good-bye to him. He had been sick for a long period and I had become well acquainted with him. Once, after our experiences at Maliangping, he let me sleep with him as I happened to be without bedclothes that night.

On the day the medicine arrived, General Ho Lung came over to inspect the lot. He turned to me and said, "Tomorrow you can go home, and we are going to prepare a farewell meeting in your honor." For some reason, however, they did not have any meeting of that kind. Probably he did not mean what he said. I received twenty dollars in traveling expenses and four dollars from Dr. Chang. The men who carried the medicine received five dollars each in tips, and Chang Yuen Fu got ten dollars.

The last few days before I left I had not been well. An epidemic of some kind had broken out and I had a touch of it. Therefore I encouraged four of the men who brought the medicine to carry me as I was afraid it would be too much of an exertion to walk that long distance. I got two bamboo poles from the Reds, and a chair-like contrivance was made. The road was very mountainous, so to help the bearers I walked a great part of the way, though I appreciated the chance to ride sometimes. The first day out I went through several small places occupied by Red troops or other departments of the Red army. They all knew me, so I did not even have to show my pass. Only the outpost at Fanghsien asked to see it. At one place I met a young man from Kingmen who was taken along when we were captured. Now he was working in one of the army departments. His sympathies had, no doubt, been with the Reds before. With regret in his voice he expressed the wish to go home. But now he did not dare. He had been away too long.

It really seemed too good to be true that I was on my way out from captivity and again to have the privilege of freedom. Freedom! What a wonderful word! Four days' journey brought me, without incident, to Shihuakai. Two missionaries from Laohokow, Mr. Nordhang and Mr. Li, were there to meet me. It certainly was kind of them to come all that way. Pastor Yin from Fancheng and Mr. Chin from the hospital at Siangyang were also there to bid me welcome. It was a joyous experience to see these men—wonderful indeed that we could meet again in this life.

We arrived at Shihuakai about five o'clock in the afternoon, but because the situation was tense, it was deemed wisest to proceed to Laohokow that night. Troops were stationed at Shihuakai preparing to confront the Reds if they happened to come once more. We still had about twenty miles to travel, but since the moon was bright we had no trouble finding our way. At three o'clock in the morning we came to Laohokow. A pass had been secured from the commanding officer at Shihuakai, so the city gates were opened without delay.

Coming into the Mission compound I told Mr. Nordhang that I did not want to enter his home, but wished to sleep outside someplace. I had my reasons: they were alive all over in my clothes. I must have looked worse than a tramp. My felt hat was soiled and faded, and I wore a shirt that was the upper part of a white dress belonging to Miss Augusta Nelson. The trousers were torn and dirty, and on my feet I had my Chinese cloth shoes—the shoes I got as a gift just before I left Fanghsien; but they were almost worn out.

In spite of my protest and general appearance my good friends took me right into their house. It was a foretaste of heaven to get into that home. I could hardly believe it was real! I had come so far—and now again I could enjoy the company of fellow missionaries. Mrs. Nordhang got up immediately and treated us to a refreshing drink. Then I had a chance to take a well-needed bath, after which I went to bed. It was difficult to go to sleep, and I think one reason was that the bed was too soft. I had been used to hard boards for such a long time that I slept better on them than on anything else.

I had intended to leave for Fancheng the same day, but was persuaded to stay because the friends, both foreigners and Chinese, had decided to have a thanksgiving service in the church. They had all been praying constantly and earnestly for my release. Now their prayers were answered and they wanted to thank God for His mercy. A well-attended meeting was held in the afternoon, and voices of thanksgiving were raised at that place and later at many more.

The news of my release soon flashed around the world. They got the news at Kuling on July 4, and from there it was sent by cable to Chicago. The message reached there also on July 4. Intercessory prayer is well pleasing in the sight of God, and therefore we are confident that those who prayed on our behalf also received a blessing and were brought closer to the Lord. In that way our experiences were not in vain. The friends at Laohokow made it very pleasant for me, and it was a pleasure to meet them all.

The third day out from Fanghsien I met a fifteen year old boy named Hsü Han Ching. He had been captured by the Red army a year before, and a ransom of five thousand dollars had been demanded. The parents paid only five hundred, so the boy was kept and placed with a squad of burglars. Early in the spring he took sick, but he managed to follow along until the middle of May. One day he fell by the roadside together with forty-five other sick ones. They were captured by the Red Spears who intended to kill them. The boy told me he had in his pocket a few dollars that he was ready to offer to them if they would use a sword instead of a spear to kill him. He had seen people dispatched by spear and dreaded it. The Red Spears, however, did not carry out their threat, but held the sick as prisoners a few days until a company of government soldiers came through. Forty-two of the prisoners were handed over to them and were promptly brought down to Shihuakai, where they were executed.

Among the three who were released was Hsü Han Ching. A farmer in the vicinity had compassion on him and let him stay in his home, where he recovered from his illness. Afterward he helped with what he could on the farm. They had heard that I would pass through the area and waited for me at a roadside inn. We rested there in the middle of the day, and Han Ching came over and spoke to me, telling me that he had seen me many times during our marches. He related everything about himself and expressed his wish to go with me. Since he was all alone he did not know where to turn, and did not dare to venture out himself. He could not go back to the Red army because he thought he might be killed by the Red Spears along the way. Thus the trip to his parents' home was also unthinkable. His home was about forty miles from Hankow on the Han River. With tears in his eyes be begged to go with me.

It was difficult to refuse, so I told him that he could go with me, but that I was unable to guarantee his safety. He had no money, so I paid his fare from Laohokow to Hankow, from where he proceeded to his home. He was my assistant on the way and I grew rather attached to him. He did wish to stay with me, but for several reasons I did not want to keep him. I hope that he will grow up to be a good man and a Christian.

On July 4 I left Laohokow by car, arriving in Fanchang the same day. I was now on our own field. The Chinese co-workers and other Christians gave me a hearty welcome; they were all glad to see me back again. At their daily prayer meetings they had constantly remembered me in their intercessions. I also met several men from Siangyang and Nanchang, and they all rejoiced because of God's wonderful mercy and power, which was certainly manifested in my case. I had very sweet fellowship with them at Fancheng, and they cared for me in a most splendid way. Pastor Wu of Kingmen also happened to be there. It was a joy to meet him.

My intention was to continue on to Kuling where my family and comrades were waiting, but rain delayed us nearly fours weeks. The road was inundated in places and the cars could not pass over it.

My unexpected stay at Fancheng gave me an opportunity to have some clothes made. Those that I wore when I came out from the Reds had to be discarded. One of the missionaries at Laohokow had let me borrow clothes that he said I could wear until I arrived in Hankow. Now I could send them back from Fancheng. Some of the Laohokow missionaries were also waiting at Fancheng, with Kuling as their destination. Some of them went back again; only two of the women remained and left with me.

How had I solved my money question? When the Reds came to Kingmen I got my two checkbooks and put them in my pocket. They noticed that I had them, but did not take them away from me. I was able to carry them the whole time. Now I had no difficulty in getting the money needed for traveling and other expenses.

Finally the roads had dried sufficiently so we could start. We made very slow progress because the road was still difficult in some places and because more than ten cars were in our company. The hundred and seventy-five miles between Fancheng and the railway we traversed in four days. Bridges were down and we often had to wade across the rivers. Where possible the cars were pushed across; where this could not be done, other cars met us on the other side. Although some areas were disturbed because of bandits, we got through without encountering any unpleasant experiences, a fortunate circumstance, since it happened repeatedly that cars were held up and people killed.

While we were stuck at one place for half a day, I met a fellow traveler who had been taken for ransom by the Reds while I was with them. He was captured at Kunhsien, but released a few days later upon paying a few hundred dollars. He had seen me and knew my name. I had not met him before, but as he related his story we felt as if we were closely akin. Common experiences drew us one toward the other. He was now on the way to Hankow with his family.

It was with a sigh of relief that we sighted the railway station. We had prepared to go to an inn and there await a train, but to our happy surprise a train was due in a few minutes. There was just enough time to purchase the tickets. That night on the train was not pleasant, but even that could have been worse. Right outside of Hankow the railway was cut by flood water, so we had to go by boat the last few miles. Hankow itself was flooded.[6] It was most unusual to see boats on the streets instead of cars.

At the Lutheran Mission Home I met two of my comrades, Miss Nelson, my fellow prisoner for five days, and Miss Johnson. What a joy it was to see again the faces of my fellow workers! There was very little time to visit, as I stayed in Hankow only half a day. My journey would not be complete until I would arrive on the mountain top of Kuling. August 4 saw me there.

Now I was again united with my dear family. How happy we were I cannot describe. God had wonderfully sustained us all during those months of uncertainty and anxiety. To Him be all the glory. It was a joy to see the rest of my comrades and to meet other friends. So many expressed how earnestly they had been praying for us. The Lord had heard the many prayers, and turned anxiety and sorrow into rejoicing and thanksgiving.

6. Latourette (*The Chinese: Their History and Culture* I, 440) says that at Hankow the Yangtze River was higher than it had been at any time in more than 60 years that records had been kept. Thousands drowned in this devastating flood of the valleys of the Yangtze and the Huai Rivers, and millions were destitute and faced with starvation. For a picture, see C. O. Anderson and R. M. Anderson, *Two Lives of Faith*, following 88.

Appendix 2

The Martyr of Three Missionaries in Central China, Province of Hupeh

January 7, 1948

Viola Larson[1]

THE DATE WAS JANUARY 7, 1948. Three Covenant missionaries were on a truck that had left Siangyang headed for Kingchow.[2] The decision was made at our summer conference to convene a mid-winter council meeting at Kingchow in January. The journey had begun bright and early at the Siangyang bus station. No busses were there when the missionaries arrived, just a two-ton truck waiting to take on passengers. In the group was Dr. Alik Berg, director and head doctor of the Bethesda Hospital, Martha Anderson,

---

1. Viola Larson was a Covenant China missionary who served her first term at Siangyang, Hupeh Province, from November, 1935 to November, 1936, and at Nanchang from November, 1936 to December, 1940. In 1946 she returned to Mainland China from the States and was stationed at Kingchow, Hupeh. After the martyr of the three missionaries, in January, 1948, she and other missionaries relocated first to Changsha, Hunan Province, and then to Kweiyang and Kweiting in Kweichow Province. In 1951 Viola went home on furlough, after which she served a term in Taiwan from 1953–1960. Upon her return to the States Viola took up residence in Berkeley, CA, where for many years she was a library assistant in the East Asiatic Library at the University of California, Berkeley. The present account is a remembrance 40 years later, written November 17, 1988 at the request of the brother of Martha Anderson, one of the martyred missionaries. Viola was waiting for the three missionaries to arrive in Kingchow, and helped to prepare their bodies for burial.

2. Pronounced "Jinjoe."

secretary-treasurer of the China Covenant Mission, and Esther Nordlund, Bible teacher and head of our Nanchang Covenant station.

Traveling by truck was not uncommon. Everyone piled into the back, and the gate was secured. If there were many passengers everyone stood, swaying in unison with the curves of the road. If only a few were on board, you had the option of sitting on your baggage, otherwise on the hard floor. Regardless of how our three comrades were riding, I am sure they were very happy. It was always a joy to attend these meetings, to be together and discuss God's work and the part we had in it. The Christian fellowship was an inspiration for all of us.

We at Kingchow were looking forward to their arrival and were making preparations for their stay. We knew in the countryside there was danger and unrest, but one could never know when or where it might strike. When traveling we simply trusted God for protection and guidance. "He shall not be afraid of evil tidings: his heart is fixed, trusting in the Lord" (Ps 112:7).

At 5 o'clock on that Wednesday, January 7th, while awaiting the arrival of our comrades, local Chinese police came to tell us the shocking news that the Siang-Fan truck had been waylaid by bandits, and that the three missionaries had been killed. The truck had brought their bodies to Kingmen, and Chinese Christians there had wrapped them in oilcloth and blankets. Chinese officials, we were told, were being very helpful in making all arrangements to bring the bodies to Kingchow.

Word came later through Chinese Christians how the tragedy occurred. When the robbers stopped the truck, the foreigners—Dr. Alik Berg, Martha Anderson, and Esther Nordlund—were made to line up. The leader of the group spoke first to Dr. Berg. "Show me your passport!" he demanded. Dr. Berg had only recently become an American citizen. When the leader saw his passport, he exclaimed, "So you're an American! America is our worst enemy." Turning to his guards he said, "Shoot him!" and a volley of shots rang out.

As Dr. Berg fell, Martha cried out in shock, "Oh-h! Oh-h No!" The leader snarled: "So you're an American too, and his friend? Then we will shoot you as well!" By this time the passengers were on their knees pleading: "Please don't kill any more!" Indifferent to their cries the leader nodded to his men, and Martha, the second victim, fell.

The captors then began discussing what to do with Esther. The passengers became more urgent, "No more! No more!" Esther, deep in anguish for her fallen friends, then turned and said to her captors, in Chinese: "You shot my friends, you can shoot me too!" Shots rang out, and Esther fell a third victim to the ground. By now the passengers were crying loudly and fearing for their own lives. But the robbers left without harming them. The grief-stricken passengers and their driver then placed the three bodies in the truck, and continued on to the next stop, which was Kingmen.

It was now Friday, January 9th, the third day since our comrades had been brutally shot. At Kingchow we missionaries were prayerfully awaiting their bodies. About dusk the truck drove up to the station gate. The wrapped bodies were removed from the truck, and laid upon three benches prepared for their arrival in a vacant room of the house adjoining the home where I lived with Mabel Olson. Chinese officials informed us not to unwrap the bodies until the next morning, as local police wanted to be present to watch and write down the number of shots fired and their location on each victim.

After supper that evening, Rev. Joel Johnson and his Chinese cook kept watch in the room until midnight. Then from midnight to dawn, Amelia Conradson and I kept the vigil. The next morning at nine, local police looked on as we untied the bodies and removed the oilcloth. We gave the police the names of each victim and told them the location and number of shots fired. All had been shot in the head, chest and arms. Dr. Berg and Martha both had broken arms. Esther had a huge, deep wound in her lower right abdomen that appeared gangrenous.

When the police and officials left, we proceeded to prepare the bodies for burial. Otelia Hendrickson and Ruth Backlund bathed and dressed Martha Anderson; Lillian Branstrom and I did the same for Dr. Berg; all four of us prepared the body of Esther Nordlund. Rev. Joel Johnson, Rev. Paul Backlund, together with Margareta Nyren of the Swedish Mission, assisted in bringing pails of water and pouring it into wash basins for our use. It was a traumatic experience for us all! It took pans and pans of clean water to wash away the caked blood on their bodies and in their matted hair. Our hearts were crushed. Tears falling freely mingled with their blood as we washed it from their wounded bodies. Though we regretted their cruel deaths, what a privilege it was to assist in preparing our dear friends for burial. This tender, loving care we gave gladly. When we had finished bathing them, combing their hair, and dressing them with clean clothes, we smiled through our tears and thanked God.

The Chinese coffins were not ready until late afternoon. Rev. Carl Branstrom and Rev. Paul Backlund painted the three coffins gray in color. On the outside, at the front end near the top, we printed their first names in large letters with black paint. At the other end, under each coffin, we placed a block of wood to raise it about 4 inches from the floor. Inside each coffin, on the bottom, we put clean rice straw for padding. Over that was placed a clean sheet, upon which we tenderly laid our comrades. From cedar boughs we made 6 wreaths and 3 crosses, decorating them with yellow and white ribbons and artificial flowers. Yellow and white are the colors for mourning in China. We placed these on each coffin and surrounded them with other greenery. Near the heads of Dr. Berg, Martha and Esther were placed burning candles. With their hands folded and resting on the clean sheet that covered them, our comrades looked peaceful with the joy of the Lord shining from their faces. It was beautiful, and we felt comforted.

It was now time to call our other missionaries to come and share these hallowed moments with our resting comrades. It was like being close to heaven—singing songs of thanksgiving and praise, reciting Scripture and praying. The Lord was near, and as we looked at the faces of Esther, Martha and Dr. Berg, it almost seemed as if they opened their eyes and smiled in agreement as we sang:

> How good is the God we adore,
> Our faithful, unchangeable Friend;
> Whose love is as great as His power,
> And knows neither measure nor end.
> 'Tis Jesus the first and the last,
> Whose Spirit shall guide us safe home;
> We'll praise Him for all that is past,
> And trust Him for all that's to come;
> And praise, and trust,
> We'll praise Him for all that is past,
> And trust Him for all that's to come.

Immediately after, the Chinese community living on the Bible Seminary grounds came to pay their respects. Pastor Daniel Chin expressed the sorrow they all felt for the missionaries and their families, but rejoiced in the hope, that in Christ, we would all meet again under better circumstances. A word of prayer was then given, with thanksgiving, for the sacrifices Esther Nordlund, Martha Anderson, and Dr. Alik Berg gave in the service of God for China. Then we sang in unison a Chinese song taken from Rom. 8:35, 37–39:

> Who shall separate us from the love of Christ?
> Shall tribulation, or distress, or persecution,
> or famine, or nakedness, or peril, or sword?
> . . . Nay, in all these things we are more than
> conquerors through him that loved us. For I
> am persuaded, that neither death, nor life, nor
> angels, nor principalities, nor powers, nor
> things present, nor things to come, nor height,
> nor depth, nor any other creature, shall be able
> to separate us from the love of God, which is
> in Christ Jesus our Lord.

Truly an apropos message!

Otelia Hendrickson, Margareta Nyren, and I remained in the room until everyone had left. Then for each comrade we did the following. We pulled back the covering sheet, made small cloth bags of lime, and placed the bags around their head, hands, and feet. Over the body were placed two sheets of paper, and between the layers we sprinkled lime the entire length of their body. After folding their hands on their abdomen, we pulled the sheet up slowly. Before we covered the head, we bid each a fond farewell from distant loved ones, ending with, "God's peace till we meet again in glory!" By this time, Rev. Carl Branstrom and Rev. Paul Backlund had come to put the heavy wooden lids on the coffins and to nail them down.

The following day we moved the coffins into the front yard for the community memorial service which was to be held in the early afternoon. We made a make-shift pulpit, and filled the area in front of the coffins with many chairs and benches. A large group of Chinese and foreign friends from surrounding churches and neighboring cities attended. With Otelia Hendrickson playing the portable organ we sang in praise to God, "How Firm a Foundation Ye Saints of the Lord." Representatives of the Missouri Synod Lutheran Church, the Catholic Church, the Episcopal Church, and the Swedish Mission Church expressed their sympathy and sorrow. Friends from the Shasi Hospital were also in attendance and took part in the service. We greatly appreciated their moral support and expressions of sympathy. The service ended with singing the doxology and praying the Lord's Prayer in Chinese. Chinese officials and local police then arranged for a truck to take the coffins of our three comrades to Hankow, also in Hupeh Province, for burial in the International Cemetery.

APPENDIX 3

A Brief Introduction of Christianity in Nanzhang County

TRANSLATED BY CAO JING

GENERAL SITUATION OF NANZHANG'S GEOGRAPHY

NANZHANG COUNTY IS SITUATED in the northwest of Hubei province, south of the Han River, neighboring Yi Cheng in the east, Bao Kang in the west, Xiangfan in the northeast, Gu Cheng in the northwest, Yuan An to the south, and Jing Men to the southeast. It has jurisdiction over 11 towns and a population of 600,000. The general feature of its 3985 square kilometer area is said to be "eight tenths mountain and a ratio of 1:1 between water and farmland." The east of the county is hilly and flat, abounding in rice and cotton. The west of the county is mountain area, rich in more than 1500 mountain products, among them natural silk, an edible fungus, and ginkgo, which was already famous throughout the country and overseas in the late Qing dynasty. There are four river systems and 48 great springs in the county, the amount of water energy reserve being 143,000 kilowatt-hours, and 23 different kinds of mineral products.

Nanzhang is a county with a long history. The famous jade, *He's Bi*, presented to the empire as Bian He in spring and autumn, comes from Nanzhang. In the famous historical novel, *Three Countries*, Mr. Shui Jing recommended Zhuge Liang to Liu Bei here, which led throughout the ages to stories on everybody's lips: *Three Visits to Thatched Cottage*, and *Restoring Royal Court*. Nanzhang is also famous for its scenic beauty, being called the "back garden" of Xiangfan, with its 7-colored waterfall, unique in Hubei.

INTRODUCTION OF THE CHURCH

General Situation

Under God's blessing and guidance, Christianity in Nanzhang has gradually developed, growing out of nothing and then from small to large. Among 11 towns in the county, two churches and two gathering groups meet publicly in two towns, and others remain unregistered. Christians are 10,000 or so. Supported by province and city Christian Councils and the Three-self Patriotic Committee, two churches have been built up, the Central Church located south of the county town in 2005, and the Dao Miao Church, 19 kilometers south of the county town in 2007. Two other gathering groups meet in private houses in the town of Wu An (one within the town, and the other south of the town). Total clergy are 6 persons: one teacher and five volunteers. "The harvest is great, the laborers few."

Two churches have complete organizations and regulations, and the other two gathering groups so far are not completely organized because of the small number of members. The contact information is as follows:

Sequence	The names of churches	Person in charge	Phone number
1	Nanzhang Evangelical Church (Central Church)	Leng Jia-quan	131 971 95 195
2	Dao Miao Branch of Nanzhang Evangelical Church	Zhang Guang-xiu	0710–535 2349
3	Gathering Group in Wu An Town	Tong Zu-xiang	01710–537 4167
4	Gathering Group in An Ji in Wu An Town	He Zhao-zhen	01710–543 1306

Introduction to Nanzhang Central Church

Time when worship began: May 1985

Total land of the church: 726.3 square meters

Time of church construction: October 2004

Capacity of the church: 500 people

Number of Christians in the church: 160

Legal person: Leng Jia-quan

Administration: Leng Jia-quan

Missionary: Leng Jia-quan

Financial Affairs Officer: Jin Ping

Church address: Nanzhang Evangelical Church

Nanzhang County, Hubei Province, P.R.China

Population of the county: 600,000

Gender proportion: men 9.5%; women 90.5 %

Educational level of church Christians:

college: 5

high school and middle school: 64

primary school: 50

illiterate: 41

Introduction to Dao Miao Branch of Nanzhang Evangelical Church

Time when worship began: September 1996

Total land of the church: 800 square meters

Number of Christians in the church: 150

Legal person: Zhang Guang-xiu

Administration: Zhang Guang-xiu

Missionary: Zhang Gung-xiu

Financial Affairs Officer: Huang Shi-ying

Church address: Dao Miao Christian Church

Nanzhang County, Hubei Province, P.R. China

Time of church construction: May 2007

Capacity of the church: 400 people

Population of the county: 600,000

Gender proportion: men 9%; women 91%

Educational level of church Christians:

high school and middle school: 38

primary school: 60

illiterate: 52

INTRODUCTION TO CHURCH HISTORY

Nanzhang Evangelical Church is the central Christian church in Nanzhang County. Early in the twentieth century missionaries from foreign churches established churches here: a total of 2 church buildings, and 11 brick and timber structures with 84 rooms. There was also one Western medical clinic and one complete primary school.

During the Great Cultural Revolution, the churches were pulled down and worship was stopped. Other house property was taken over by some units and gradually pulled down also. The last building in the yard of the county government was burned down in 1988. In May of 1985, 5 old sisters started to worship together, led by the old pastor's wife in her own house. With the growing of the church under God's grace, in December of 2000 all the Christians led by Brother Leng Jia-quan bought four private houses (totaling five unfired brick houses and one yard, taking in 410.3 square meters) in Chuan Wan Village in the town of Cheng Guan, receiving help from the County Religious Bureau, Xiangfan Christian Church, the

Province Christian Council, and the Christian Three-self Patriotic Committee. In December of 2002 they bought another 316 square meters south of the house property, giving the church now a total land acquisition of 726.3 square meters.

In May of 2003 the Christian Three-self Patriotic Committee of Nanzhang County was officially established. Since the houses the church bought were too old to stand, in October of 2004 they began to erect the church building. The Province Christian Council and Christian Three-self Patriotic Committee promised to sponsor this in the amount of 80,000 RMB. In October of 2005 the church was basically completed, and the Hong Kong Lutheran Church sponsored the facilities within the building. In May of 2007, they erected another church building in Dao Miao. Up to now, the Province Christian Council and the Christian Three-self Patriotic Committee have been helping them financially, but they still owe a sum of project money in the amount of nearly 100,000 RMB. Please pray for them and wish Christianity in Nanzhang a more thriving future.

Recorded May, 2008

Appendix 4

Covenant Missionaries in China

THE FOLLOWING BIOGRAPHIES OF Covenant missionaries to China build on information contained in the Covenant annuals, *Aurora* and *Our Covenant*; Peter Matson's book, *Our China Mission* (Chicago: Covenant Book Concern, 1934, 115–120); an unpublished doctoral dissertation of Earl C. Dahlstrom, "The Covenant Missionary Society in China" (Hartford Seminary Foundation, 1950, 211–231); and a missionary list preserved in the F. M. Johnson Archives and Special Collections in Brandel Library, North Park University, Chicago. It is supplemented and corrected from books and articles published by the Evangelical Covenant Church, and from personal recollections of my own and others. Missionaries in the biographies are located at stations and other places where their presence has been documented, but owing to the nature of missionary work, where travel is common, relocations occur, and evacuations become necessary, some missionaries were doubtless elsewhere for longer or shorter periods of time.

ELLEN ACKERSON[1]

Ellen Ackerson was born in Skåne, Sweden on June 20, 1878, and came to the United States in 1880. After a conversion experience at Northfield, Minnesota in 1892, Ellen joined the First Covenant Church of Minneapolis. She graduated from the nursing program at Swedish Hospital, Minneapolis as a trained nurse in 1906. In 1907 she accepted the call of the Mission Covenant Church to go as a missionary to China, and arrived in China in

---

1. See *Aurora* (1924) 46.

early 1908 with her sister Amelia (later Mrs. Amelia Conradson).[2] Support was given by the First Covenant Church in Minneapolis. Upon arrival, Ellen became involved in medical and women's work, after 1914 joining the staff of Bethesda Hospital in Siangyang. In March, 1927, she was forced to leave Siangyang with the Matsons and other missionaries because of the communist uprising, going to Hankow and then to Shanghai.[3] But in September, 1928 she was able to return with Edla Matson and Judith Peterson to Siangyang, where in 1934 she was superintendent and instructor of nurses at Bethesda Hospital.[4] Ellen was at Siangyang in April, 1939 when Oscar Anderson arrived.[5] She spent four terms in China, where her work was highly valued. Because of failing health she returned to the United States on furlough in early 1940, and retired from active missionary service in 1941. Her final years were lived out in Minneapolis. She died Dec 4, 1950.[6]

Amelia Ackerson—see **Amelia C. Conradson**
Alma E. Anderson—see **Alma E. Mortenson**
Esther N. Anderson—see **Esther N. Peterson**

C. OSCAR ANDERSON[7]

Oscar Anderson was born at Slaka, Östergötland, Sweden on April 26, 1893. He came to the United States in 1913, settling in Arlington, Illinois. Soon after matriculating at North Park College in 1916, he committed himself to Christ and heard the call to go to China. Anderson graduated from North Park Theological Seminary and went to China, arriving in December, 1921. Upon arrival he worked a half-year at Nanchang and took another half year of language study in Peking (1922–23), and after visiting other Covenant stations began work with his wife at Icheng (1924–1927). Oscar had married Ruth Engstrom the summer of 1924 at Kuling. The Andersons had to leave China in February, 1927 when many Covenant missionaries went

---

2. The sisters arrived in Shanghai on February 10, 1908; *The Chinese Recorder* 39 (1908) 174.

3. Appended note in a letter from Peter Matson to the Mission Council dated Feb 19, 1927.

4. P. Matson, *Our China Mission*, 93, 118.

5. C. O. Anderson and R. M. Anderson, *Two Lives of Faith*, 113.

6. *Our Covenant* 26 (1951) 109–10.

7. See *Aurora* (1922) 108.

home, but Oscar would not resign,[8] and the two of them returned to work at Kingmen (1929–1931).

On April 17, 1931 Oscar was kidnapped at Kingmen along with Augusta Nelson and Esther Nordlund by a group of communist soldiers. Augusta Nelson and Esther Nordlund were released after five days, but Oscar was held for 75 days, being released only after the Covenant paid a ransom of 67 cases of medical supplies valued at $2000.

In the fall of 1931 conditions had worsened in the interior of China, particularly in Hupeh Province and in Kingmen where the communists were still around. But Oscar after his release was able to make several visits in the district between 1933 and 1936 when a general exodus of the Red armies from south and central China made for a few years of relative peace.[9] In the fall of 1932 he was assigned to Kingchow, where he did relief work, taught in the seminary, and did evangelistic work.[10] Ruth and the children spent the winter in Kuling.[11] The Andersons remained at Kingchow until going home on furlough in 1936.

Oscar returned to China in the winter of 1938 on the first American vessel to sail into Shanghai after the city became occupied by the Japanese,[12] but he and his companions had to get to the Covenant field via Indo China.[13] During his last term in China (1938–1945), Oscar was at Siangyang, separated from his family, who stayed in Chicago and lived in the Missionary Home in North Park. During the war years, when Kingchow was cut off from the rest of the field by the Japanese army, Oscar functioned as chairman of the mission in Siangyang. His health was impaired during this time, and he went through a serious operation in Chengtu, China, a few months before returning to the United States in 1945. Upon returning home he did extensive itinerating, although his health was often not good. In February, 1949 he had to undergo more surgery, which left him in a weakened condition. Oscar died November 28, 1950 at Swedish Covenant Hospital, Chicago. He was 57 years of age.[14] Oscar was remembered as a fine evangelistic missionary, an able administrator, and one who lived out the Gospel he was preaching.

8. C. O. Anderson and R. M. Anderson, *Two Lives of Faith*, 35.

9. Ibid., 92–93.

10. Ibid., 92.

11. Ibid., 88.

12. Ibid., 112.

13. *The Covenant Weekly* (January 24, 1939) 4.

14. C. O. Anderson and R. M. Anderson, *Two Lives of Faith*, 162.

RUTH M. ANDERSON[15]

Ruth Anderson was born Ruth M. Engstrom in St. Paul, Minnesota, on March 27, 1893. She studied at a business college and then three years at North Park Bible Institute. Ruth sensed God's leading to missionary service in China, and on September 18, 1923 sailed from San Francisco to China. In the summer of 1924, Ruth married Oscar Anderson at Kuling. Ruth worked with her husband at Icheng during their first term (1924–1927), and their second term (1929–1931) began at Kingmen, although in May, 1930 Ruth and the children left for Hankow and then Shanghai, which is where they were when Oscar was kidnapped in April, 1931. The Andersons went to Kingchow in the fall of 1931, and remained there until going home on furlough in 1936. During Oscar's last term in China (1938–1945), Ruth stayed in Chicago tending to the children and their education. Ruth was said to be a courageous and brave woman, outwardly as calm as anyone, even when Oscar's life was in danger.

MARTHA J. ANDERSON

Martha Joanna Anderson was born in Chicago Heights, Illinois, on December 1, 1906. She was the daughter of the Rev. and Mrs. Adolph Anderson of the Salem Covenant Church in Minneapolis. Martha graduated from Minnehaha Academy in Minneapolis in 1925, and North Park College and Bible Institute in 1937. She was dedicated for missionary service at the Covenant Annual Meeting in 1937, which was held in Minneapolis. She went to China, arriving there in late 1938 with Oscar Anderson and others. She spent a year studying Chinese in Hong Kong.[16] From 1939–1945 she served at Siangyang,[17] and was secretary-treasurer of the Covenant Missionary Society in China and the Bethesda Hospital at Siangyang. On January 3, 1945, she left Siangyang with other missionaries and was evacuated on an American Air Force plane based at Laohokow.[18] In July, 1945 Martha went home to the United States via India.[19] In 1947 she returned to China and

---

15. See *Aurora* (1924) 47.

16. *The Covenant Weekly* (January 24, 1939) 4.

17. Judith Peterson, in a letter to the Rev. Gust Johnson dated May 21, 1940, said that Martha Anderson had just arrived in Siangyang a few days before she left on April 10. She had a long and difficult trip from Hong Kong. The missionary register has her beginning her work in China in 1939.

18. C. O. Anderson and R. M. Anderson, *Two Lives of Faith*, 133.

19. *Our Covenant* 20 (1945) 113–14.

assumed her previous position in Siangyang.[20] Martha was one of the three Covenant missionaries killed by bandits on January 7, 1948,[21] and was buried in a small International Cemetery in Hankow.

ALBERT E. ANDRÉ

Albert Ephriam André (originally Shoberg) was born in Malmö, Sweden, on January 10, 1877, and came with his parents to the United States in 1879. At 15 or 16 he went out as a missionary to India under Frederik Franson and the Scandinavian Alliance Mission. Returning to the United States, he traveled extensively, winning friends and giving interesting missionary lectures. In 1898 André married Beda Elovson, and the two of them then accepted the call of the Mission Covenant Church to go to China, where Albert began evangelistic work in Fancheng in 1899. In 1901 he and Beda returned to the United States because of Beda's health, but in 1902 they were back in China, working in Fancheng from 1902–1907. André built the mission station at Fancheng, working there until August 1907, when again they had to return to America due to Beda's poor health. In 1908 the Andrés resigned from service in the Covenant, and for a few years Albert served the Elim Covenant Church in Minneapolis. He later divorced his wife and remarried, making his home now on the East Coast. André had various jobs after the end of World War I, one of which was curator of the Oriental Department of the Brooklyn Museum. In 1934 André suffered a stroke, and then had a brain operation, which left him very weak. He never recovered, dying at Kingston NY in June, 1944. He was buried in Minneapolis beside his first wife, who died in 1933.

BEDA ANDRÉ

Beda André was born Beda Elovson in Värmland, Sweden, on May 7, 1872. She spent a term as a missionary in India under the Scandinavian Alliance Mission. In 1898 she married Albert André, and the same year the two of them went out under the Covenant Board to China. In 1899 she was doing women's work in Fancheng. The two of them returned to the United States in 1901 because of Beda's poor health, but were back at Fancheng in 1902, and remained there until 1907 when summoned home by the Covenant

20. The "Martha" traveling to China with Ann Kulberg in September-October, 1947, was probably Martha Anderson, who is mentioned in a letter from Ann Kulberg Carlson, dated October 9, 1947.

21. An obituary is contained in *Our Covenant* 23 (1948) 155–56.

Board. The Andrés resigned as Covenant missionaries in 1908 and moved to Minneapolis, where they became estranged and were finally divorced. Beda died in Minneapolis in April, 1933.

GUNNAR ARNELL

Gunnar Arnell was born in the parish of Anneboda, Småland, Sweden on August 19, 1883. Converted during his teen years, he became active in the Mission Covenant Church in Jönköping. In June 1902 he emigrated to the United States and arrived in Tacoma, Washington, and in August of the same year he joined the Mission Covenant Church in Tacoma. From early childhood he had a desire to dedicate his life to missionary service. Gunnar studied one term at North Park College in Chicago, and after hearing about the need for missionaries in China, he asked to be sent out. The churches in Tacoma and Seattle promised support, and the Mission Covenant extended a call to him for service in China. He was ordained at Tacoma on July 31, 1904.

Gunnar sailed for China with the Rev. Joel Johnson and Victoria Welter (later Mrs. Victoria Sjöquist), arriving in Hankow on September 7, 1904. Dr. John Sjöquist came down to Hankow to escort them to Siangyang. During the long houseboat trip up the Han River Arnell was stricken with typhus fever, and was unconscious upon arrival in Siangyang on October 2, 1904. He died five days later, on October 7, 1904, and was buried in the Fancheng cemetery. He was only 21 years of age.[22]

PAUL S. BACKLUND

Paul Backlund was born November 17, 1905, at Deer Lodge, Montana. The family later moved to Chicago, settling in the North Park community. Paul graduated from North Park College and Seminary in 1934, and continued his studies at the University of Chicago, where he earned a B.S. degree in 1937. Paul served Covenant churches in Donaldson, Indiana and the Bronx, New York City. He was called as a missionary to China and ordained in 1937 at the Covenant Annual Meeting in Minneapolis, and went to China in 1938. Backlund worked first at the Kikungshan American School for missionary children, located now on Cheung Chau Island, Hong Kong (1938–40). He was there in May, 1940.[23] In the fall of 1940 he went to

22. *The Chinese Recorder* 35 (1904) 647.
23. Reported in a letter from Judith Peterson to the Rev. Gust Johnson, dated May

Siangyang and worked there with Oscar Anderson (1940–45).[24] Backlund visited Nanchang in the fall of 1942, and at Christmas, 1942 was in Siangyang witnessing a baptismal service.[25] On January 3, 1945 he left Siangyang with other missionaries on a boat to Laohokow, where the group was then evacuated by an American Air Force plane.[26]

Backlund married Ruth Strang in Chicago on November 28, 1946, and the two went to China in the spring of 1947,[27] where they were stationed at Kingchow (1947–48). Paul and Ruth were at Kingchow when the bodies of the three murdered Covenant missionaries arrived there in January, 1948. Paul assisted in the memorial service, and helped prepare the bodies for burial. Paul and Ruth returned to the United States in early 1949 because of Ruth's poor health,[28] after serving briefly at a new covenant field opened up in Kweichow Province. In 1950 Paul was pastor of the Mission Covenant Church in Cheyenne, Wyoming. At some earlier time Paul taught English to the young George Lindbeck, son of Lutheran China missionaries, who went on to become professor at Yale Divinity School. Paul lived his last years in Turlock, California, where he was a resident of Bethany Home.

RUTH BACKLUND

Ruth Backlund was born Ruth Strang at Nappanee, Indiana, on March 27, 1916. Converted at the United Brethren Church in Donaldson, Indiana, she later joined that church as a member. Ruth attended North Park Bible Institute (1936–1937), and later graduated as a nurse from St. Joseph's Hospital in South Bend (1943–1946). She married Paul Backlund on November 28, 1946, at the North Park Covenant Church, and then sailed with her husband to China in the spring of 1947. In their short stay in China the Backlunds were stationed at Kingchow (1947–48). When the bodies of the three martyred missionaries arrived in Kingchow in January, 1948, Ruth, together with Otelia Hendrickson, Lillian Branstrom, and Viola Larson, washed the bodies and prepared them for burial. Ruth returned home with Paul in 1949

21, 1940. In Oscar Anderson's biography (p. xxiii) it is said that Backlund's initial arrival in China was in 1940.

24. C. O. Anderson and R. M. Anderson, *Two Lives of Faith*, 125.

25. Backlund, "Glimpses of China Today," 94.

26. C. O. Anderson and R. M. Anderson, *Two Lives of Faith*, 133.

27. Oscar Anderson met Paul in Silverhill, Alabama in February, 1947 on his way back to China; cf. C. O. Anderson and R. M. Anderson, *Two Lives of Faith*, 155.

28. *The Covenant Weekly* (February 18, 1949) 5; *Our Covenant* 24 (1949) 23.

after serving briefly in Keichow Province, and in 1950 she and Paul were at the Mission Covenant Church in Cheyenne, Wyoming.

Ebba Beckus—see **Ebba Fondell**

ALEXIS (ALIK) FRIEDRICH BERG

Alik F. Berg was born at Sangnitz, Estonia, on May 31, 1904, and attended school in Petrograd / St. Petersberg (Russia), Riga (Latvia), Weymouth College (England) and Dorpat (Estonia). Converted in England in 1919, he then became active in Christian Endeavor in Helsingfors (Helsinki), and was also a lay preacher. Alik then went on to study medicine at the University of Dorpat (1922–23), Göttingen University in Germany (1923–1924), and at Helsingfors (Helsinki), Finland (1926–1930). He did postgraduate work at several hospitals in Finland, and was a private practitioner and part-time military physician from 1934–1938. After taking a course in Tropical Medicine and Hygiene at London University in 1938, Alik went as a medical missionary to China in 1939, serving under the auspices of the Norwegian Lutheran Mission (Norske Kinamissionsförbund). Dr. Berg served on the staff of Froeyland Memorial Hospital in Laohokow, Hupeh Province (1940–1946). He was also acting superintendent of the Bethesda Hospital in Siangyang for four months. Alik and Signe of the Norwegian Mission in Laohokow were in Kunming when Oscar Anderson came through in late August of 1945, working at the American Army post office.[29] The Covenant Annual Meeting called Alik and his wife, Dr. Signe Berg, to be Covenant missionaries for one term in 1946. Alik became head doctor and director of the Bethesda Hospital in Siangyang (1946–48).[30] Dr. Alik Berg was one of three Covenant missionaries murdered in China on January 7, 1948.[31] He was a learned man, having published works on ectopic pregnancies and the Friedman pregnancy test, and able to speak eight languages, including Chinese.

SIGNE BERG

Signe Berg, wife of Alik Berg, was born October 31, 1909 in Tammerfors, Finland. She took her first medical degree (cand. med.) at the University of

---

29. C. O. Anderson and R. M. Anderson, *Two Lives of Faith*, 144.
30. *Our Covenant* 23 (1948), 156.
31. An obituary appears in *Our Covenant* 23 (1948) 156.

Helsingfors (Helsinki) in 1931, her second degree (lic. med.) at the same university in 1937, and then became a private practitioner at Jeensun, Finland in 1937–1938. Signe was a member of the Mission Covenant Church of Finland (Fria Missionsförbundet), but went to China in 1939 under the auspices of the Norwegian Lutheran Mission (Norske Kinamissionsförbund). She served on the staff of Froeyland Memorial Hospital in Laohokow, Hupeh Province, China, from 1940–1945, and on the staff of Bethesda Hospital in Siangyang from 1945–1947, where for a time she was acting superintendent. The Covenant Annual Meeting called her and her husband, Dr. Alik Berg, in 1946 to be Covenant missionaries to China for one term. In 1947 Signe returned to Finland to attend to her mother, who was seriously ill, and was not in China when Alik was murdered by bandits in January, 1948. Signe was in the United States in August and September of 1948, speaking in the churches. In October she returned to China.[32] In 1950 she was at the Henry Ford Memorial Hospital in Detroit, Michigan. In 1952 Signe went with other Covenant missionaries to serve in Formosa (Taiwan).

ELIZABETH H. BJÖRKGREN[33]

Elizabeth Björkgren was born in Worcester, Massachusetts, on April 13, 1892. Her parents moved to Canada where she received her education and taught for some years in the public schools, before going to Moody Bible Institute in Chicago. There she intended to prepare herself for missionary service in China. Elizabeth was the first representative of the Covenant in Canada to go out as a missionary to China, and received support from the Covenant churches in Canada. She came to China in 1921, and served one term in the Nanchang district and at the girls' school in Nanchang (1921–27). In 1927, when a large number of missionaries evacuated from the interior of China, she returned to Canada and resigned from the Covenant staff. She then married a Mr. Rosengren, and the two of them settled in Wetaskiwin, Alberta, a small city 43 miles south of Edmonton. Elizabeth was active in the Wetaskiwin Covenant Church for many years. By 1947 she and her husband had moved to Calgary, Alberta.

32. *Our Covenant* 23 (1948) 49–50.
33. See *Aurora* (1922) 112.

CARL A. BRANSTROM

Carl Branstrom was born at Skellefteå, a town in Norrland, Sweden, on April 3, 1906. He came to the United States in October 5, 1923, settling in Jamestown, New York. Branstrom attended North Park College and Theological Seminary for seven years, graduating in 1932. He got his A.B degree at Tarkiol College, and later did two years of graduate work at McCormick Theological Seminary in Chicago. In 1933 he accepted the call to become a Covenant missionary to China, and went to China the same year. He received support from the Broadway Covenant Church in Minneapolis, Minnesota, and the First Mission Covenant Church of Jamestown, New York. He studied Chinese at Peking for a year, and then spent his first term at the Covenant head stations in Nanchang (1934), Fancheng (1935), and Kingmen (1936–39). Carl focused on evangelism. He married Lillian Almquist in Kuling, China, on July 10, 1935. The Branstroms went home on furlough in 1939, during which time Carl pursued further study,[34] and then they returned to China in late 1940 and were stationed at Nanchang (1940–45). They had to flee to Szechuan from the Japanese in the mid-1940s,[35] and returned to the United States via India in 1945.[36] The Branstroms were in Red Oak, Iowa in July of 1946.[37]

The Branstroms returned to China in 1947,[38] and began working in Kingmen (1947–48). In January, 1948, Carl and Lillian were in Kingchow when the bodies of the three murdered Covenant missionaries arrived. Carl assisted in the memorial service, and both he and Lillian helped prepare the bodies for burial. After evacuating Kingchow in 1948 the Branstroms served briefly in a new Covenant field opening up in Kweichow Province. In September, 1949 they were in Hong Kong, wondering if they should return to the United States. In July, 1950 Carl was resting on Cheung Chan Island with sinus trouble.[39] When they returned to the United States in about

---

34. A picture of Carl and Lillian Branstrom with their two small girls appeared in *The Covenant Weekly* Swedish (Feb. 28, 1939) 3.

35. Carl Branstrom and Edward Nelson were down in Kweiting, presumably at this time. Edward Nelson was in China from 1946–1949. Branstrom gives a report of Kweichow and Kuanghsi (Kwangsi?) Provinces in southwest of China in "From Temples of Idols to the Temple of God," 72–83. Oscar Anderson (C. O. Anderson and R. M. Anderson, *Two Lives of Faith*, 133) says the Branstroms left Nanchang in the fall of 1943, going over the mountains to Chungking, and that it was a difficult trip.

36. Ibid.

37. C. O. Anderson and R. M. Anderson, *Two Lives of Faith*, 151.

38. Oscar Anderson met them in Silverhill, Alabama on their way back to China; cf. C. O. Anderson and R. M. Anderson, *Two Lives of Faith*, 155.

39. Letter from Ann Kulberg Carlson to her parents in "Mission to China," dated

1951, they lived in the Missionary Home in North Park. Later they moved to Eagle Rock, CA.

LILLIAN BRANSTROM

Lillian Branstrom was born Lillian Almquist in Essex, Iowa, on June 11, 1903. She received her education at Iowa State Teachers' College (extension course; 1922), and then entered nurses training, graduating from Lord Lester Hospital in Omaha, Nebraska (1927), and taking a post-graduate course at Cook County Hospital, Chicago (1929). Lillian attended Moody Bible Institute Evening School in 1930–1932, and North Park College in 1933–1934. She went to China under the Covenant Board in 1934, and spent her first year in Kingchow, working in the dispensary.[40] Support came from the Fremont Covenant Church in Fremont, Iowa, her home church, and the neighboring Essex Covenant Church. On July 10, 1935, Lillian married the Rev. Carl Branstrom in Kuling, China. The two of them then served at Fancheng (1935), Kingmen (1936–1939), and Nanchang (1940–45). Lillian returned from the United States with Carl in 1947, taking up work again in Kingmen (1947–48). She was present with her husband when the bodies of the three martyred missionaries arrived at Kingchow, and together with Viola Larson, Otelia Hendrickson, and Ruth Backlund washed the bodies and prepared them for burial. She and Carl were in Kweichow Province after evacuating from Kingchow in 1948, and in the next year were in Hong Kong. Lillian is remembered as a very able missionary, courageous in times of danger, and resourceful in times of need.

Alma Carlson—see **Alma Carlson Himle**

ARVID CONRAD CARLSON[41]

Arvid Carlson was born in Tjärstad, Östergötland, Sweden, on August 12, 1893. He sailed for America in 1910, and upon arrival studied for a time in Rushfield, Minnesota. He then moved to Wesley, Iowa, where he joined the Congregational Church. Carlson came to Chicago and attended North Park Academy, from which he graduated in 1920, and North Park Theological Seminary (1921). He was ordained in Kingsburg, California on October

---

July 25, 1950.

40. C. B. Nelson, "Our Medical Missionary Work in China," 69.

41. See *Aurora* (1922) 107–8.

16, 1921, and went to China the same year. Arvid did evangelistic work in the Kingmen district (1921–27) until the communist uprisings forced him and his wife to leave in 1927. Carlson had married Esther Hanson at Kuling, China on July 18, 1923. After the Carlsons went home in 1927, they did not return to China, which was deemed unfortunate since Arvid was considered to be particularly well qualified for the China mission field and was remembered for his evenness of temper, friendly spirit, and exemplary Christian character. At home Carlson served churches in Illinois, Minnesota, and Iowa. In 1947 the Carlsons were living in Warren, Minnesota, where Arvid was serving the Warren church.

Edla Carlson—see Edla Matson

ESTHER CARLSON

Esther Carlson was born Esther Hanson in Seatonville, Illinois on January 20, 1897. She received missionary training in the Training School of Home and Foreign Missions, Chicago, and nurses training at Swedish Covenant Hospital, Chicago. She graduated from Swedish Covenant in 1921. After graduation, Esther practiced nursing briefly in Turlock, California, and then went out as a missionary to China in 1922. She married Arvid Carlson at Kuling on July 18, 1923. The Carlsons worked at Kingmen from 1923–1927, where Esther was a nurse and did women's work. The communist uprising forced them to return home in 1927, after which they resigned from the China staff and decided to serve in the homeland rather than return to China.

VIRGINIA CARLSON

Virginia Carlson arrived on the China field in September, 1947,[42] serving there only briefly before evacuating to Hankow with other missionaries after the murder of the three missionaries. In early 1948 she was studying Chinese at the Language School in Wuchang, and in November was at the American School Kikungshan that had now relocated to Hong Kong.[43]

42. *Our Covenant* 22 (1947) 96.
43. A. L. Dwight, "Where Is the Dispersion?" 3.

HERMAN J. CONRADSON[44]

Herman Julius Conradson was born at Hablingbo, Gottland, Sweden on July 12, 1881. He moved to America in 1906, and received theological training at North Park College and Theological Seminary, graduating from the seminary in 1911. After graduation he served the First Mission Church in Jamestown, New York as assistant pastor, and then returned to Gottland, where he worked for some time in his home province. Conradson returned to the States and was ordained as a missionary to China at Jamestown, New York on September 15, 1912. He left for China almost immediately, arriving there in 1912. Herman worked for two years in Siangyang, and was then transferred to Kingman. He married Covenant missionary Amelia Ackerson on March 24, 1915. The two worked together at Kingmen until 1921, when they went home on furlough. At Kingmen and its many outstations Herman did evangelistic and educational work, having a close relationship with Joel Johnson.[45] During their first furlough in 1922–23, Herman studied part of the time and earned his B.A. degree from St. Olaf College in Northfield, Minnesota (1923).

In 1923 the Conradsons returned to Siangyang, where Herman was in charge of the schools and the church in Siangyang. In September, 1926, the Conradsons left Kuling to return to Siangyang, but on the evening of his arrival Herman was invited out for a meal, after which he was stricken by a severe attack of cholera, which was rampant that year all over China. People were dying like flies.[46] Two western-trained Chinese doctors, together with Ellen Ackerson, Amelia's sister, who was a nurse at Bethesda Hospital, did all they could for him, but on September 10th he died.[47] Herman was buried in the small foreign cemetery in Fancheng.[48]

AMELIA C. CONRADSON

Amelia Conradson was born Amelia C. Ackerson in Northfield, Minnesota on August 26, 1883. She studied at Carlton College in Northfield, after which she became a schoolteacher and later a bookkeeper. Amelia accepted

44. See *Aurora* (1924) 46; (1927) 123–26.

45. P. Matson, *Our China Mission*, 78.

46. C. O. Anderson and R. M. Anderson, *Two Lives of Faith*, 31.

47. Covenant records say he became ill the evening of his arrival at Siangyang from Kuling, which was on September 9th, and died on September 10, 1926 at 8 a.m. in the morning. Peter Matson in a published obituary (*The Chinese Recorder* 57 [1926] 899) puts the date of his death on September 8th.

48. *Our Covenant* 1 (1927) 74–75.

the call of the Mission Covenant to go to China as a missionary in 1907, arriving in China in the spring of 1908.[49] She married the Rev. Herman Conradson on March 24, 1915. Her work in the Siangyang and Kingmen districts was chiefly educational and evangelistic, where in both places she was a teacher and in charge of the girls' schools. After Herman died in 1926, she continued to serve in China, and from 1932–1939 was head of the Bible training school for young women in Siangyang, which had been built up by Edla Matson.[50] Amelia returned to the United States on furlough in early 1940, and then remained there, becoming a parish worker in the First Covenant Church in Jamestown, New York (1944–47). In May, 1947 she returned to China and took up work in Kingchow (1947–48). Amelia was in Kingchow when the bodies of the three martyred missionaries arrived in January, 1948, and kept watch with Viola Larson the night after the bodies arrived and before they were prepared for burial. After the death of Martha Anderson she became Treasurer of the Covenant Mission. She also served briefly in the newly opened field in Kweichow Province. In 1950 she was in Hong Kong leading women's groups.[51] Amelia is said to have won many souls for Christ in China, and endeared herself to countless people through her unselfish service and love for the Chinese people.

EARL C. DAHLSTROM

Earl Dahlstrom was born in Rockford, Illinois on January 31, 1914. He received his education at North Park College (1936), the University of Chicago (A.B. in 1938), North Park Theological Seminary (1940), and the Kennedy School of Missions, Hartford Seminary Foundation, in Hartford, Connecticut (M.A. 1949). Dahlstrom was ordained in 1940 at the Covenant Annual Meeting in Duluth, Minnesota, and after serving Covenant churches in Wisconsin, Illinois, and Connecticut, he went to China in 1940 to teach at the Kikungshan School, an American school for missionary children now located on Cheung Chau Island, Hong Kong.[52] Earl arrived in Hong Kong on August 31, 1940,[53] but taught for only one semester, as uncertain politi-

49. Amelia arrived with her sister Ellen in Shanghai on February 10, 1908; cf. *The Chinese Recorder* 39 (1908) 174.

50. P. Matson, *Our China Mission*, 118.

51. Letter from Ann Kulberg Carlson to people in Cromwell, CT, dated July 11, 1950.

52. The school after opening in 1913 was located at Kikungshan, a Lutheran retreat center north of the Covenant field on the border of Hupeh and Honan Provinces; see Swenson, "Notes on Kikungshan."

53. Dahlstrom, "Impressions of an Initiate in China." Judith Peterson in a letter to

cal events necessitated the sending of children home to America. He then
went to Shanghai, and for a time was a student and teacher at St. John's
University,[54] where classes were conducted in English. Shanghai at the time
was partially controlled by the Japanese. Then Earl's health failed, and he
had to return to the United States in 1941. On September 12, 1942 he married Rosalie M. Jones. On September 30, 1946 Earl and Rosalie sailed for
China, where Earl began teaching again at the Kikungshan School. This
school was operated by the Lutheran Missions in China, but served as a
school for children from many different missions. By June, 1948 Earl was
again in poor health, and within a month was flying home to the Mayo
Clinic for treatment.[55] After returning to the United States, Earl earned a
doctorate from Hartford Seminary Foundation, where his dissertation was
on "The Covenant Missionary Society in China" (1950). He then became
a professor at North Park Theological Seminary, where he remained until
retirement.

ROSALIE DAHLSTROM

Rosalie Dahlstrom was born Rosalie M. Jones at Marquette, Kansas on Sep-
tember 2, 1920. She was the daughter of Covenant pastor J. Arvid Jones.
Rosalie graduated from North Park College (1940), and from Northern
Illinois State Teacher's College in De Kalb (B.E. 1942). On September 12,
1942, she married the Rev. Earl C. Dahlstrom, and at the Covenant Annual
Meeting of 1946, held at Jamestown, New York, Rosalie was dedicated for
missionary service to China. Earl and Rosalie sailed from San Francisco on
September 30, 1946, arriving in Shanghai on October 16. She was with him
at the American School Kikungshan (1946–48). In 1948 they returned to
the United States.

---

the Rev. Gust Johnson, dated May 21, 1940, said they were waiting for Earl Dahlstrom
in Hong Kong. An earlier trip was cancelled due to unsettled conditions (Gust E. Johnson, *The Covenant Weekly* July 30, 1940, 4).

54. For a picture of the laying of a cornerstone at St. John's University on January 1,
1915, see *The Chinese Recorder* 46 (1915) opposite p. 203; a picture of the new science
building at St. John's appears in *The Chinese Recorder* 51 (1920) opposite p. 594.

55. Ann Kulberg Carlson in a letter in her "Mission to China," dated June 20, 1948,
said Earl would probably never be able to return to China, and he did not return.

ALBERT L. DWIGHT[56]

Albert L. Dwight was born Albert L. Johnson in Shibboleth, Kansas, (near Lund) on December 23, 1887. He was converted in Lund, after which he graduated from the Western Normal School in Stockton, California. He then taught school for four years. Albert attended the Bible Institute of Los Angeles (Biola), completing his course in July, 1915. He then accepted the call as a missionary to China. Albert had married Elna Lundell on January 1, 1915, and the two of them went to China in the fall of 1915. In their first term they served under the name of Albert and Elna Johnson, but then changed their name to Dwight. Albert and Elna did evangelistic work at Fancheng, Icheng, and Siangyang during the years 1915 to 1936; in the early years Albert went out on itineration with Victor Nordlund. In 1918 Albert moved to Fancheng, taking charge of the district and of Icheng and its out-stations.[57] Albert Dwight and Victor Nordlund built the Icheng station.[58] The Dwights went home in 1927 with other Covenant missionaries, but on October 5 1928 were on the steamer *President Adams* sailing from San Francisco with Oscar and Ruth Anderson, Mabel Olson, and I. W. Jacobson headed for China.[59] They went home on furlough in 1936, and only Albert returned to China in 1938.[60] In early 1940 he was at Kingchow.[61] The city at the time was in Japanese hands, and communication was cut off. Albert was expatriated home on the *Gripsholm* in 1942, and remained in the United States between 1942 and 1945, during which time he served as a Covenant pastor. Albert and Elna returned to China in 1945, remaining until December, 1949, when they went home. They were the last Covenant missionaries to leave Mainland China. Albert Dwight was remembered as a missionary with good judgment and common sense, unquestioned loyalty to Christ, and a deep love for the Chinese. His son Norman and wife Martha later served as Covenant missionaries to Taiwan. The Dwights were members of the Hilmar Covenant Church in Hilmar, California.

56. See *Aurora* (1924) 47.

57. P. Matson, *Our China Mission*, 78.

58. Ibid., 119.

59. C. O. Anderson and R. M. Anderson, *Two Lives of Faith*, 39.

60. P. Matson, "The Siang Fan District," 29; *The Covenant Weekly* (January 24, 1939) 4.

61. John Peterson, "Kingchow and Shasi," 54.

ELNA S. DWIGHT

Elna Dwight was born Elna Sophia Lundell at Davey, Nebraska on September 25, 1887. She graduated from the Western School of Commerce in Stockton, California, and taught for two years at the Bible Institute of Los Angeles. Elna married the Rev. Albert L. Dwight on January 1, 1915 in Turlock, California, and went with him to China in the fall of that year. The two served together in China from 1915 to 1936, at Fancheng, Icheng, and Siangyang. In 1936 they went home on furlough, and Elna remained with the children when Albert returned to China in 1938. The two returned to China in 1945, coming home finally in December, 1949.[62] Elna was a quiet person, but was remembered as a consecrated and courageous Christian, not shrinking from duty.[63] She died on Dec 20, 1952 at the age of 65.

RUTH EDLUND

Ruth Edlund was born in Chicago on November 10, 1912. She was educated at Calumet High School, the University of Chicago, Swedish Covenant Hospital (R.N. 1935),[64] Moody Bible Institute, Evening School (1937–1940), and Loyola University (B.S. 1944). At Loyola she completed a course in public health nursing.[65] An active member of the Bethany Mission Covenant Church in Chicago, Ruth was accepted for missionary service to China in June, 1943. But on account of the war, and a lack of transportation facilities, she was unable to sail to China until June 2, 1946. Once in China, Ruth was a nurse on the staff of Bethesda Hospital in Siangyang. Ruth later served in Kweiting in southwest China. In September, 1949, she was in Hong Kong, getting ready to go to Japan.[66] After returning to the United States, Ruth made her home in the North Park community of Chicago.

62. *Our Covenant* 25 (1950) 107.

63. *Our Covenant* 28 (1953) 116.

64. Ruth is pictured with her graduating class of 1935 in *The Covenant Weekly* (June 4, 1935) 5.

65. *Our Covenant* 19 (1944) 73.

66. Letter of Ann Kulberg Carlson in her "Mission to China," dated September 10, 1949.

ELLEN M. FALK[67]

Ellen Falk was born in Chicago on March 10, 1893. At age 15 she made a commitment to Christ, and in 1911 joined the Englewood Mission Covenant Church, Chicago. Ellen studied at Moody Bible Institute Evening School for three years, and then took nurses training at Swedish Covenant Hospital, from which she graduated in 1921. In 1921 she went to China as a missionary, being supported by the Young People's Society of the Englewood Covenant Church. Ellen served as a nurse and did dispensary work at Nanchang and Icheng from 1921 to 1927. Due to the communist upheaval in 1927 she returned to the United States, and in 1932 or 1933 married a Dr. Masterberg. The two then made their home in the Seattle, Washington vicinity.

ELMER W. FONDELL

Elmer William Fondell was born at Dawson, Minnesota on August 20, 1898. He was converted in 1909 and became a member of the Mission Covenant Church in Dawson. He graduated from Macalester College in St. Paul, Minnesota (1922) and North Park College and Theological Seminary (1925). Elmer accepted the call for Covenant missionary service in 1925, and sailed for China in that year, working first as an educational missionary at Siangyang. Because of the unrest at Siangyang, he then went to teach at the Shanghai American school, and after that at the American school in Kuling. In March, 1927 he left Siangyang with the Matsons and other missionaries because of the communist uprising, going to Hankow and then to Shanghai.[68] Elmer married Ebba Beckus in Shanghai on May 18, 1928. Because of ill health, Elmer returned to the United States in 1930, and two years later resigned from the China staff. He then served Covenant churches in Haxton, Colorado (1933–1939), and Paxton, Illinois (1939–1942), after which he was called to be Professor of Missions and Evangelism at North Park College and Theological Seminary.

EBBA C. FONDELL

Ebba Fondell was born Ebba Cecelia Beckus in Beloit, Wisconsin, on November 11, 1892. She was converted at confirmation age, and then joined

67. See *Aurora* (1922) 110.

68. Appended note in a letter from Peter Matson to the Mission Council, dated Feb. 19, 1927.

the Mission Covenant Church in Beloit. Ebba graduated from Beloit College in 1916, and later took special studies at the University of Wisconsin. For some years she taught language and history in high school. In 1922 she accepted the call to go to China as an educational missionary, serving in Siangyang and Fancheng. She married the Rev. Elmer Fondell in Shanghai on May 18, 1928. Ebba taught with Elmer at the Kuling school for one year, and then returned with him to the United States in 1930. Ebba was remembered as a very able woman and a well-balanced Christian worker.

Esther Franzen—see **Esther R. Kjellberg**

FREDERICK P. GEORGE[69]

Frederick George was born in the parish of Fryele, Småland, Sweden, on October 31, 1889. He emigrated to the United States in 1910, and was converted in Chicago that same year. He began studies at North Park College in the fall of 1911, and continued there for seven years while at the same time serving various Covenant churches. Frederick accepted the call to go as a Covenant missionary to China, and arrived in China in the fall of 1918, where he taught in government schools at Siangyang. A year after arrival in China he contracted peritonitis, and died on October 21, 1919, the anniversary of his day of arrival.[70] He was buried in the small cemetery in Fancheng. His loss was keenly felt, as he had a winning personality, a burning enthusiasm to fulfill his calling, and an unfailing devotion to the Lord. Frederick had also made great strides in language studies. He won the confidence of students at the Siangyang schools, and his death was said to have aroused new interest in the Covenant China mission, with a score of young men and women offering themselves subsequently for service there.

HJALMAR J. GRAVEM[71]

Hjalmar Gravem was born in Minneapolis, Minnesota on January 20, 1890. Converted at Elkorn, Manitoba, Canada in 1913, he then attended Christian and Missionary Alliance training schools at Saint Paul, Minnesota, and Nyak, New York. He then joined the Elim Covenant Church in Minneapolis, and was married to Helen Nelson in 1922. Ordained the same

---

69. See *Aurora* (1921) 113.

70. *Aurora* (1921) 113; P. Matson, *Our China Mission*, 78.

71. See *Aurora* (1923) 105.

year, Hjalmer and Helen were sent to China and arrived in 1922. Hjalmar and Helen did evangelistic work at Nanchang from 1922 to 1927. In 1927 they went home on their first furlough, and from 1927 to 1933 Hjalmar undertook missionary work in and around International Falls, Minnesota. The Gravems returned to China, and served again at Nanchang from 1934 to 1941. Helen returned with the children to the United States in 1941, living in Minneapolis. In 1944, during the war, Hjalmar was commissioned captain in the Marine Corps as liason officer for work in China. He was discharged in 1946, and returned alone to his former field in Nanchang. In September, 1949 the Gravems were in Hong Kong.[72] Hjalmar and Helen Gravem returned home in June, 1950.[73] Hjalmar Graven was known as an evangelistic missionary, and it is said "his joy was to take a group of Chinese coworkers and go out to towns and villages, doing missionary work in un-evangelized districts."[74] Hjalmar Gravem died on December 12, 1950.[75]

HELEN GRAVEM[76]

Helen Gravem was born Helen Nelson at Russell Minnesota on September 5, 1898. Her education consisted of two years at a business college, and two years at Minnehaha Bible Institute. In 1922 she was married to the Rev. Hjalmar Gravem, and on November 19, 1922 was commissioned for missionary work in China. She was stationed with her husband at Nanchang. In May, 1940 she and her family were in Hong Kong.[77] In 1941 Helen returned home with the children to Minneapolis. Helen was remembered as a very well balanced, capable missionary. She was a member of Mission Covenant churches in Russell and Minneapolis (Elim), Minnesota.

JUDITH HAGSTROM[78]

Judith Hagstrom was born in Kalmar, Sweden, on August 16, 1874. While still quite young, she emigrated to the United States and settled in Chicago,

72. Letter of Ann Kulberg Carlson in her "Mission to China," dated Sept. 10, 1949.

73. *Our Covenant* 25 (1950) 107.

74. *Our Covenant* 26 (1951) 104.

75. Ibid., 103–4.

76. See *Aurora* (1923) 105.

77. Reported in a letter from Judith Peterson to the Rev. Gust Johnson, dated May 21, 1940.

78. See *Aurora* (1909) 83–86.

where she joined the First Covenant Church. Judith became active in the Young Women's Association of First Covenant. In 1903 she entered nurses training at Swedish Covenant Hospital, and graduated from there in 1905. In that same year she was called by the Evangelical Mission Covenant to go out as a missionary to China. After a brief visit to her parents in Sweden, Judith arrived in China in the early part of 1906. She immediately started language study and medical work in Siangyang, and in two short years endeared herself to both Chinese and missionary comrades. The stress of the work and the severe climate in China caused her to become seriously ill. On the advice of a Covenant medical doctor it was decided that Judith should return to the United States in the company of Hilda Rodberg, who was also a nurse. By the time they reached Shanghai her condition worsened, and on April 22, 1908 she died.[79] Judith was laid to rest in the Bubbling Well Cemetery in Shanghai.[80]

ELSA HAMMERLIND[81]

Elsa Maria Hammarlind was born on November 22, 1894 at Bringetofta, Småland, Sweden. She arrived in the United States in 1909 and settled in Sioux City, Iowa, where she joined the Covenant Church. Later she moved to Grand Rapids, Michigan, and became active in the work of the Mission Covenant Church there. Elsa pursued studies at North Park College in 1912–1914, and graduated from the Nursing School at Swedish Covenant Hospital in 1917. She went to China as a missionary in 1920, receiving support from the Grand Rapids Mission Church. Elsa's work in China was medical and evangelistic, being carried on at Icheng (1922–1927)[82] and Nanchang (1933–45). During her first furlough to the United States in 1932, Elsa took a postgraduate course at the Cook County Hospital in Chicago, and at a T.B. Sanatorium. Her last term in China was from 1933 to 1945, where she was in charge of the dispensary at Nanchang.[83] After the bombing of the hospital at Siangyang in March, 1939, she and a Chinese nurse were particularly helpful to many refugees that came there from other districts.[84] Late in February, 1945 Elsa reluctantly agreed to leave Nanchang and went

---

79. *The Chinese Recorder* 39 (1908) 296; Olsson (*By One Spirit*, 753 n. 74) says she died while being repatriated.

80. For a picture of missionaries at her grave, see *Aurora* (1913), 101.

81. See *Aurora* (1921) 91. In some early sources her name is spelled "Hammarlind."

82. P. Matson, *Our China Mission*, 119.

83. C. B. Nelson, "Our Medical Missionary Work in China," 69.

84. E. C. Matson, "Life under the Shadows of Death," 28.

through Siangyang on her way to Laohokow to be evacuated. With her was Minglan, a Chinese girl whom she had adopted. In August of 1945 Elsa was working for the American Red Cross at Kunming when Oscar Anderson passed through there.[85] At Kunming she left Minglan in an orphanage for a year while in the United States. In 1948 Elsa also worked with Otelia Hendrickson at a large orphanage in Changsha.[86]

Elsa was able to return to Kingchow with Joel Johnson before the end of 1948, and in February it was reported that they intended to stay there, but they did not remain long. Soon after the communists came and they were forced to evacuate. By February, 25, 1949 Joel and Elsa were on their way to Chunking in southwest China. Elsa was in Hong Kong in September of 1949, and had decided that if she could not return to China she would go to Japan.[87] She never went to Japan, however. In July of 1950 she and Viola Larson were preparing to move to Chuen Wan, a village outside Hong Kong,[88] and in September, 1951 she was still in the Hong Kong area.[89] Elsa then worked in Formosa (Taiwan) beginning in 1952, and when she returned to live in North Park and retire from missionary service, she brought Minglan with her. Elsa is remembered as having done excellent work in Nanchang, where she gained the love and admiration of the whole city. She died in January, 1970 at 76 years of age.

E. OTELIA HENDRICKSON[90]

Esther Otelia Hendrickson was born in Minneapolis on November 28, 1891. She moved to Portland, Oregon in 1899, and completed nurses training in 1915 at the Good Samaritan Hospital, Portland, OR. Otelia left for China as a Covenant missionary on October 20, 1920, arriving there in November with Victor Nordlund and seven other new missionaries. Her work was chiefly that of a medical missionary, being also an instructor of nurses. She served at Kingmen (1920–25), Shasi (1931–38), and Siangyang (1941–45). Otelia was a pioneer in hospital ministry at Kingmen, and the

---

85. C. O. Anderson and R. M. Anderson, *Two Lives of Faith*, 144.

86. Personal communication from Minglan Hammerlind Wong, Mar. 6, 2014.

87. Letter of Ann Kulberg Carlson in her "Mission to China," dated Sept. 10, 1949.

88. Letter from Ann Kulberg Carlson to people in Cromwell, CT, in her "Mission to China," dated July 11, 1950.

89. Letter from Ann Kulberg Carlson to President Theodore W. Anderson in her "Mission to China," dated Sept. 6, 1951.

90. See *Aurora* (1921) 91.

first superintendent of nurses in the Kingmen hospital.[91] In May, 1925 she returned home to take a four-month course in theoretic and practical obstetric training at Chicago Lying-In Hospital and Dispensary, receiving a diploma in August, 1926. During that summer she also received a Sunday School Teacher's Certificate from North Park College. She could not return to China in 1927 because of conditions there, so from 1927 to 1930 she took a position at the University of Oregon and did public health work. From February 1930 to September, 1931 she served the First Covenant Church in Seattle as a church missionary. On October 10, 1931, Otelia sailed for China and spent her second term at the Kang Teng Chinese hospital in Shasi,[92] owned and operated by Dr. Edmund Li and his sister, Dr. Elizabeth Li. Both were Christians committed to run their hospital on Christian principles. She was home on furlough from 1938–40. In 1940 she was at Bethesda Hospital in Siangyang, but in May was expected at Kaoshan where missionaries from the ruined city of Kingmen were living.[93] At Easter, 1941 she was again in Siangyang.[94] On January 3, 1945, Otelia left Siangyang on a boat with other missionaries headed for Laohokow, where they were evacuated by an American Air Force plane based there.[95] In March, 1945 she was at Anking in Shensi Province, being advised by the American Consul to evacuate to the southwest due to a Japanese offensive.[96] In June of 1945 Otelia was at Chungking, helping Oscar Anderson get a room at the China Inland Mission home on his way out of China.[97]

After a furlough to the United States (1945–46), Otelia returned to China in May, 1947, where she was stationed briefly in Kingchow. She was present when the bodies of the three martyred missionaries arrived in Kingchow in January, 1948 and together with Ruth Backlund, Lillian Branstrom, and Viola Larson washed the bodies and prepared them for burial. She left Kingchow for Hankow to attend the committal service for the martyred missionaries, and then went to Changsha with Elsa Hammerlind to help out at a large orphanage there. In mid-November she was in Chungking. After Christmas she began conducting classes for nurses besides teaching

91. Judith M. Peterson, "Bethesda Training School for Nurses," 137.

92. C. B. Nelson, "Our Medical Missionary Work in China," 69.

93. Reported in a letter from Judith Peterson to the Rev. Gust Johnson, dated May 21, 1940.

94. C. O. Anderson and R. M. Anderson, *Two Lives of Faith*, 126.

95. Ibid., 133.

96. Letter from E. Rice at the American Embassy, Sian, Shensi Province, to Otelia Hendrickson, dated Mar. 26, 1945.

97. C. O. Anderson and R. M. Anderson, *Two Lives of Faith*, 141.

and helping in the health program of a war orphan Bible school. She was a member of the Nurses Association of China.

In September, 1949 Otelia left Chungking for Japan, where she then worked for more than two years as a Covenant missionary.[98] In 1950 she was working with Virginia Ohlson in the Japanese Nurses Christian Fellowship.[99] Otelia died on January 5, 1981 at the Cresta Loma Convalescent Home in San Diego. Otelia was remembered as a good nurse with teaching and administrative ability well above the ordinary.

ALMA CARLSON HIMLE

Alma Himle was born Alma Carlson in Västergötland, Sweden, on March 23, 1870. She graduated from a Minneapolis hospital and then attended Moody Bible Institute in Chicago. In 1897 she went to China under the auspices of the Mission Covenant Church, and was engaged in the dispensary and in women's work at Fancheng until 1899, when she married the Rev. T. H. Himle of the Norwegian Hauge Synod Mission, after which she severed her connection with the Mission Covenant. Alma and her husband worked for many years at Hsin Ye, Honan (Henan), a neighboring mission station to the north of the Covenant field. In 1909 the Himles left China, and Mr. Himle served in Santa Rosa, California until 1917, when he returned to China to help consolidate three Norwegian synods. Alma remained with the children in Santa Rosa. Alma suffered an attack of typhoid contracted T.B, and died on September 8, 1918 before her husband returned home. She was buried in Santa Rosa. Her husband then served a church in LaCrosse, Washington, and was director of a Lutheran Old People's Home at Coeur d'Alene, Idaho. He died September 25, 1925, and was buried in Northfield, Minnesota.

ISAAC W. JACOBSON

Isaac Wilhelm Jacobson was born at Sjögestad, Östergötland, Sweden, on March 10, 1877. He emigrated with his parents to the United States in 1888, and settled in Pilot Mound, Iowa. Isaac entered North Park College and Theological Seminary in 1898, and graduated in 1902. He was ordained as a missionary to China at the Covenant Annual Meeting held in Galesburg, Illinois in 1902, and went to China in the fall of that year. Isaac opened up

98. Letter of Ann Kulberg Carlson in her "Mission to China," dated Sept. 10, 1949.
99. Letter from Judith Peterson to the Rev. Ralph Hanson, dated Dec. 26, 1950.

the Nanchang district in the winter of 1902–03, built up the mission station at Nanchang, and established outstations in centrally located places in the district. In May, 1907 he married Anna Lassesen of the neighboring Norske Kinamissionsförbund (Norwegian Lutheran China Mission), after which she joined the Covenant mission. Isaac also served in Siangyang, Kingmen, and Kingchow, and for several years was chairman of the China conference. Isaac joined the staff at the Kingchow seminary and preparatory school in about 1912.

In 1920 Isaac and family went home on furlough. In 1922 they returned to Nanchang, staying until the general evacuation of 1927. On October 5, 1928 just Isaac returned to China with the Oscar Andersons, the Dwights, and Mabel Olson.[100] During the Sino-Japanese war Isaac was at Kingmen, although by early 1940 the station had been destroyed by Japanese bombs. Anna was at home with the children. The Japanese relocated Isaac Jacobson, Joel Johnson, and Mabel Olson to Hankow, where they were interned until repatriated to the United States in 1942 on the exchange steamers *SS Conte Verde* (Italian) and *Gripsholm* (Swedish). After returning home, Isaac was engaged in deputation work and taught for three years at the Covenant Bible Institute in Prince Albert, Canada. Isaac and Anna spent their last years in the North Park community of Chicago. Isaac was recognized as a competent linguist, a translator of Swedish hymns into Chinese, a good teacher, and a very able missionary. Isaac and Anna's son, Harald Jacobson, worked in the naval service at Chungking during the period of American evacuation of China,[101] and was later a high-ranking person in China affairs in the United States government, stationed in Washington, D.C.

ANNA JACOBSON

Anna Jacobson was born Anna Lassesen at Romsdalen, Norway, on May 28, 1874. She received a good education in the local gymnasium and normal training school, and then spent a year at a Ladies Training Home in London. In 1902 Anna went to China as a missionary under the Norske Lutherske Kinamissionsförbund (Norwegian Lutheran China Mission Association). In May, 1907 she married the Rev. Isaac Jacobson, and then came over into the service of the Mission Covenant Church, where the two worked in the populous Nanchang district. She also served with her husband at Kingchow. Anna was involved in women's work and with the girls' school. She went

100. C. O. Anderson and R. M. Anderson, *Two Lives of Faith*, 39; P. Matson, *Our China Mission*, 93.

101. C. O. Anderson and R. M. Anderson, *Two Lives of Faith*, 142.

home with Isaac in 1927, and did not return, conditions being chaotic in China at the time, particularly with regard to the bringing up of children. Anna spent a considerable amount of time separated from her husband, but neither of them ever spoke of this as a sacrifice, although undoubtedly it was. During Isaac's last two terms in China, Anna was in Chicago caring for and seeing to the education of their children. Anna died on October 25, 1954 after a lengthy illness.[102]

ALFRED J. JOHNSON[103]

Alfred Johnson was born in Chicago on January 30, 1898. In 1916 he came to faith in the Lord and united with the Mission Church in Ravenswood, Chicago. After high school he spent two years at an architectural school, and then attended North Park College and Theological Seminary. Alfred accepted the call of the Covenant to go as a missionary to China in 1921, and after marrying Ruth Hedberg in October, 1921, the two sailed from San Francisco on the *SS Nanking* to China. After arriving, they were briefly at Kingmen,[104] but in 1922 took up evangelistic and educational work in the Icheng district. There was a problem with bandits around Icheng in 1924, and Alfred was also suffering from severe asthma attacks, which made necessary their return to the United States in 1927. Alfred then resigned from the China staff. In the following years he served Covenant churches in Chicago, Kansas, and Nebraska, and was chaplain at Covenant Home, Chicago. Alfred and Ruth lived their later years in the North Park community of Chicago. Their son Gordon became a high-ranking person in China affairs for the United States government during WW II, serving in the Navy in Chungking.[105]

RUTH A. JOHNSON[106]

Ruth Johnson was born Ruth Hedberg in Onsby, Skåne, Sweden, on December 29, 1896. She came to faith in the Lord in 1915, after which she became active in the Humbolt Park Mission Covenant Church of Chicago. Ruth attended a business college, and then Moody Bible Institute for three years. In

---

102. *Our Covenant* 30 (1955) 42.

103. See *Aurora* (1922) 113.

104. J. S. Johnson, "The Kingmen District," 46–48.

105. C. O. Anderson and R. M. Anderson, *Two Lives of Faith*, 142.

106. See *Aurora* (1922) 113.

1921 she married the Rev. Alfred Johnson, and the two of them went out as Covenant missionaries to China in that year, doing evangelistic work in the Icheng district. In 1927 Ruth returned home with her husband, and the two did not return to China.

Albert Johnson—see **Albert Dwight**
Karen E. Johnson—see **Karen E. Karlstedt**

HILDA G. JOHNSON[107]

Hilda Johnson was born in Providence, Rhode Island, on August 19, 1896. She graduated from high school in Providence and from Rhode Island Normal School. Hilda was converted in 1916, and became a member of the Covenant Congregational Church of Providence. Until 1922 she was a schoolteacher in Providence. During 1923–1924 Hilda studied at North Park College, after which she went out under the Covenant as a missionary to China, sailing on December 6, 1924 in the company of Judith Peterson. She was a teacher and did children's work in Fancheng and Siangyang. When the communists started their northward march and began an intense propaganda campaign against missionary work, Hilda had to evacuate with the other missionaries. She spent the summer and fall of 1927 in Shanghai, and the next year relocated with other Covenant missionaries to Hankow. The uncertainty of the future and the climate in China broke her health, and Hilda was forced to return to the United States in 1928. Upon arrival home, she began teaching school again in Providence, Rhode Island.

HILMA M. JOHNSON

Hilma Maria Johnson was born in Väfnesunda, Östergötland, Sweden, on November 18, 1872. She graduated from Lunnevad High School and then emigrated to the United States, arriving there in 1891. Her early years were spent in Chicago, but then she moved to Denver, where she was converted in 1898. During 1900–1901 she pursued studies at North Park College, and then went out as a China missionary in the latter part of 1901, receiving support from the student body at North Park. Her consecration for China service in November, 1901 was by Covenant leaders C. A. Bjork and David Nyvall.[108] She sailed for China from San Francisco on Dec 3, 1901, and ar-

---

107. See *Aurora* (1925) 116.
108. *Our Covenant* 35 (1962) 102.

rived in Siangyang on Feb 14, 1902. Hilma served for four decades as a China missionary:[109] at Siangyang, Fancheng (where in 1915–16 she was in charge of women's work and had a girls' school); at Kingmen in the 1920s; and in the late 1930s and early 1940s at Kingchow. In March, 1927 she left Siangyang with the Matsons and other missionaries because of the communist uprising, going to Hankow and then to Shanghai.[110] Her work was chiefly educational and evangelistic. In 1934 she was in Hankow, serving as treasurer of the Covenant China Mission.[111] In 1938 she was back at Kingchow, and had a very narrow escape with another woman when Japanese bombs were dropped near the mission compound.[112] Hilma returned home after more than 40 years of missionary service in October, 1941, having had only two furloughs. In 1947 she was living in the North Park community in Chicago, and from 1955 was a resident of Covenant Home, Chicago. Hilma died in Chicago on Oct 7, 1962 at 89 years of age.

JOEL S. JOHNSON

Joel Sigfrid Johnson was born in Norra Vram, Skåne, Sweden, on February 16, 1876. He arrived in the United States in 1891. Joel graduated from North Park College in 1902, and after that studied in Joliet, Illinois, during which time he also served the Lockport Covenant Church (1900–1904). Joel went to China as a Covenant missionary in 1904, where he engaged in evangelistic and educational work in Siangyang and Kingmen. He began his work in Siangyang, but then went to build the station at Kingmen and open some 15 outstations in this large and populous district. He also had a prominent part in building the Kingchow Seminary.[113] On January 20, 1914, Joel married Adine Wenberg in China. During the communist disturbances of 1927, Joel and his family went home, and Joel served as Foreign Mission Secretary of the Covenant (1927–1930). He then served as pastor of the Chicago Heights Mission Church (1931–1933). In 1935 Joel went back to China, once again taking up work in Kingmen. During the war with Japan the Kingmen station was severely bombed, and practically destroyed. While Joel was in Kingmen in early 1940, Adine lived in the Missionary Home in North Park. When the Japanese came to occupy Kingmen, Joel

---

109. Olsson, *By One Spirit*, 446.

110. Appended note in a letter from Peter Matson to the Mission Council, dated Feb. 19, 1927.

111. P. Matson, *Our China Mission*, 118.

112. E. C. Matson, "Life under the Shadows of Death," 24.

113. P. Matson, *Our China Mission*, 116.

and Isaac Jacobson were removed to Hankow where they were interned for two years. The two were repatriated to the United States in 1942 on the exchange steamers SS *Conte Verde* (Italian) and *Gripsholm* (Swedish). Joel returned to China in September, 1946, taking up work at Kingchow. In 1947 he was in Siangyang.[114] He was in back in Kingchow when the bodies of the three martyred Covenant missionaries arrived in January, 1948. Together with Paul Backlund, Joel helped prepare the bodies for burial, painting the coffins grey and nailing down the heavy lids. When the missionaries were evacuated from Kingchow after the tragedy of January, 1948, Joel asked to remain in Shasi with the Swedish missionaries. He did for a time, and then was in Hankow. He and Elsa Hammerlind were permitted to return to Kingchow by the end of 1948, but did not stay there long. On February 25, 1949 they had fled the communists and were on their way to Chungking.[115] Joel returned to the United States in April, 1949[116] and took up residence with his family at the Covenant Missionary Home in North Park. In 1951 he and Adine moved to Seattle, where they spent their last years. Joel died at 96 on February 5, 1973.[117] Joel was a premier Covenant missionary, having good administrative ability and being practical, artistic, and a good builder. He was also an engaging speaker.

ADINE R. JOHNSON

Adine Johnson was born Adine Wenberg in Batavia, Illinois on September 29, 1884. She graduated from Columbia Conservatory of Music,[118] and was a music instructor, choir director, and organist in Batavia for five years, then in Sioux City for three years. Adine went to China in the fall of 1913, and on January 20, 1914 was married to the Rev. Joel S. Johnson. Adine was a music teacher, and it was not long before the Kingmen station became known as having the best singing in the entire Covenant field. Adine organized a choir, which is said to have sung exceptionally well. In 1922 she had a piano shipped to Kingmen: 32 men were required to transport it from the river port of Shipai. In 1927 she and Joel left China, and while Joel served as Foreign Mission Secretary of the Covenant, the two made their home

114. In a letter of Ann Kulberg Carlson in her "Mission to China," dated Nov. 6, 1947.

115. J. S. Johnson, "Flight in the Winter"; A. L. Dwight, "Covenant Work in China," 55.

116. *Our Covenant* 24 (1949) 23.

117. *The Seattle Times* (Jan. 18, 1964) 2.

118. *The Covenant Companion* (Mar. 25, 1966) 22.

in Batavia, Illinois. In 1935, when Joel returned to China, Adine moved to Chicago to take charge of the children's education. She did not return to China. Adine died on July 22, 1968 in Seattle. Joel and Adine's son, Winston, became an accomplished musician, serving as Professor of Music at North Park College and organist of the North Park Covenant Church.

OSCAR E. JOHNSON

Oscar Johnson was born in Vånga parish, Östergötland, Sweden, on October 15, 1883. He grew up in a Christian home where his father was both a teacher and a preacher. As a young man Oscar emigrated to the United States, settling in Providence, Rhode Island. In the fall of 1904 he entered North Park College, and graduated from North Park Theological Seminary in 1907. Oscar then accepted a call from the Covenant Church in Helena, Montana, but his desire was to go out as a missionary. He was accepted by the Mission Covenant Board to go to China, and was ordained at the Mission Covenant Church in Lakeview, Chicago, on August 2, 1908. A few weeks later he went to China, serving his first term in evangelistic work at Fancheng and Kingmen. In 1911 he married Justine Nilsson, who had come to China as a Covenant missionary in 1909. Oscar gained many friends in China, but because of his wife's poor health, the two had to return to the United States in the spring of 1913. Justine stayed in California, and Oscar went on to Chicago to take up further studies at North Park College, hoping to go on to medical school and then return to China as a medical missionary. But his stay at North Park was short. On October 31, 1913, he was found dead in his room. It was a great shock to his wife and friends. Justine, after a visit to Sweden where she regained her health, served as a nurse at several hospitals on the West Coast, at first as head nurse at Emanuel Hospital, Turlock, California.

JUSTINE E. JOHNSON

Justine Emelia Johnson was born Justina Nilsson on August 15, 1880 in Sunne, Sweden. She emigrated to the United States in 1899. Justine graduated from a nursing program at a hospital in Providence, Rhode Island, and then held the position of head nurse there for several years. In 1909 she was called as a missionary to China, and went out the same year. In 1911 she married the Rev. Oscar E. Johnson. The two achieved great success in the Kingmen district, but Justine's health failed, and on medical advice the two went home on furlough in 1913. For health reasons, Justine went to

California, and Oscar continued on to Chicago to study at North Park College. After Oscar's untimely death in 1913, Justine was heartbroken, and her condition worsened. She resigned as a missionary, and went to Sweden. But gradually her health was restored and she returned to America, where she took the position of head nurse at Emanuel Hospital, Turlock, California, a position she held for many years. She later assumed a similar position in Alameda, California. Justine was admired as a very capable nurse, energetic and enthusiastic in all that she did.

PAUL R. JOHNSON[119]

Paul Johnson was born near Waverly, Minnesota on March 22, 1899. After graduation from Watertown High School, he continued his education at a business school. Paul wanted to take further studies at Minnesota State University, but World War I intervened, and he was drafted into the army, serving until the end of the war. He then studied for two years at Moody Bible Institute with the aim of going out as a missionary. In August, 1921 Paul married Elin A. M. Swanson, and that year the two went out as Covenant missionaries to China. During their first term, they served at Siangyang, where Paul did evangelistic work and was manager of Bethesda Union Hospital. In 1927, because of upheavals in China, the two went home on furlough. While in the United States, Paul received his B.S. degree (1930). The two returned to China in 1934, where they were stationed at Icheng doing evangelism, but in April, 1939, after Japanese bombs had destroyed the city and the mission station at Icheng, the Johnsons moved up to Siangyang.[120] In the summer of 1940 they had to return home on account of Elin's illness. Paul began medical studies, and graduated as a medical doctor in 1945. That same year he returned to China, serving at the Bethesda Hospital in Siangyang. His ship had been torpedoed on the return voyage, but limped into Gibralter, where he managed in some way to secure air transportation to India, and then to China.[121] Paul was not long in Siangyang. In April, 1945 he was with Oscar Anderson in Chengtu, helping him recover from his surgery.[122] It was a strenuous time, but things had improved with the Japanese withdrawal from the Covenant field. Elin joined her husband in China in 1946, but once again she became ill, and the two of them had to

119. See *Aurora* (1922) 109.

120. C. O. Anderson and R. M. Anderson, *Two Lives of Faith*, 113.

121. Ibid., 116

122. Ibid., 140.

return home in 1947, where they were granted indefinite leave of absence from the Covenant field at the Covenant Annual Meeting in Seattle (1947).

ELIN A. M. JOHNSON[123]

Elin Johnson was born Elin Swanson in Solg, Härjedalen, Sweden, on April 2, 1898. She studied at Linsele, and then for two years at Uppsala. In 1916 she emigrated to the United States, settling in Minneapolis. Elin studied English in the Evening School of Minnehaha Academy, and Bible at the Northwestern Bible School in Minneapolis. She also received nurses' training at the Swedish Hospital in Minneapolis. In 1921 Elin married the Rev. Paul R. Johnson, and that same year the two of them went out under the Covenant Board to China, where they worked at Siangyang and Icheng. Elin's health was not the best in China, and she became an invalid at home in the United States in 1940 and again in 1947. Elin was nevertheless remembered as a fluent speaker and one having great natural gifts.

REUBEN N. JOHNSON[124]

Reuben Johnson was born in Chicago on August 26, 1896. He studied at North Park College (1911–1916), a short time at Moody Bible Institute, and then worked for a time in his father's business in Chicago. J. N. Johnson, called "Shuttle Johnson," invented and held the patent on a shuttle for sewing machines, and as a result had a successful business.[125] Reuben went to China as a Covenant missionary in 1920, arriving there October 30 with Victor Nordlund and seven other new missionaries. He took up work in Fancheng and Kingchow. He married Ida Ostrōm at Kingchow on November 14, 1924,[126] after which the two lived in Kingchow.[127] Reuben was a good accountant and bookkeeper, serving as treasurer for the Covenant China Mission and for the theological seminary and middle school in Kingchow. During the upheaval in 1927 Reuben and Ida returned with other missionaries to the United States, and did not go back to China. Reuben began

123. See *Aurora* (1922) 109–10.

124. See *Aurora* (1921) 92.

125. His obituary appeared in *The Covenant Weekly* Swedish (Feb. 14, 1939) 8.

126. A picture of Reuben and Ida at the time of their marriage in Kingchow appeared in *The Covenant Companion* Old Series (June, 1925) 17.

127. The Ravenswood Covenant Church of Chicago built this house at the cost of $3000. A picture of the house appeared in *The Covenant Companion* Old Series (March, 1926), 15.

working again in his father's business, and after his father's death took over the business. The Johnsons were active in the Ravenswood Mission Covenant Church in Chicago.

IDA J. JOHNSON[128]

Ida Johnson was born Ida Oström in the parish of Nederluleå, Norrbotten, Sweden, on April 13, 1890. She was converted in 1910 and emigrated to the United States in 1912, settling in Chicago. There she joined the large Covenant Tabernacle on Chicago's South Side. For about a year Ida studied at North Park College (1917–1918), and then took nurses' training at Swedish Covenant Hospital, graduating from there in 1921. She was called to missionary service in China, and went soon after, arriving in China in 1921. She took up work at Kingchow and Shasi, where she became school nurse at the Kingchow Theological Seminary and middle school. Ida married the Rev. Reuben Johnson at Kingchow on November 14, 1924. The two left China in 1927, and upon their return to the United States made their home in the Ravenswood community of Chicago. Ida was remembered as an excellent nurse and mission worker in China.

KAREN E. KARLSTEDT[129]

Karen Karlstedt was born in Annerstad, Småland, Sweden, on March 25, 1895. She emigrated to the United States in 1910, taking up residence in Chicago. In the spring of 1912 she was converted, and joined the Edgewater Mission Covenant Church. For a year and a half she attended North Park College, and then entered nurses' training at Swedish Covenant Hospital, from which she graduated in 1921. That same year she went to China as a missionary under the Covenant Board. She was a nurse and did dispensary work in the Kingmen district until 1927, when the communist persecution forced her and other Covenant missionaries to evacuate. Karen had been engaged to the Rev. Frederick P. George, whose missionary career ended suddenly in 1919 (see Frederick P. George). In 1928 she married Albin Johnson of the Portage Park Covenant Church in Chicago, and the two of them subsequently became active in that church.

128. See *Aurora* (1922) 114.
129. Ibid., 112.

ESTHER R. KJELLBERG[130]

Esther R. Kjellberg was born to Swedish parents in Oslo, Norway, on December 11, 1898. She came with her parents to the United States in 1902. After graduating from high school and Minnesota State University, she taught for some years. Esther was a member of the Salem Covenant Church in Minneapolis. She went out as a Covenant missionary in 1923 to China, where she did educational work at Kingmen (1923–1927). In 1927, because of the communist uprising, Esther was forced to leave Kingmen and return to the United States. She went to Stockholm, Sweden, where she married the Rev. Elof Franzen in 1929. Esther then entered the service of the Swedish Mission Covenant. The two of them returned to China in 1932, and served for many years in the Swedish Covenant field at Macheng, which was also in Hupeh Province (1932–1938). They returned home in 1938, and were planning on going back to China in 1946, but because of Esther's poor health, they were unable to do so.

ANN KULBERG

Anna Kulberg, from Beverly, MA, was announced as a new recruit to the China field in September, 1947.[131] She arrived in Shanghai, after a stop in Japan and Hong Kong, on September 23, 1947.[132] But she did not remain in China for long. In early 1948 she was studying Chinese at the Language School in Wuchang,[133] and in June was heading for Kuling.[134] Then in September, 1949 was on the *St. Paul* plane evacuating China missionaries.[135] Soon after she was teaching children at the American School Kikungshan, now located on Cheung Chau Island, Hong Kong. She and others were working on a songbook.[136] If the situation in China did not improve, she planned to go to Japan.[137] In September, 1951 she and Viola Larson had tickets on the M/S *Tidaholm*, a Swedish-American Line Freighter sailing from Goteborg, and was to arrive in New London, CT in another 18 days.[138]

130. *Aurora* (1924) 48.

131. *Our Covenant* 22 (1947) 96.

132. Letter in Ann Kulberg Carlson, "Mission to China," dated Sept. 23, 1947.

133. Hanson, "Current Situation in China," 5.

134. Letter in Ann Kulberg Carlson, "Mission to China," dated June 20, 1948.

135. Letter in Ann Kulberg Carlson, "Mission to China," dated Sept. 10, 1949.

136. Letter in Ann Kulberg Carlson, "Mission to China," dated Nov. 7, 1949.

137. Ibid.

138. Letter to President Theodore W. Anderson in Ann Kulberg Carlson, "Mission

Anna Larson—see **Anna Nelson**

LEONARD J. LARSON[139]

Leonard John Larson was born in Worthington, Minnesota, on March 29, 1894. He graduated from high school in Worthington, and then from North Park College and Theological Seminary in 1918. Leonard received his B.A. degree from Wheaton College (Illinois) in 1920. During his time at North Park and Wheaton he served Covenant churches in Blue Island and Elgin, Illinois. Leonard and his wife Alice went to China under the Covenant Board in 1920, arriving there October 30 with Victor Nordlund and seven other new missionaries. He was stationed at Kingchow, serving there chiefly as a teacher in the middle school and in the theological seminary. He became principal of the middle school after C. J. Nelson became sick and returned home in 1923.[140] During this time, which was three years, he made a valuable contribution to the educational work. Leonard and his family went home on furlough in 1926, a year before their term was up, and Leonard began studies at the University of Chicago. His intent was to return to China to begin a normal school for the training of elementary school teachers,[141] but due to the unrest in China in 1927, he was advised to stay home and enter into pastoral work in the United States. He then served churches in Nebraska and Kansas, and did not return to China.

ALICE N. LARSON[142]

Alice Natalia Larson was born Alice Natalia Bloomgren in Kirion, Iowa, on August 23, 1893. She was brought up in Worthington, Minnesota, where she also received her schooling. Alice became an active member of the Worthington Mission Covenant Church. During 1919–1920 she pursued studies at North Park College, and on September 23, 1920, married the Rev. Leonard J. Larson in Worthington. Alice and Leonard went to China as Covenant missionaries in 1920, and were stationed at Kingchow (1920–1926). They traveled on the *S. S. China*, which left San Francisco for Shanghai, stopping in Honolulu and Yokohama enroute. The trip took 21

---

to China," dated Sept. 6, 1951.

    139. See *Aurora* (1921) 90.

    140. L. J. Larson, *Son of Prayer*, 91.

    141. Ibid., 92.

    142. See *Aurora* (1921) 90.

days. Alice took part in the missionary work among women, and taught English at the Kingchow Middle School. In 1926 she and Leonard left for the United States, and did not return to China.

VIOLA M. C. LARSON

Viola Larson was born near Nekoosa, Wisconsin on November 21, 1910. She was converted in a small country school house,[143] and after moving to Chicago in 1928, joined and became active in the Ogden Park Covenant Church. Viola attended Moody Bible Institute Evening School (1931–1932) and North Park College (1932–1935).[144] She accepted the call of the Covenant Church to go as a missionary to China, and in 1935, after the Covenant 50-year Jubilee in Chicago, she and Mildred Nelson sailed with the Peter Matsons to China. Time was spent on the ocean voyage learning Chinese from Mr. Matson. Viola located in Siangyang, and together with Mildred Nelson continued her study of Chinese there (1935–1936). Viola was an evangelistic missionary, and in 1936–1940 she served in the district of Nanchang. While there she made several trips into the Nanchang mountains, walking or riding horseback. She recalled having to be sure she arrived home before dark so the gatekeeper of the city would let her in.

When Peter Matson returned to the United States in 1940, Viola left Nanchang on foot for Shanghai, arriving there in December of that year. In February, 1941 she sailed for the United States on the last ship to leave China. After arriving home, Viola volunteered for mission work in the mountains of Virginia, where she labored for two years (1941–1943).[145] Then she studied Chinese for a year at the University of California, Berkeley.[146] Viola returned to China in June 1946, stationed now in Kingchow. She was present in Kingchow when the bodies of the three martyred missionaries arrived there in January, 1948. She, Otelia Hendrickson, Ruth Backlund, and Lillian Branstrom washed the bodies of their comrades and prepared them for burial.

After this traumatic event, Viola relocated first to Changsha, in Hunan Province, then to Kweiyang and Kweiting in Kweichow Province, and later to Hong Kong. In 1949 she was in Hong Kong with the Lutheran Mission and

143. V. Larson, "Why We Went to China."

144. A picture of Viola Larson and Millie Nelson at the graduation from North Park appeared in *The Covenant Weekly* (June 25, 1935) 2. Both were going to China in the fall.

145. *The Covenant Companion* (April, 2005) 32.

146. *Our Covenant* 19 (1944) 73.

with Elsa Hammerlind,[147] and in July, 1950 was preparing to move with Elsa Hammerlind to Chuen Wan, a village outside Hong Kong. Viola had been holding services in factories in the area.[148] In 1951 she returned home on furlough,[149] after which she went as a Covenant missionary in Taiwan, serving in Feng Yuan, where she started a church among mainland refugees in her upstairs apartment (1953–1960).[150] After returning to the United States, Viola took care of her mother for a year, and then began working in 1961 as an assistant librarian in the East Asiatic Library of the University of California. A member of the Berkeley Covenant Church, Viola nevertheless spent much time with Chinese Christians in San Francisco. Viola later moved to Chicago, where she became a member of the Trinity Covenant Church in Oak Lawn, and was also involved in the Calvary Covenant Church on Chicago's south side. Her last years were spent with her sister Violet at Covenant Home, Chicago, and later at Covenant Village, Northbrook. Viola was an extraordinary missionary, excellent in the Chinese language, integrating exceptionally well with the Chinese people, and courageous in journeys on the China field.

Anna Lassesen—see **Anna Jacobson**
Dora Lindahl—see **Dora Nordlund**

IVAN H. LINDGREN[151]

Ivan Lindgren was described as having appeared suddenly on the Covenant horizon, like a Nova star in the heavens, and then to have disappeared just as suddenly. Born in Ed, Värmland, Sweden, on January 5, 1892, he studied at the Gothenberg gymnasium and then emigrated to the United States in 1914. Ivan pursued studies at Moody Bible Institute, and for a time was a member of the Bethany Covenant Church in Chicago. He was called and sent to China as a Covenant missionary in 1920, arriving on October 30 with Victor Nordlund and seven other new missionaries. He was stationed for a short time at Siangyang and Kingmen, where he did evangelistic work.

147. Letter of Ann Kulberg Carlson in her "Mission to China," dated Sept. 10, 1949.

148. Letter from Ann Kulberg Carlson to people in Cromwell, CT, dated July 11, 1950.

149. She and Ann Kulberg had tickets on the M/S *Tidaholm*, a Swedish-American Line Freighter sailing from Goteborg on Sept 27, 1951; cf. Carlson, "Mission to China," Letter to President Theodore W. Anderson, dated Sept. 6, 1951.

150. *The Covenant Companion* (April, 2005) 32.

151. See *Aurora* (1921) 92.

But being dissatisfied with the work, his comrades, and with the Chinese, he resigned from the Covenant staff in 1922. He remained in China for a while, nursing a sick Swedish man, and then in 1923 returned to the United States. Later he went to Sweden, and rumor had it that he served with the Pentecostals. Later he returned to the United States and joined the Episcopalians. By the 1940s one could find no trace of him whatsoever.

Ellen M. Masterberg—see **Ellen M. Falk**

GERTRUDE MARSH

Gertrude Marsh arrived on the China field in September, 1947,[152] serving there only briefly before evacuating to Hankow with other missionaries after the murder of the three missionaries (see Appendix 2). In early 1948 she was studying Chinese at the Language School in Wuchang.[153] On October 1, 1948, Gertrude went with other missionaries from Hankow to Changsha, and then relocated to Kweiyang in Kweichow Province,[154] where she remained until having to leave the Chinese mainland.

PETER MATSON

Peter Mattson,[155] pioneer Covenant missionary to China, was born in Lindenäs, Dalarna, Sweden, on March 27, 1868. He emigrated to the United States in March, 1879, and the family settled on a farm in Alexandria, Minnesota. He received his early education in the pioneer country of northern Minnesota. In January, 1885 he accepted Christ as Savior. On a summer day, two or three years later, he knelt by a haystack and promised the Lord he would give half his income to missions or become a missionary himself. In the fall of 1888 he entered "Skogsbergh's School" in Minneapolis, and then in 1889 the Swedish Department of the Chicago Theological Seminary. Peter was called by the Covenant for missionary service to China, and ordained on September 8, 1890 at the Covenant Annual Meeting in Galesburg, Illinois. A few weeks later he sailed for China in the company of an older family, the Rev. and Mrs. Karl P. Wallen. He arrived in Shanghai on October 28, 1890. Matson chose Hupeh

152. *Our Covenant* 22 (1947) 96.
153. Hanson, "Current Situation in China," 5.
154. Marsh, "A Nine-Day Journey in China"; "Views from Modern China."
155. For this earlier Swedish spelling, see *Aurora* (1908) 61.

Province as the Covenant field, and for nearly 50 years gave leadership to the Covenant missionary enterprise there.

In 1892 Matson took up residence in Fancheng, and in 1893 married Kristina Svensson of the Swedish Mission Covenant. Her health in China was not good for most of her remaining years in China. She died on December 29, 1922. Peter married Edla Carlson 18 months later while home on furlough. The ceremony took place on July 21, 1924 in Seattle, Washington. Peter and Edla served together in China until 1939, when they returned to the United States. Peter was 72 years old. At once he began speaking wherever he could for the evangelism of China.[156] During the last 8 months of his life he was inactive, and died on May 30, 1943.[157] A few days before his death he concluded that his task was done, and Edgar Swanson reported that it was then that he submitted his resignation. It had never been presented to the board of mission or acted upon.[158] Matson was buried in Ridgewood Cemetery, just north of Chicago, and a monument not far from the cemetery entrance marks his grave.

CHRISTINE MATSON[159]

Christina Matson was born Kristina Svensson in the parish of Alster, Värmland, Sweden, on October 9, 1864. She graduated from the Normal School at Karlstad, and then served as a teacher in the public school at Stora Kil until 1890, when she entered the Bible Institute of the Mission Covenant in Sweden. Her aim there was to prepare herself for missionary service in China. Marcus Cheng recalled the lasting impression Christine made upon him as a young boy in Sweden.[160] After spending a few months of language study in London, Christine went to China, arriving in Hankow in November, 1891.[161] On May 18, 1893, she married Peter Matson, and transfered to the American Mission Covenant staff, but her health was not good in China, and on December 29, 1922 she died.[162] She was buried in the small missionary cemetery in Fancheng on Feb 7, 1923.[163] She was preceded in

---

156. Matson's itineration is reported in an unsigned letter to the First Covenant Church of St. Paul, MN, dated Dec. 23, 1941.

157. *Our Covenant* 18 (1943) 130–31.

158. Swanson, "Missionary Peter Matson," 35.

159. See *Aurora* (1924) 113–15.

160. P. Matson, *Sowing in Tears, Reaping in Joy*, 11.

161. Ibid., 9.

162. An obituary appears in *The Chinese Recorder* 54 (1923) 495.

163. V. Johnson, *The Momentous Years*, chap. 6.

death by two young sons (1894; 1899), and a third died after her.[164] She was survived by one son, Paul, and two daughters, Esther and Ragnhild. Chinese Christians erected a memorial to her in Siangyang.

Christine endeared herself to her missionary comrades and the Chinese, and her loss was keenly felt by all of them, as well as by her husband of 30 years. Despite poor health, Christine had a profound impact on the missionary work in Fancheng and Siangyang, particularly among Chinese women. She was the pioneer of schools for girls.[165] She also wrote a number of articles in Covenant papers, informing people at home of the missionary work that was being carried on. Christine was possessed with a benevolent spirit, and was a very fluent writer in Swedish, which she used to deepen and create new interest in the China missionary enterprise. A contemporary called her "the best known and most loved lady in the Mission Covenant."

EDLA C. MATSON[166]

Edla C. Matson was born Edla C. Carlson at Fridened, Sweden, on January 28, 1883. She arrived in the United States in 1887, settling in St. Paul, Minnesota. In 1897 a commitment to Christ was made, and Edla joined the First Covenant Church of St. Paul. She later moved to Chicago Heights, Illinois, transferring her membership to the Chicago Heights Mission Church. Edla attended Moody Bible Institute (1919–1920), took private lessons in music, and in 1925 pursued studies in Religious Education at Auburn Theological Seminary, Auburn New York. She went out as a Covenant missionary to China in 1920, arriving there October 30 with Victor Nordlund and seven other new missionaries. She was stationed at Siangyang. In 1924 she had her first furlough, and during the stay at home, on July 21, 1924, she married the Rev. Peter Matson. Matson's first wife, Christine, died in China in 1922. From this point on Edla worked as an evangelistic and educational missionary at Siangyang, until she returned home with Peter in 1939. At Siangyang she built up a Bible training school for young women in the early 1930s.[167] Peter Matson died three years after their return to the United States. Edla was a very able missionary, energetic, persistent, and possessed of a warm spirit. In later years she lived in the North Park community of Chicago, and

---

164. Swanson, "Missionary Peter Matson," 34.

165. L. J. Larson, "Educational Work in China," 49; P. Matson, *Our China Mission*, 115.

166. See *Aurora* (1921) 91.

167. P. Matson, *Our China Mission*, 119.

attended the North Park Covenant Church. She died at Covenant Village, Mount Miguel, Califorai.

ESTHER M. MATSON

The eldest daughter of Peter Matson, Esther Marie Matson was born at Fancheng on October 7, 1897. After finishing elementary school in China, Esther graduated from Johnson High School, St. Paul, Minnesota, and then took a teacher's education course at Northfield, Minnesota, after which she taught briefly in consolidated schools. Esther then went to North Park College and Theological Seminary, graduating from there in 1919. That same year she returned to China, where she was stationed at Siangyang with her parents, doing educational work. The combination of China's climate and the passing of her mother in 1922 led to a complete breakdown, and Esther had to return to the United States. The doctors unanimously advised her against returning to China. After a time of complete rest she regained her health, and studied for two years at the Pestalozzi-Froebel Teachers College in Chicago. She then taught at Olivet Institute in Chicago, and later at a private boarding school in Peekskill, New York. From 1930 to 1943 Esther was employed by North Park College, working half of the time in the College Bookstore, and half of the time as a clerk in the Registrar's Office. After this Esther moved to Minneapolis, where she was employed at Augsburg Publishing House.

RAGNHILD C. MATSON

Ragnhild Christine Matson, a younger daughter of Peter and Christine Matson, was born at Siangyang on June 7, 1902. She graduated from the American school for missionary children at Kikungshan, Honan Province (1923), and later came to the United States where she received nurses' training at Swedish Covenant Hospital. She graduated from there in 1927, and then attended North Park Bible Institute, from which she graduated in 1930. Ragnhild was then commissioned for missionary service to China, and went to China in 1930, receiving support from the Beulah Covenant Church in Turlock, California. In China she served as a medical missionary at the Bethesda Hospital in Siangyang, where she was involved in the training school for nurses (1931–1937). She then went home on furlough, and returned to China in 1940, the year Peter and Edla Matson left the China field for good. Since it was difficult to get to the Covenant field at the time, she was engaged as a nurse in Shanghai, working especially among

Jewish refugees, until war broke out between Japan and the United States. In December 1941, Shanghai was under Japanese rule.[168] Ragnhild was then placed with other Americans in a concentration camp, where she suffered from malnutrition and her weight plummetted from 140 to 100 pounds. She was finally repatriated on the exchange liner *Gripsholm*, and arrived in New York on December 1, 1943. Ragnhild remained in the United States until her death.

ALMA E. MORTENSON

Alma Mortenson was born in the parish of Refteled, Småland, Sweden, on May 11, 1883. She arrived in the United States in 1904, and received nurses' training in Seattle, Washington. Alma went to China as a Covenant missionary in 1911, serving in the dispensary and doing women's work in the Nanchang district until 1926–27, when the communist uprising forced her and other missionaries to evacuate. She then returned to the United States, where she married Emil Anderson. The two became active in the Portage Park Covenant Church.

ANNA MUNSON

Anna Marie Munson was born in Helsingborg, Skåne, Sweden, on June 29, 1879. She came to the United States in 1885. Anna attended a Bible school in Minneapolis (1900–1902), and then continued her studies in Toronto, Canada. She went out as a missionary to China in 1906 under the auspices of the China Inland Mission. Returning home, she then attended North Park College (1912–1913), and was recommended by her home church in Wakefield, Nebraska to go out as a China missionary under the Covenant. She went to China in 1913, where she was involved in evangelism, education, and women's work at Siangyang, until her marriage in 1919 to the Rev. John Enoch Gillström, who served with the Swedish Mission Covenant. The two labored together in China until 1921, when they moved to Sweden. In Sweden they traveled extensively, lecturing and preaching (1921–1925). Then in 1926 they moved to Canada, where her husband became pastor of the Calgary Mission Church; from 1933–1945 he was a traveling missionary in Canada. After her husband died in 1945, Anna continued living

---

168. Peter Matson expresses concern for her in a letter to the First Covenant Church, St. Paul, MN, dated Dec. 23, 1941.

in Calgary, carrying on Christian work among the Chinese in Calgary and vicinity.

AUGUSTA NELSON

Augusta Nelson was born April 11, 1881 at Enslöv, Halland, Sweden. She emigrated to the United States in 1903, settling in Lowell, Massachusetts. Augusta pursued studies at North Park College (1906–1907), and then entered nurses training at Swedish Covenant Hospital in 1907, graduating in 1910. The Mission Covenant Church called her as a missionary to China in 1910. She arrived in China in 1911, just in time for the great revolution, when the Manchu Dynasty was brought down and a republic was established. Augusta served with distinction in the Chinese Red Cross (1911–1912; 1927–1928), for which she was accorded special honor and recognition by the Chinese government. When the communists captured her at Kingmen in 1931 they found the medal of merit she had been given and were impressed enough to speak to her about it.[169] Her work with the Covenant was chiefly medical, carried out at Singyang (at Bethesda Hospital she became superintendent of nurses); Nanchang (dispensary work); Kingmen (dispensary work); and Kingchow (dispensary work). Support came from the Young People's Societies of Iowa. Augusta had to leave the field with others in the evacuation of 1927, but in September, 1928 was on her way back to China, returning to Kingmen and working also in Kingchow.[170] Augusta lived through two civil wars in China, tended the wounded, was kidnapped once and held 5 days for ransom (1931), and served for five years as a missionary in Japanese occupied Kingchow. It was said due to her tact and firmness the mission property at Kingchow was kept from being completely destroyed by the Japanese. Augusta was a nurse at Kingchow in the late 1930s[171] and early 1940s. She was particularly helpful to the hundreds of refugees that crowded into the seminary building after the summer of 1938.[172] The Japanese allowed her to stay because she was a Swedish subject, but her actions were watched and circumscribed. Augusta went home to the United States in 1946, arriving in San Francisco on July 18. She then went to Sweden for a visit. Augusta was remembered for her skill, faithfulness, and sympathy in her China missionary labors.

169. C. O. Anderson and R. M. Anderson, *Two Lives of Faith*, 171.

170. P. Matson, *Our China Mission*, 93.

171. Augusta was in charge of the dispensary at Kingchow in 1936; cf. C. B. Nelson, "Our Medical Missionary Work in China," 69.

172. E. C. Matson, "Life under the Shadows of Death," 28.

C. BARTON NELSON

Carl Barton Nelson was born in Minneapolis on April 26, 1905. He attended high school in Minneapolis, and continued his education at the University of Minnesota (B.S. 1927; B.M. 1929; M.D. 1930). Dr. Nelson credited his conversion to the influence of godly parents. He then became a member of the First Covenant Church, Minneapolis. Nelson was called to be a Covenant medical missionary to China in 1930, getting support from the Salem Covenant Church, Minneapolis. He married Muriel E. Johnson on August 14, 1930 in St. Paul, and the same year the two went to China. Their work was at the Bethesda Hospital in Siangyang, where Barton was superintendent of the men's hospital (1931–1935). Barton was well liked by Chinese and missionary comrades alike. Muriel, who was a trained nurse, took an active part in the medical work as long as her health permitted. But her health failed, and the two had to go home on furlough in 1935. When she was better, they returned to China in the fall of 1939, working again at the Bethesda Hospital in Siangyang. They stayed only a year.[173] In 1940 they had to go home because of Muriel's failing health, and did not return to China. At home Dr. Nelson carried on a medical practice in Minneapolis. He resigned from the China staff in 1942.

MURIEL E. NELSON

Muriel (Molly) Nelson was born Muriel Johnson on August 14, 1905 at St. Paul, Minnesota. She graduated from the Nursing School of the University of Minnesota. On August 17, 1930, she married Dr. C. Barton Nelson, and in the same year the couple went out as Covenant medical missionaries to China. Muriel worked untiringly doing women's work at the Bethesda Hospital in Siangyang,[174] but because of failing health, she and her husband went home on furlough in 1935. Her health gradually improved and they returned to China, although with the Sino-Japanese War raging in 1937, travel at first was difficult, and later became almost impossible. In May–June, 1938 she was in Hong Kong, where she was in the hospital for an operation. The Nelsons came to Bethesda Hospital in Siangyang in the fall of 1939, and were there in early 1940. But Muriel's health worsened and they were forced to return to the United States, where they settled in Minneapolis.

---

173. C. O. Anderson and R. M. Anderson, *Two Lives of Faith*, 120.
174. P. Matson, *Our China Mission*, 119.

CARL J. NELSON[175]

Carl Johan Nelson, the first full-time Covenant educational missionary to China, was born at Kearney, Nebraska on February 23, 1880. He graduated from Luther Academy, Wahoo, Nebraska (1895), and from Carlton College, Northfield, Minnesota (B.A. 1904), and then served for a time as pastor of Covenant churches in Denver and Boulder, Colorado, and as assistant pastor of First Covenant Church, Minneapolis. In June, 1906 Carl married Emma M. Anderson, and in the autumn of 1906 the two went out as Covenant missionaries to China. They arrived in Shanghai with the Matsons on October 18, 1906.[176] A year later Emma gave birth to a daughter Frances.[177] Carl was unusually qualified for his work in China. He had a brilliant, well-trained mind, coupled with a childlike faith in God. For a time he worked in the high school at Siangyang (the "Siangyang Academy"), but then in 1911, when a preparatory school was added to the seminary in Kingchow, he began teaching there. In 1915 he became dean of what was now a middle school for boys, turning it into one of the best schools in China. In 1923, when Carl had completed two full terms of exceptional service in China as teacher, guide, and friend of a great number of Chinese students, his health failed, and they had to return home. Shortly after his arrival in the United States he was taken to a hospital in San Francisco and operated on for gallstones and other complications. On August 23, 1923 Carl died, and was buried in Swedeburg, Nebraska.

EMMA M. NELSON

Emma Marie Nelson was born at Swedeberg, Nebraska, on March 13, 1881. She studied music in Oklahoma City, and received her college education in the same city at Epworth University. In June, 1906 she married C. J. Nelson, and in the autumn of that year they went out as missionaries to China. Emma worked chiefly at head stations in Siangyang and Kingchow, teaching music, English, and religious subjects in the middle schools. Her work as a teacher of music and singing, at a time when singing at Christian worship services in China was as poor as it could be, was of especial value. Together with her husband and children, Emma returned to the United States in 1923. Her husband Carl had an operation in San Francisco, and died in August of that

175. See *Aurora* (1924) 123–25.

176. *The Chinese Recorder* 37 (1906) 652.

177. The girl was born on Dec. 14, 1907, in Siangyang; *The Chinese Recorder* 39 (1908) 173.

year. Emma then devoted herself to bringing up her five children. Despite poverty and infantile paralysis of one of the children, she succeeded in giving them a good education. In the late 1940s Emma was living in Chicago. Emma Nelson was remembered as an unselfish, heroic Christian lady.

EDWARD G. NELSON

Edward George Nelson was born at Farmington, Connecticut, on February 5, 1914. He received his education at Farmington High School, North Park Junior College (1936), North Park Theological Seminary (1940), Hamline University (1943), and the University of California, Berkeley (1943–1945). During his time of preparation for ministry, he served an internship at the Tabernacle Church in Seattle, Washington, as student pastor at Tishilwa, Illinois, and served as pastor also in Rush City and Harris, Minnesota. Edward was called to be a missionary to China at the Covenant Annual Meeting in June 20, 1943, and was ordained at the meeting. In 1943 he was studying Chinese language at the University of California, Berkeley.[178] On October 27, 1943, in Rockford, Illinois, he married Mildred Nelson, who was also with him studying Chinese at Berkeley.[179] Mildred had been a Covenant missionary in China since 1935. Not being able to go to China immediately, the couple served for one year in 1945 as Covenant missionaries to Alaska. They returned home just in time to get ready to go to China in June, 1946. When they arrived at Siangyang, Edward surprised the Chinese by responding to their welcome in Chinese. Millie and Ed had a beautiful home in Siangyang, its dining room all Swedish designs.[180]

Edward went with Carl Branstrom to Kweiting in southwest China sometime after 1946.[181] When the Covenant missionaries were forced to leave China, Edward and Mildred transferred to Hong Kong in the summer of 1949, where they were at the American School. In two weeks they were headed to Japan. Subsequently, they joined other Covenant missionaries in Formosa (Taiwan) in 1952. When they finally returned to the United States, they made their home in Bedford, New Hampshire. Edward Nelson during his short stay in China was nevertheless a premier missionary, working to plant the Gospel firmly into the Chinese culture, and endearing himself in a

178. *Our Covenant* 18 (1943) 129.

179. *Our Covenant* 19 (1944) 73.

180. In a letter from Ann Kulberg Carlson in her "Mission to China," dated Nov. 6, 1947.

181. Branstrom, "From Temples of Idols to the Temple of God."

multitude of ways to the Chinese people. He was also resourceful, creative, and excelled in brush painting and in other Chinese arts.

MILDRED G. NELSON

Mildred Genevieve was born in Kewanee, Illinois on February 2, 1909, later moving with her family to Rockford, Illinois in 1920. In the Rockford Mission Chapel Sunday school she was "instructed in the ways of the Lord," and became interested in the work of foreign missions. By the time she graduated from the 8th grade she wanted to be a missionary to China.[182] Mildred joined the First Mission Covenant Church in Rockford. In 1930, at a Young People's Conference at Cedar Lake, Indiana, she responded to a message by Theodore W. Anderson, President of the Covenant, by offering herself as one who would go wherever God wanted her to go. Mildred entered North Park College in February, 1930, and after her graduation in 1935[183] was sent to China as a Covenant missionary, sailing with the Peter Matsons and Viola Larson. Upon arrival, she began work as an educational missionary in Siangyang, where she stayed until 1941, when she went home to the United States on furlough. From 1939 to 1941 she had charge of the Bible Training School for Women begun by Edla Matson, although in November, 1938, it had to be closed because of the Japanese bombings and moved to Nanchang.[184] From 1942 to 1943 she did deputation work at home, and attended Wheaton College in Illinois (1942–1943). On October 27, 1943, Mildred married the Rev. Edward G. Nelson in Rockford, Illinois. Not being able to return to China immediately, the Nelsons studied Chinese at the University of California until 1945, when they were sent to Alaska to substitute for missionaries home on furlough. In 1946 they returned from Alaska, and in June of that year left for China, where they took up residence at Siangyang. In November, 1947 she and Ed were in Siangyang.[185] Besides her missionary duties, Mildred was the treasurer of the China mission. Mildred was an extraordinary missionary, gifted with a dynamic and winsome personality;

---

182. Mildred Nelson, "Why We Went to China."

183. A picture of Millie Nelson and Viola Larson at their graduation from North Park appeared in *The Covenant Weekly* (June 25, 1935) 2. Both were to go to China in the fall.

184. Conradson, "The Young Women's Bible Training School," 120–21.

185. In a letter of Ann Kulberg Carlson in her "Mission to China," dated Nov. 6, 1947.

a good speaker; an excellent cook of Chinese food;[186] and one who endeared herself to the Chinese people among whom she lived and worked.

KARL M. NELSON[187]

Karl Magnus Nelson was born in Nora parish, Ångermanland, Sweden, on August 19, 1890. He studied at the Herösand gymnasium, and while still a young man emigrated to the United States, where he arrived on Christmas Eve, 1905. He lived with his uncle, Peter Nordlund, in Menominee, Michigan until 1909. Karl graduated from North Park College (1912), received his S.B. degree from the University of Chicago, and then an M.D. degree from Rush Medical College in Chicago (1919). He finished his internship in 1920, and the same year accepted the call to go to China as a Covenant medical missionary. He sailed for China, and upon arrival with the Victor Nordlund and seven other new missionaries on October 30, began work at the Bethesda Union Hospital in Siangyang. He became superintendent of Bethesda Hospital. On December 6, 1920 Karl married Anna Larson in Kingchow. The two went home on furlough in 1926, and were unable to return to China because of communist revolutionary activity in 1927–1929. It was a great loss to the China mission. In August, 1927, Dr. Nelson located himself in Princeton, Illinois, and during the next 20 years built up a medical practice there. He held numerous offices, including church chairman in the Mission Covenant Church of Princeton, and was chairman of the Board of Trustees of the Princeton Children's Home. He also held offices in the Princeton community, and in 1947 was elected mayor of Princeton. Karl and Anna's son, F. Burton Nelson, became a Covenant pastor, a professor at North Park Theological Seminary, and an internationally known scholar of the German theologian and martyr, Dietrich Bonhoeffer.

ANNA NELSON

Anna Nelson was born Anna Larson in Chicago on October 7, 1890. She attended Park Manor Grade School, Watson's Business College, and Englewood Training School for Nurses, from which she graduated in 1918. Anna became a member of the South Side Covenant Tabernacle in 1907. Having developed an interest in China missions about 1911, she was sent to China by the Mission Covenant Church in September, 1919, arriving in

---

186. Mahnke, "Millie Nelson, Goffstown, New Hampshire."

187. See *Aurora* (1921) 92.

Shanghai on October 8. Anna was stationed at Siangyang, where she served as a nurse. On December 6, 1920 she married Dr. K. M. Nelson, who had just arrived from America, at Kingchow, in the home of the John Petersons. Anna then labored together with her husband at the Bethesda Hospital in Siangyang. In 1926 they returned to the United States on furlough. The next year the Communist upheaval made it impossible for the Nelsons to return to China, so they resigned from the China staff, and settled in Princeton, Illinois. Anna Nelson is reported to have done a splendid work in China, being also an ideal mother for her children.

Justine Nilsson—see **Justine Johnson**

VICTOR L. NORDLUND[188]

Victor Leonard Nordlund was born in the parish of Skog, Helsingland, Sweden, on January 19, 1869. He emigrated to the United States in 1889 and settled in Youngstown, Ohio, where he joined the First Covenant Church of Youngstown. In 1891 he went out as a missionary to China with the Scandinavian Alliance Mission (under Frederick Franson), laboring in Shansi, Shensi, and Kansu Provinces. Support came from the Englewood Mission Covenant Church in Chicago. On April 5, 1895 Victor married Maria Nelson, who was also in China with the Scandinavian Alliance Mission. Their marriage took place in Fancheng, Hupeh, where the Covenant had its mission.[189]

Victor returned to the United States in 1899 and studied for two years in the Swedish Department of the Chicago Theological Seminary (1900–1901). He and Maria were back to China in 1912, this time under the board of the Mission Covenant Church, supported again by the Englewood Covenant Church in Chicago. They began work in Fancheng, where they had been married in 1895, and spent seven years,[190] with Victor focusing on evangelism. The couple went home on furlough in 1918. Victor returned alone to China with his daughter Esther on October 30, 1920, bringing with him seven new missionaries. For two years Victor and Esther served at the Nanchang station and in the Nanchang district. In 1922 Victor built a house at Nanchang.[191] During this time he was also going to Icheng to do evangelistic work. Maria died at home on September 9, 1922. Victor served in

---

188. See *Aurora* (1921) 89.

189. E. Nordlund, *The Life and Work of Victor Nordlund*, 47.

190. Ibid., 108.

191. *The Covenant Companion* Old Series (April, 1925) 26.

the China until 1926, when Communist activities forced him to go home. Since he was unable to return to China the following year, the Covenant asked him to go to Alaska, which he did. For two years he served at the Covenant mission station in Unalakleet (1927–1929). After he returned from Alaska, his health gradually failed and he was unable to return to China. He did pulpit supply in several churches at home. Victor died from a heart attack on April 10, 1937, at which time he was pastor of the Cragin Mission Church in Chicago. Victor was remembered as a gifted evangelist and very much a man of prayer. Victor and his wife Maria are buried in Ridgewood Cemetery just north of Chicago.

MARIA NORDLUND

Maria Nordlund was born Maria Nelson in the parish of Stroo, Skåne, Sweden, on June 28, 1866.[192] She emigrated to the United States in 1889, and in 1891 went to China as a missionary under the auspices of the Scandinavian Alliance Mission, serving in Shensi, Kansu, and Shansi. In April, 1895 she married Victor L. Nordlund, also with the Scandinavian Alliance Mission, in Fancheng, Hupeh Province. The two returned home in 1899 and were in Chicago in 1900–1901, when Victor was studying at the Chicago Theological Seminary. Victor and Maria then went out to China in 1912 as missionaries of the Mission Covenant Church, and labored for seven years at Fancheng. Maria was involved in women's work. After their furlough in 1918, Victor returned with his daughter Esther to China in 1920; Maria stayed at home to attend to the children's education. But Maria became ill and died on September 9, 1922.[193] She was buried at Montrose Cemetery in Chicago, but her remains were later transferred to Ridgewood Cemetery in Des Plaines. Maria was remembered as a great contributor to the cause of mission, one important fruit being the nurture of three children who became China missionaries: Mildred, Esther, and Joel Nordlund.

ESTHER V. NORDLUND[194]

Esther Victoria Nordlund, daughter of Covenant missionaries Victor and Maria Nordlund, was born at Kingchow on October 31, 1896. She traveled

192. For more on Maria Nelson Nordlund, see Esther Nordlund's biography (*The Life and Work of Victor Nordlund*, 45–56).

193. A published obituary in *The Chinese Recorder* 54 (1923) 613, puts the date of her death on Sept. 8, 1922.

194. See *Aurora* (1921) 90.

to the States in 1909 to get her education, at which time she also joined
the Englewood Mission Church on Chicago's south side. In 1911 Esther
transferred her membership to the Covenant Church in Youngstown, Ohio,
which later took on her support when she herself went out as a China missionary. Esther graduated from North Park College in 1917, and received
her teacher's certificate from Wheaton College (Illinois) in 1920. Esther
was called to be a Covenant missionary to China in 1920, and went there
the same year as an evangelistic and educational missionary, working with
women and at the girls' schools. She served at all the head stations on the
Covenant field, including Icheng.[195] For two years, in 1927–1929, when the
Communist uprising drove Christian missionaries from that part of China,
Esther served with her father at the Covenant mission station in Unalakleet,
Alaska.[196] When she returned to China with her sister Mildred in 1931, she
gave herself chiefly to women's work at the mission station at Fancheng. In
1931, when serving at Kingmen, she, Augusta Nelson, and Oscar Anderson
were kidnapped in April and held for ransom. Esther and Augusta were
released five days later and allowed to return to their stations, but Oscar
was held for 75 days, and a large ransom consisting of medical supplies
had to be paid by the Covenant to secure his release. In early 1940 Esther
was in Fancheng. For a time she was also head of the Covenant station at
Nanchang. Esther left Nanchang on January 3, 1945 with other missionaries from Siangyang on a boat headed for Laohokow to be evacuated by an
American Air Force plane.[197] In March, 1947, after being in the homeland
for two years,[198] Esther returned to China, but because of unrest in the field
due to war with the Japanese, she established a Chinese language school
for missionaries in the Philippine Islands.[199] Later in 1947 she returned to
China. Esther was one of three Covenant missionaries murdered by bandits
in January, 1948.[200] With the others she was laid to rest in a small foreign
cemetery in Hankow. Esther had no difficulty with the Chinese language,
having learned it from childhood. She was remembered as a fine missionary
and an able Bible teacher.

195. P. Matson, *Our China Mission*, 119.

196. *Our Covenant* 23 (1948) 157–58.

197. C. O. Anderson and R. M. Anderson, *Two Lives of Faith*, 133.

198. *Our Covenant* 20 (1945) 113

199. *Our Covenant* 23 (1948) 157.

200. An obituary appeared in *Our Covenant* 23 (1948) 157–58.

JOEL C. NORDLUND

Joel Clemens Nordlund was born at Williams Bay, Wisconsin, on July 13, 1902. The son of Covenant missionaries Victor and Maria Nordlund, Joel spent most of his childhood in China and received part of his education there. He graduated from North Park College and Theological Seminary, and received his Ph.B degree from the University of Chicago. While in seminary he served as student pastor of Covenant churches in Iowa and North Dakota. Joel was then sent as a Covenant missionary to China, arriving there in 1929. In 1929–1934 he did evangelistic work in the Siangfan district, at Icheng, and at Nanchang.[201] On June 25, 1931 he married Dora Lindahl, who had just come as a missionary to China, in Kuling, but on July 17, 1933 Dora died. Joel went home on furlough in 1934, and did not return to China. In subsequent years he pastored Covenant churches in Silverhill, Alabama; Cragin, Chicago; Renova, Pennsylvania; and Osage City, Kansas. While in Silverhill Joel was remarried to Alida Desieria. Joel later served churches in California.

DORA NORDLUND

Dora Nordlund was born Dora Lindahl in Minneapolis, Minnesota, on May 30, 1906. When she was four years old her parents moved to Mound, Minnesota, and there she grew up. Dora studied at the Bible Institute of Minnehaha Academy, and then took three years of nurses' training at the Nurses' Training School of the University of Minnesota. At the Covenant Annual Meeting in Princeton, Illinois, in June 1929, she was commissioned for missionary service in China, and on September 8 was consecrated at Minnehaha Academy. She sailed for China in early October, 1929, and upon arrival began nursing and women's work at Siangyang and Fancheng. In 1931 she married the Rev. Joel Nordlund in Kuling. When arriving at the mountain retreat in the early summer of 1933, she was not well, but it was hoped that cooler climate there would do her good. It was not to be. On July 17, 1933, Dora died, leaving behind a baby boy of two months, David Lee. Dora was buried in the cemetery at Kuling.

---

201. P. Matson, *Our China Mission*, 119.

MILDRED E. NORDLUND

Mildred Nordlund, daughter of China missionaries Victor and Maria Nordlund, was born at Sian-Fu, Shensi (Shaanxi), China, on December 24, 1904.
She received a portion of her education in Shanghai, and then went to the
United States in 1918 to complete her education. Mildred graduated from
North Park College (1922), and from Rush Medical School, Chicago (M.D.
1929). She then went out to China as a medical missionary in 1930. Accompanied by her sister Esther, she traveled via Sweden. Her service in China
was from 1931–1936, and 1937–1945, at the Bethesda Hospital in Siangyang. She became superintendent of the women's hospital at Bethesda,[202]
and was there when Oscar Anderson arrived in April, 1939.[203] During the
Sino-Japanese war Mildred rendered valuable service to the armed forces
and civilian population. Mildred left Siangyang with other missionaries
on January 3, 1945, headed for Laohokow on a boat where they would be
evacuated by an American Air Force plane.[204] During her furlough in 1947
she was serving in hospitals and medical schools in the eastern part of the
United States. She did not return to China. Mildred was remembered as a
splendid medical missionary, an interesting speaker, and a woman of strong
character.

MABEL E. OLSON

Mabel Emelia Olson was born in Milwaukee, Wisconsin, on September 15,
1883. She graduated from Sioux City High School and Commercial Department in 1902, then taught in the Commercial Department of the Central
Holiness University, University Park, Iowa, and after that graduated from
a three-year Bible course at the same university. Mabel became a member
of the First Covenant Church in St. Paul, Minnesota, and was called to be
a Covenant missionary to China in 1913. She went to China, arriving in
1913. Her work in China was as an evangelistic and educational missionary
in Fancheng, Siangyang, Kingmen, and Kingchow. She also did women's
work, and for some years was principal of the Concordia Middle School for
Girls in Fancheng.[205] In March, 1927 she had to leave Siangyang with the
Matsons and other missionaries because of the communist uprising, going

---

202. Ibid.
203. C. O. Anderson and R. M. Anderson, *Two Lives of Faith*, 113.
204. Ibid., 133.
205. P. Matson, *Our China Mission*, 118.

to Hankow and then to Shanghai.[206] On October 5, 1928 she was on the steamer *President Adams* with the Oscar Andersons, the Dwights, and I. W. Jacobson bound for China.[207] She was in Kingchow doing women's work in the early 1930s,[208] and in Kingmen in the fall of 1935,[209] also in early 1940, although at this time the station was largely destroyed as a result of Japanese bombs. She returned with Oscar Anderson and others in the winter of 1938.[210] In December, 1941 Mabel and other Covenant missionaries were in Hankow, which was under Japanese rule.[211] Mabel was among the Covenant missionaries interned by the Japanese, and was repatriated home from China on the exchange liner *Gripsholm* in 1942. She returned to China on May 5, 1946 and began working in Kingchow.[212] Mabel was in Kingchow when the bodies of the three martyred missionaries arrived there in January, 1948. She came home in early 1949.[213] She was said to be very zealous for the Lord, and never spared herself in her missionary labors.

JEMIMA E. OLSON[214]

Jemima Olson was born in Minneapolis, Minnesota, on March 25, 1897. From early childhood she committed her ways to the Lord, and in 1916 became a member of the First Covenant Church in St. Paul, Minnesota, the church that supported her when she later went out as a missionary to China. Jemima graduated from the University of Minnesota in 1918 (B.A.), and then taught school in Long Prairie and Bemidji, Minnesota. She was accepted for China missionary service by the Covenant, and went to China in 1921. Her work in China was chiefly educational, for which she was well suited, both by natural gifts and by training. Jemima served for one term in Siangyng and Fancheng. At Fancheng she was principal of the Concordia Middle School for Girls. But her health was not the best in China, and

206. Appended note in a letter from Peter Matson to the Mission Council, dated Feb. 19, 1927.

207. C. O. Anderson and R. M. Anderson, *Two Lives of Faith*, 39.

208. Ibid., 91, 94.

209. J. S. Johnson, "The Kingmen District," 48.

210. *The Covenant Weekly* (January 24, 1939) 4.

211. Letter from Peter Matson to the First Covenant Church, St. Paul, MN, dated Dec. 23, 1941.

212. Reported also in a letter from Judith Peterson to the Rev. Ralph Hanson, dated July 4, 1946.

213. *The Covenant Weekly* (Feb. 18, 1949) 5.

214. See *Aurora* (1922) 111.

because of this, and because of troubled conditions in China at the time, she came home in 1927, and did not return to China. At home her health was restored, and she began to do missionary work in northern Minnesota. In 1932 Jemima married the Rev. James Schrieber of the Oakhills Fellowship, Bemidji, and subsequently was engaged in missionary work there. Jemima combined a brilliant mind with a humble spirit, making her a splendid missionary.

ERNEST L. OSCARSON[215]

Ernest Leonard Oskarson was born at Frödinge, Småland, Sweden, on July 5, 1895. He emigrated to the United States in 1911, settling in Wasau, Nebraska. His conversion took place in Falun, Wisconsin. He came to the Free Church Bible School, then in connection with Moody Bible Institute, from the First Covenant Church in Tacoma, Washington, and after graduation from that school spent a year or more at North Park College. Oscar married Sigrid Skoglar in Chicago on June 13, 1923. The two sailed for China, via Sweden, in the latter part of that year. Ernst served from 1923 to 1927 as builder and repairman at Bethesda Hospital in Siangyang, and for a time was manager of the hospital. Ernst was a first-rate carpenter, and won the admiration of Chinese carpenters in Siangyang for his work. Ernest and Sigrid went home to the United States with other Covenant missionaries in 1927, and did not return to China. Ernest then served Covenant churches in Kansas and Colorado, and in the late 1940s was living on a farm in Boulder, Colorado, farming and doing carpentry work.

SIGRID E. OSCARSON

Sigrid E. Oscarson was born Sigrid Elisabeth Skoglar in Vimmerby, Kalmar Lan, Sweden, on February 20, 1899. She arrived in the United States in 1920, and located in Sterling, Colorado. Sigrid attended the Free Church Bible School in Chicago, and on June 13, 1923 married the Rev. Ernest Oscarson in Chicago. The two went out as missionaries to China in the latter part of 1923, taking up work at the Covenant station in Siangyang. She and Ernest returned home in 1927, and because of the trouble in China at the time, and also because they had small children, they did not feel they could return to China.

215. See *Aurora* (1924) 45.

THEODORE PEDERSEN[216]

Theodor Pedersen was born at Struer, Denmark, on August 20, 1884. He came to Iowa in 1889, and pursued studies for some time at the Swedish Bible Institute, Minneapolis, Minnesota (Free Church). In 1909 he married Hannah Carlson, and the two went out as missionaries to Mongolia with the Scandinavian Alliance Mission (under Frederick Franson). During the revolution of 1911 they had to leave Mongolia and go to Shanghai, where they came in contact with Covenant missionaries. The Pedersens were invited to the Covenant field, and in 1913 became full members of the Covenant staff. They became involved in evangelistic work in Siangyang and Nanchang. After serving one term, they went home on furlough in 1919. Theodore stayed with relatives in Essex, Iowa, assisting in harvesting. On July 5, 1919 he became dizzy, his heart stopped beating, and he died, not quite 35 years of age. He had been healthy and strong, but suffered from varicose veins, and dates for his hospitalization and an operation had been set. His wife Hannah remained for a time in Essex, and then moved to Chicago.

HANNAH E. PEDERSEN

Hannah Elizabeth Pedersen was born Hanna Elisabeth Carlson in the parish of Bringetofts, Småland, Sweden, on September 29, 1885. She emigrated to the United States in 1900, and settled in Iowa. In 1909 she married the Rev. Theodore Pedersen, and they went out as missionaries to Mongolia that year under the Scandinavian Alliance Mission. After leaving their field due to revolutionary activity in 1911, and coming into contact with Covenant missionaries in Shanghai, they were invited to the Covenant field and were accepted in 1913 as full members of the Covenant staff. She did evangelistic work with her husband Theodore at Siangyang. In 1919 they went home on furlough, where her husband passed away in Essex, Iowa on July 5. Hannah stayed for a time in Essex, Iowa, but then moved to Chicago to be near her daughter, who was attending North Park College. For a number of years Hannah was in charge of the Covenant cafeteria at North Park.

216. See *Aurora* (1921) 114.

ESTHER C. PETERSON[217]

Esther C. Peterson was born in Chicago on January 13, 1890. She was converted at age 12, and later went on to study at a business college and at
Moody Bible Institute (one year). She entered nurses' training at Swedish
Covenant Hospital, graduating from there in December, 1920. Esther accepted the call to go out as a Covenant missionary to China in 1921. She
spent one term in China, serving as a nurse in the Nanchang district. In
1927 she returned home with other Covenant missionaries on account of
the civil war, and did not return to China. Esther cared for her mother until June 25, 1947, when her mother passed away. Esther was active in the
Covenant Tabernacle Church on Chicago's south side, as well as in other
churches, after her return.

JOHN PETERSON[218]

John Peterson was born in the parish of Enslöv, Halland, Sweden, on September 18, 1879. He was converted at age 12, and from early childhood
had an interest in missionary work. He wanted to go to Congo. In 1902 he
emigrated to the United States, and 10 days after his arrival, entered the
Swedish Department of the Chicago Theological Seminary (the "Risberg
School"). He graduated from there in 1905. During this period he briefly
served churches in Dawson, Minnesota (one summer), and the Covenant
church in Michigan City, Indiana (18 months). John then accepted the call
of the Mission Covenant to go out as a missionary to China, and he arrived in Siangyang in February, 1906. During his first term he was stationed
at Fancheng (1906–1910) and Nanchang (1910–1912), doing evangelistic
work. On December 3, 1908 he married Esther N. Anderson in Shanghai.
Esther had just arrived in China in November. In 1914–1915 John filled
in for Peter Matson at Siangyang, doing evangelistic work there. Then in
1915 he was elected to be the Covenant's representative at the Kingchow
Theological Seminary, which had opened in 1909 and was run jointly by
the American and Swedish Mission Covenant. He taught there for 35 years,
from 1915 to 1940. John and Esther went home on furlough in 1932, and
only John returned to China; Esther remained at home with the children,
in 1938 living with them in the Missionary Home in North Park.[219] John returned to the United States for good in 1940. While in North Park he taught

---

217. See *Aurora* (1922) 111.

218. See *Aurora* (1924) 45.

219. C. O. Anderson and R. M. Anderson, *Two Lives of Faith*, 110.

at North Park Seminary and worked as archivist at Covenant Headquarters. In 1943 he also taught for a year at the Covenant Bible Institute in Prince Albert, Canada. During his furloughs John studied at McCormick Theological Seminary and the University of Chicago. John Peterson died on May 4, 1953 after a year of poor health.[220] He was an exceptional teacher at the Kingchow Seminary and gave valuable service to the school and to the Covenant missionary work in other ways. He was remembered as a saintly man, humble and friendly, and a living testimony for God.[221]

ESTHER N. PETERSON

Esther Natalia Peterson was born Esther Natalia Anderson in the parish of Enslöv, Halland, Sweden, on September 10, 1885. She emigrated to the United States in 1903, settling in Lowell, Massachusetts. From 1906 to 1908 she studied at North Park College, and was commissioned for missionary service to China at North Park on May 24, 1908. Esther arrived in China in November, 1908. On December 3 she was married to the Rev. John Peterson, who had arrived in China two years earlier. Esther served at Covenant mission stations in Fancheng, Nanchang, Siangyang, and Kingchow, where she did women's work. She truly loved the Chinese, and they loved her in return. In part because of disturbed conditions in China, and because of John's work at the Kingchow seminary, she was separated from her husband and left to care for the children alone, but she willingly accepted this. She and John went home on furlough in 1932, and when John returned to China she stayed in Chicago caring for the children and attending to their education. John returned home in 1940. In December, 1942 Esther suffered a stroke that partially paralyzed her, impairing her speech and her ability to write.

JUDITH PETERSON[222]

Judith Peterson was born in Rockford, Illinois, on September 21, 1893. After a conversion experience in 1909 she joined the Mission Tabernacle Church in Rockford. Judith graduated from Michael Reese Hospital in Chicago on October 15, 1916, and before going to China in 1924, worked as a private duty nurse (1916–1918), was an army nurse at Camp Dix, New Jersey (1918–1919), and filled important positions at the Swedish American

---

220. *Our Covenant* 28 (1953) 110–11.
221. Ibid., 111.
222. See *Aurora* (1925) 115.

Hospital, Rockford (1919–1921) and the California Lutheran Hospital
(1921–1923). After hearing Peter Matson speak about Covenant mission
work in China, Judith felt called to be a missionary nurse in China.[223] She
then took some Bible courses at North Park College, after which she was
commissioned as a Covenant missionary on November 23, 1924. She left for
China 3 days later, and upon arrival in China worked for the most part at
the head stations in Kingmen and Siangyang (1924–1949). Her service was
almost entirely medical, her first years being in Kingmen. She evacuated
the field with other missionaries in 1927, but was able to return in September, 1928.[224] In 1934 she was superintendent and instructor of nurses
at Bethesda Union Hospital in Siangyang,[225] and was at the hospital when
Oscar Anderson arrived in April, 1939.[226] In May, 1940, on her way home
via Hong Kong, she reported that traveling was difficult because many of
the steamers had stopped running.[227] While in the United States during the
war years, Judith worked for the American Red Cross in Rockford, training
nurses' aides. In 1946 she was back in China,[228] and in 1947 again Director
of Nursing at Bethesda Hospital in Siangyang. Judith's Chinese name was
Pei Hsiao Chieh ("Miss Pei").[229]

With the advance of communist forces in central China, Judith was
forced to evacuate with other missionaries in October, 1949. She then went
to Japan and worked in this newly opened Covenant mission from 1950
to 1952.[230] In 1952 she transferred to Formosa (Taiwan) to work with Ed
and Millie Nelson, and to help Dr. Signe Berg and Elsa Hammerlind establish a medical clinic. She was in Formosa from 1952–1954. Judith had
to leave Formosa due to health problems, and after a period of hospitalization in Chicago and recuperation in Rockford was called to become the
first nurse at the Covenant Palms retirement community in Miami, Florida
(1956–1962).[231] Judith passed away in July 1977 at 83 years of age. She was
remembered as a devoted missionary, an interesting speaker, intelligent

---

223. C. E. Anderson, *Growing Up Anderson*, 249.

224. P. Matson, *Our China Mission*, 93.

225. Ibid., 119.

226. C. O. Anderson and R. M. Anderson, *Two Lives of Faith*, 113.

227. Judith Peterson in a letter to the Rev. Gust Johnson, dated May 21, 1940.

228. Letter received by [the Rev. Ralph Hanson], now the Secretary of Foreign Missions, from Judith Peterson, dated July 5, 1946.

229. R. Matson, "Letter from Bethesda Hospital, Siangyang, China."

230. Her arrival in Japan in December 1950 is reported in a letter to the Rev. Ralph
Hanson, dated Dec. 26, 1950.

231. C. E. Anderson, *Growing Up Anderson*, 253–54.

conversationalist, and able administrator, winning the love and respect of the Chinese as well as all her missionary coworkers.

HILDA N. RODBERG

Hilda Nathalia Rodberg, the first trained missionary nurse to be sent out by the Covenant to China, was born in Braham, Minnesota on April 25, 1872. Her father was J. P. Rodberg, a pioneer Covenant preacher.[232] After studying at Carlton College, Northfield, Minnesota, Hilda entered nurses' training at Swedish Covenant Hospital to prepare herself for missionary work in China. She was the first nurse to graduate from the Nursing School of Swedish Covenant Hospital in Chicago. Hilda accepted the call of the Mission Covenant to go out as a China missionary, and sailed for China, arriving in Siangyang at the end of 1901.[233] She and Dr. Sjöquist worked together as a medical team in Siangyang, which at the time was recovering from the Boxer Rebellion (1900). Peter Matson wanted a hospital in Siangyang, but in 1903 there was only a dispensary; nevertheless, 1400 patients were treated by Dr. Sjöquist and Hilda Rodberg in that year. The dispensary continued until 1914, when Bethesda Union Hospital was opened.

Dr. Sjoquist and Hilda Rodberg worked with primitive equipment, but were said to have performed many miracles of healing. When more nurses were called by the Covenant to go to China, Hilda began to do educational and evangelistic work at Siangyang, Nanchang, and Kingmen, where she became indefatigable in her work for the education of girls.[234] Hilda went home on furlough in 1909, and after returning went to Nanchang, then two years later relocated to Kingmen (1912),[235] where she was affectionately referred to as *Lo Sioo tsie* ("Miss Rodberg"). Hilda evacuated with other missionaries in 1927. In October, 1928, she was living with her sister Anna in Turlock, CA.[236] Hilda returned to Kingman in 1929, but in May became very ill and had to seek medical help in Hankow.[237] Hilda's contribution to the China missionary enterprise was considerable. She died on February 11, 1931,[238] and was buried in the small foreign cemetery in Hankow.

232. See *Aurora* (1908) 123–24.

233. P. Matson, *The Chinese Recorder* 62 (1931) 248.

234. L. J. Larson, "Educational Work in China," 50.

235. J. S. Johnson, "The Kingmen District," 50–51

236. C. O. Anderson and R. M. Anderson, *Two Lives of Faith*, 39.

237. Ibid., 41, 48.

238. In Matson's obituary (*The Covenant Companion* Old Series [April 4, 1931] 4) her date of death is put at Feb. 11, 1931; in Covenant records it is put at February 12.

ANNIE SANDERS

Annie Sanders was born in Småland, Sweden, in 1853, and emigrated to the United States in her early youth. She attended Frederick Franson's short Bible courses, and was then sent out as a missionary to China in 1891 under the Scandinavian Alliance Mission. Support came from the Covenant Tabernacle in Chicago where August Skogsbergh was pastor. She was then promised support if she joined the Covenant China Mission, which she did in 1895, going to do women's work at the Covenant station in Fancheng. But she was there only until 1897–98, when she decided to return to the Scandinavian Alliance Mission and take up work in northern China. There she served faithfully until her untimely death on May 30, 1903. She was alone at her station, and having come down with a slight illness, took the wrong medicine, which caused her death. Annie learned the Chinese language quickly and become a splendid missionary.

Jemima E. Schreiber—see **Jemima E. Olson**

JOHN SJÖQUIST

John Sjöquist, pioneer Covenant medical missionary to China, was born Johan Sjökvist at Hvitsand, Värmland, Sweden, on January 30, 1863. He studied at Ahlberg's Mission Institute, Arebro (1884–1886), and then emigrated to the United States in 1887, where he spent the following two years studying at Chicago Theological Seminary. For two years after that he studied at Carleton College, Northfield, Minnesota. John then served briefly as a pastor in Superior, Wisconsin. He accepted the call to go to China as a Covenant missionary in 1893, and on April 14 arrived in Shanghai.[239] After three years on the field doing evangelistic work,[240] the Covenant Board called him home in 1896 to pursue medical studies, which he then did at Rush Medical College, Chicago. He graduated from Rush in June, 1900 and after marrying Maria Swanson on July 11, went a second time to China, arriving there in January, 1901. This time he came as a medical missionary. With him and his wife Maria was Hilda Rodberg, the first graduate of Swedish Covenant Hospital. Maria became ill on the voyage to Fancheng, and died soon afterwards, on November 13, 1901. In 1904 John married Victoria Welter. Dr. Sjöquist worked for the most part in Siangyang, first at a dispensary-infirmary he and Hilda built up, and then at Bethesda Hospital, which opened in 1914.

239. *The Chinese Recorder* 24 (1893) 252.
240. P. Matson, *Our China Mission*, 115.

Dr. Sjoquist demonstrated for the first time in that part of China the efficacy of western medicine and surgery.[241] He went home on furlough in 1909, but then returned with Victoria to Bethesda Hospital, where the two worked together until John was diagnosed with a weak heart in 1917. He told Victoria he could go at any moment, but remained faithfully at his work until the end came. John died on August 15, 1917.[242] He was buried next to his first wife Maria in the Fancheng cemetery. His beautifully inscribed gravestone survives in what remains of the cemetery, where I saw it in October, 2014. Dr. Sjöquist was remembered as a wise, original man with a brilliant mind, and an excellent physician, missionary statesman, and friend of all. He made an outstanding contribution to the Covenant Mission.

MARIA E. SJÖQUIST[243]

Maria Elisabeth Sjöqvist was born Maria Elisabeth Svenson in Altona, Illinois, on May 12, 1869. She moved with her parents to Holdrege, Nebraska in 1887. She was converted at age 13, and began almost immediately to share her faith and become active in Christian work. On July 11, 1900, she married Dr. John Sjöquist, and went with him to China as a Covenant missionary the same year. The Sjöquists were in Wuchang when their first daughter was born. In the fall of 1901 they left for Fancheng, but Maria became ill on the voyage, and died after their arrival in Fancheng, on November 13, 1901. Maria was the first Covenant missionary to die in China and be buried on Chinese soil, although some missionary children had died in China before her, and were buried in the small Fancheng cemetery. Her daughter, Ruth, stayed with her father for a few years, but then she too died.

VICTORIA SJÖQUIST

Victoria Sjöquist was born Victoria Welter in Malmö, Skåne, Sweden, on November 24, 1878. She emigrated to the United States, and graduated from North Park College and Theological Semnary in 1903. Victoria went out as a Covenant missionary to China in 1904. On September 1, 1904 she married Dr. John Sjöquist, and served in China until 1918, a year after her husband's death. Victoria's work was evangelistic and with women, mostly

241. K. M. Nelson, "Glimpses from Our Medical Work in Siangyang," 26.

242. See obituary by Peter Matson in *The Chinese Recorder* 48 (1917) 731–32; also Victoria Sjöquist in *Förbundets Veckotidning* (October 9, 1917) 4.

243. See *Aurora* (1903) 36–41, with a picture.

in the Bethesda Hospital at Siangyang where Dr. Sjöquist worked. In 1918 she returned to the United States with the children and made her home in Chicago. While living in Chicago she became active in the Covenant Women's Auxiliary, serving for a time as secretary of foreign missions in that organization. The care of her children prevented her from returning to China. A few years later she married Mr. Robert Cronholm, and moved to his farm in Wisconsin. Victoria was remembered as a very active and energetic missionary.

KARL P. WALLEN

Karl Petter Wallen was born in Uppland, Sweden, on August 18, 1864. He emigrated to the United States in 1888 and studied for two years in the Swedish Department at the Chicago Theological Seminary. In 1890 Karl was ordained and commissioned with Peter Matson by the Mission Covenant Church for missionary service to China. He went with his wife to China in 1890, and they settled at Fancheng in the spring of 1893, doing dispensary and evangelistic work.[244] They served there until 1897, when they returned home and resigned from the Covenant staff. In 1900 Karl was serving a Swedish Episcopal Church in Pawtucket, RI, and subsequently was practicing massage in Providence, RI, where the couple had settled.

MIA WALLEN

Mia (or Maria) Wallen was born in Uppland, Sweden, on October 16, 1867. She emigrated to the United States and in 1890 married the Rev. Karl P. Wallen. That year she was dedicated by the Mission Covenant for missionary service to China, and upon arrival in China became involved in evangelism at Fancheng (1893–1897). In an early picture of her and her husband with Peter Matson, she has a small child on her lap.[245] In 1895–96, when Matson had to return to the United States to address a lack of administrative orderliness in the Covenant executive board, and plead for more monetary support, Mia Wallen had some harsh words for the Covenant Board,[246] and in 1897 she and her husband returned home and resigned from the Covenant staff.

---

244. P. Matson, *Our China Mission*, 115; "The Siang Fan District," 23.

245. John Peterson, "Our Pioneer Missionary in China," 16.

246. Olsson, *By One Spirit*, 753 n. 54.

APPENDIX 5

Modern Place Names in China

Anhwei Province	Anhui Province
Anking	Anqing
Anluh	An Lu
Chengtu	Chengdu
Chungking	Chongqing
Hankow	Hankou
Honan Province	Henan Province
Hongkew (Shanghai)	Hongkou (Shanghai)
Hupeh Province	Hubei Province
Ichang	Yichang
Icheng	Yicheng
Kiangsi Province	Jiangxi Province
Kingchow	Jingzhou
Kingmen	Jingmen
Kiukiang	Jiujiang
Kuling	Guling
Kweichow Province	Guizhou Province
Kweiting	Guiding
Kweiyang	Guiyang
Laohokow	Laohekou
Nanchang (Hupeh)	Nanzhang (Hubei)

Nanchang (Kiangsi)	Nanchang (Jiangxi)
Nanking	Nanjing
Peiping / Peking	Beijing
Shasi	Shashi
Shensi Province	Shaanxi Province
Sian	Xian
Siangfan	Xiangfan
Siangyang	Xiangyang
Szechuan Province	Sichuan Province
Yangtze River	Chang Jiang ("Long River")

Bibliography

Almquist, August J. "A Brief Review of the Work of the Covenant Hospital and Home of Mercy, 1886–1936." *The Covenant Weekly* (April 21, 1936) 4, 6.

Anderson, C. Oscar. "Chinese Co-Workers." In *Half a Century of Covenant Foreign Missions*, edited by P. Matson et al., 92–95. Chicago: Evangelical Mission Covenant Church of America, 1940.

Anderson, C. Oscar, and Ruth M. Anderson. *Two Lives of Faith: The Autobiographies of C. Oscar Anderson and Ruth M. Anderson.* Edited by J. Edward Anderson et al. Denver: World Press, 1974.

Anderson, Craig E. *Growing Up Anderson: Part I—Beginnings.* Punta Gorda, FL: ShoreBird, 2013.

Anderson, Theodore W. "Foreword." In *Half a Century of Covenant Foreign Missions*, edited by P. Matson et al., 7–8. Chicago: Evangelical Mission Covenant Church of America, 1940.

Backlund, Paul S. "Glimpses of China Today." *Our Covenant* 19 (1944) 91–97.

———. "Traveling in China." *The Covenant Weekly* (April 30, 1948) 3.

Berg, Signe. "And God Answered Prayer." *The Covenant Weekly* (April 22, 1949) 5.

Branstrom, Carl A. "From a Missionary's Diary." *Our Covenant* 20 (1948) 63–70.

———. "From Temples of Idols to the Temple of God." *Our Covenant* 26 (1951) 72–83.

Broomhall, Marshall. *Robert Morrison: A Master-Builder.* New York: George H. Doran, 1924.

Bruce, J. Percy. "Massacre of English Baptist Missionaries and Others in Shansi." *The Chinese Recorder* 32 (1901) 132–37.

Candlin, G. T. "Chinese Hymnology—(Rev. J. Lees)." *The Chinese Recorder* 24 (1893) 167–73.

Carlson, Ann Kulberg. "Mission to China." Unpublished letters from 1947 to 1951.

Chéng, Marcus. *After Forty Years: Autobiography of Rev. Marcus Cheng B.A.* Philadelphia: China Inland Mission, 1947.

———. "Literary Work." In *Half a Century of Covenant Foreign Missions*, edited by P. Matson et al., 116–18. Chicago: Evangelical Mission Covenant Church of America, 1940.

Chin, Tze-show. "A Personal Testimony." In *Half a Century of Covenant Foreign Missions*, ed. P. Matson et al., 168–70. Chicago: Evangelical Mission Covenant Church of America, 1940.

———. "Siangyang Station Destroyed." *The Covenant Weekly* (October 8, 1948) 1.

Conradson, Amelia C. "The Young Women's Bible Training School." In *Half a Century of Covenant Foreign Missions*, edited by P. Matson et al., 119–21. Chicago: Evangelical Mission Covenant Church of America, 1940.

The (Covenant) Hymnal. Chicago: Covenant Press, 1950.

Dahlstrom, Earl. "The Covenant Missionary Society in China." Ph.D. diss., Hartford Seminary Foundation, 1950.

———. "Impressions of an Initiate in China." *Our Covenant* 16 (1941) 31–44.

Darroch, John. "Current Events as Seen through the Medium of the Chinese Newspapers." *The Chinese Recorder* 43 (1912) 23–33.

———. "Evangelistic Tracts and Literature." *The Chinese Recorder* 42 (1911) 328–343.

———. "The Influence of Religious Tract Societies in China." *The Chinese Recorder* 43 (1912) 398–410.

D'Elia, Paschal M. S. J. "Dr. Sun Yat-sen and Christianity." *The Chinese Recorder* 62 (1931) 75–88.

Dwight, Albert L. "China Missions Suffer." *The Covenant Weekly* (January 16, 1948) 3.

———. "Covenant Work in China." *Our Covenant* 23 (1948) 53–58.

———. "Gleanings from China." *The Covenant Weekly* (February 4, 1949) 3.

———. "Gleanings from China." *The Covenant Weekly* (March 18, 1949) 3.

———. "Into the Highways and Hedges." *The Covenant Weekly* (December 16, 1948) 2.

———. "A Land of Fluctuations." *The Covenant Weekly* (August 6, 1948) 2–3.

———. "Revival Movements." In *Half a Century of Covenant Foreign Missions*, edited by P. Matson et al., 96–103. Chicago: Evangelical Mission Covenant Church of America, 1940.

———. "Where Is the Dispersion?" *The Covenant Weekly* (November 3, 1948) 5.

Dwight, Norman. "Waldenström Goes to China and the 'Doers of the Word' Seminary." *Pietisten* 23/2 (2008) 11.

Ekeland, T. et al. *White unto Harvest: A Survey of the Lutheran United Mission: the China Mission of the Norwegian Lutheran Church of America*. Minneapolis: Board of Foreign Missions, Augsburg Publishing House, 1919.

Evans, Mrs. R. K. "City Evangelistic Work among Women." *The Chinese Recorder* 48 (1917) 32–36.

Fedde, Nathaniel. "Bethesda Union Hospital." In *White unto Harvest: A Survey of the Lutheran United Mission, the China Mission of the Norwegian Lutheran Church of America*, 138–41. Minneapolis: Board of Foreign Missions, Augsburg Publishing House, 1919.

Fitch, G. F. "Hymns and Hymn-Books for the Chinese." *The Chinese Recorder* 26 (1895) 466–70.

Fu, Chie-yu. "Witnessing for Christ." In *Half a Century of Covenant Foreign Missions*, edited by P. Matson et al., 174–75. Chicago: Evangelical Mission Covenant Church of America, 1940.

Glover, Archibald E. *A Thousand Miles of Miracle in China*. 20th ed. London: China Inland Mission, 1944. (1st ed., 1904).

Grainger, A. "The Street-Chapel." *The Chinese Recorder* 52 (1921) 593–99.

Hammerlind, Elsa.[1] "The Chinese Mother." In *Half a Century of Covenant Foreign Missions*, edited by P. Matson et al., 108–11. Chicago: Evangelical Mission Covenant Church of America, 1940.

---

1. The name in some sources is spelled "Hammarlind."

Hanson, Ralph P. "China's Crisis and Challenges." *The Covenant Weekly* (January 7, 1949) 3.

———. "Current Situation in China." *The Covenant Weekly* (April 16, 1948) 5.

[Hedstrand, G. F.]. "The Chinese Cromwell." *The Covenant Companion* Old Series (January, 1925) 7–8.

[———]. "Gist of China Conference Oral Reports." *The Covenant Weekly* (July 1, 1949) 3.

———. "An Interview with Marcus Cheng." *The Covenant Weekly* (December 14, 1948) 1–2.

Jacobson, Isaac W. "Christian School Work." In *Half a Century of Covenant Foreign Missions*, edited by P. Matson et al., 63–69. Chicago: Evangelical Mission Covenant Church of America, 1940.

———. "The Nanchang District." In *Half a Century of Covenant Foreign Missions*, edited by P. Matson et al., 32–40. Chicago: Evangelical Mission Covenant Church of America, 1940.

———. "Peasant Uprising against Communism in China." *The Covenant Weekly* (May 27, 1949) 2.

———. "Present Conditions on Our Field in China." *Our Covenant* 17 (1942) 75–83.

Johnson, Gust E. "Welcome Home." *The Covenant Weekly* (August 21, 1942) 3.

Johnson, Joel S. "Flight in the Winter." *The Covenant Weekly* (March 11, 1949) 3.

———. "Gospel-Band Experiences." *The Covenant Weekly* (January 16, 1948) 3.

———. "Kingchow Greetings." *The Covenant Weekly* (June 11, 1948) 3.

———. "Kingchow Tidings and Comments." *The Covenant Weekly* (January 7, 1949) 2.

———. "The Kingmen District." In *Half a Century of Covenant Foreign Missions*, edited by P. Matson et al., 46–52. Chicago: Evangelical Mission Covenant Church of America, 1940.

Johnson, Vernoy. *The Momentous Years: A Biography of Ruth Alice Hedberg Johnson and Alfred Joseph Johnson*. Chicago: n.p., 1996.

Larson, Leonard J. "Educational Work in China." *Our Covenant* 1 (1927) 38–50.

———. *Son of Prayer: Autobiography of Leonard J. Larson*. Edited by Muriel Larson Forsberg and Sharon Forsberg Welge. Kansas City, MO: n.p., 2000.

Larson, Viola. "Why We Went to China." *Our Covenant* 10 (1936) 88–89.

Latourette, Kenneth Scott. "American Catholic Missionaries in China." *The Chinese Recorder* 56 (1925) 96–98.

———. *The Chinese: Their History and Cultur*. Vols. I–II. 2nd ed. New York: Macmillan, 1943. (Orig. pub. 1934.)

Little, Edward S. *The Story of Kuling*. [Shanghai]: Chinkiang Literary Association, 1899.

Lundbom, Jack R. "All Great Works of God Begin in Secret." In *Exploring Bible, Church and Life: Essays in Celebration of the 100th Anniversary of the Lutheran Theological Seminary, Hong Kong*, edited by Simon Chow et al., 289–99. Theology and Life 36. Hong Kong: Lutheran Theological Seminary, 2013. Reprinted in Lundbom, *Theology in Language, Rhetoric, and Beyond*, 150–63. Eugene, OR: Cascade Books, 2014.

Mahnke, Susan. "Millie Nelson, Goffstown, New Hampshire." *Yankee* (September, 1979) 136–48.

Marsh, Gertrude. "A Nine-Day Journey in China." *The Covenant Weekly* (November 12, 1948) 2.

———. "Views from Modern China." *Our Covenant* 24 (1949) 41–52.

Matson, Edla C. "The Covenant Women's Evangelistic Auxiliary." In *Half a Century of Covenant Foreign Missions*, edited by P. Matson et al., 86–91. Chicago: Evangelical Mission Covenant Church of America, 1940.

———. "Life Under the Shadows of Death." *Our Covenant* 14 (1939) 21–29.

———. *Peter Matson: Covenant Pathfinder in China.* Chicago: Covenant Press, 1951.

Matson, Peter. "China Reminiscences." *Our Covenant* 15 (1940) 19–29.

———. "Hilda Nathalia Rodberg." *The Chinese Recorder* 63 (1931) 248.

———. *Our China Mission: The Story of the Mission Covenant's Work in China.* Chicago: Covenant Book Concern, 1934.

———. "Pioneer Days in Fancheng." In *Arise—Shine, Year Book 1940*, 53–55. Minneapolis: Board of Foreign Missions of the Norwegian Lutheran Church of America, 1940.

———. "Recollections from China." *Our Covenant* 9 (1935) 39–50.

———. "Shadow and Light in Hupeh." *The Chinese Recorder* 58 (1927) 802–3.

———. "The Siang Fan District." In *Half a Century of Covenant Foreign Missions*, edited by P. Matson et al., 22–31. Chicago: Evangelical Mission Covenant Church of America, 1940.

———. *Sowing in Tears, Reaping in Joy* (Chicago: Covenant Book Concern, 1923).

Matson, Peter, and C. O. Anderson. "The Icheng District." In *Half a Century of Covenant Foreign Missions*, edited by P. Matson et al., 41–45. Chicago: Evangelical Mission Covenant Church of America, 1940.

Matson, Peter, et al., eds. *Half a Century of Covenant Foreign Missions.* Chicago: Evangelical Mission Covenant Church of America, 1940. Reissued under the title *Covenant Frontiers.* Edited by P. Matson et al. Chicago: Evangelical Mission Covenant Church of America, 1941.

Matson, Ragnhild. "Letter from Bethesda Hospital, Siangyang, China." *The Covenant Weekly* (February 6, 1934) 1.

———. "Out of Bondage." *The Covenant Weekly* (December 10, 1943) 1, 9.

[McIntosh, Gilbert]. "Sun Wen: Revolutionary and Idealist." *The Chinese Recorder* 56 (1925) 213–14.

Nelson, C. Barton. "Heal the Sick." In *Half a Century of Covenant Foreign Missions*, edited by P. Matson et al., 122–27. Chicago: Evangelical Mission Covenant Church of America, 1940.

———. "Our Medical Missionary Work in China." *Our Covenant* 10 (1936) 68–72.

Nelson, Carl J. "The Twenty-fifth Anniversary of the 'Sin Tao Hues.'" *The Chinese Recorder* 47 (1916) 132–33.

Nelson, Edward G. *China in Your Blood.* Chicago: Covenant Press, 1953.

———. "The Covenant Church in China and Southeast Asia." *Our Covenant* 32 (1957) 17–19.

Nelson, K. M. "Glimpses from Our Medical Work in Siangyang." *Our Covenant* 1 (1927) 23–37.

Nelson, Mildred. "Why We Went to China." *Our Covenant* 10 (1936) 87–88.

Nelson, Murial (Mrs. C. Barton). "The Missionaries' Home." In *Half a Century of Covenant Foreign Missions*, edited by P. Matson et al., 150–51. Chicago: Evangelical Mission Covenant Church of America, 1940.

Nordlund, Esther V. *The Life and Work of Victor Leonard Nordlund, 1869–1937.* San Fernando, La Union, Philippines: Ilocano Printing Co., 1940.

Nordlund, Mildred. "A China Experience." *The Covenant Companion* (January 1, 1981) 10–11.

———. "Flash Pictures of War Time China." *Our Covenant* 21 (1946) 86–97.

———. "Medical Work among Women." In *Half a Century of Covenant Foreign Missions*, edited by P. Matson et al., 128–33. Chicago: Evangelical Mission Covenant Church of America, 1940.

Norris, F. L. "Music in the Chinese Church." *The Chinese Recorder* 40 (1909) 179–89.

Olson, Mabel E. "Judge Finds Christ." *The Covenant Weekly* (July 2, 1948) 3.

———. "Women's Work." In *Half a Century of Covenant Foreign Missions*, edited by P. Matson et al., 80–85. Chicago: Evangelical Mission Covenant Church of America, 1940.

Olsson, Karl A. *By One Spirit*. Chicago: Covenant Press, 1962.

Osnes, E. "Conference in Siangyang and Fancheng." *The Chinese Recorder* 37 (1906) 469–70.

Pedersen, Theodore. "Bethesda Union Hospital." *The Chinese Recorder* 46 (1915) 261.

Peterson, John. "Kingchow and Shasi." In *Half a Century of Covenant Foreign Missions*, edited by P. Matson et al., 53–57. Chicago: Evangelical Mission Covenant Church of America, 1940.

———. "Kingchow Theological Seminary." In *Half a Century of Covenant Foreign Missions*, edited by P. Matson et al., 70–79. Chicago: Evangelical Mission Covenant Church of America, 1940.

———. "Our Pioneer Missionary in China." In *Half a Century of Covenant Foreign Missions*, edited by P. Matson et al., 15–19. Chicago: Evangelical Mission Covenant Church of America, 1940,

———. "A Solemn Baptismal Act of 162 Officers and Soldiers." *The Chinese Recorder* 70 (1939) 384–86. (Reported also in *The Covenant Weekly* [April 25, 1939] 4.)

Peterson, Judith M. "Bethesda Training School for Nurses." In *Half a Century of Covenant Foreign Missions*, edited by P. Matson et al., 134–39. Chicago: Evangelical Mission Covenant Church of America, 1940.

Salters, Audrey, ed. *Bound with Love: Letters Home from China 1935–1945*. St. Andrews: Agequod, 2007.

Scherer, James A. "The Lutheran Church in China: A Brief History." *Currents in Theology and Mission* 17 (1990) 390–92.

———. "The Lutheran Missionary Pioneers: Who Were They?" *Currents in Theology and Mission* 17 (1990) 343–65.

Sköld, Joh. "Tankar vid 25-års Jubileet in Kingchow." *Hemåt* (1917) 107–15.

Smith, A. H. "The Relation of the Chinese Revolution to Human Progress." *The Chinese Recorder* 44 (1913) 9–13.

Springweiler, Max. *Pioneer Aviator in China*. Translated by Larry D. Sall. Dallas: CAT Association and The Air America Association, 1998.

Sturton, Stephen D. "The Outreach of the Tao Fong Shan Christian Institute." *The Chinese Recorder* 67 (1936) 626–29.

Svenska Ev. Missionsförbundets I Amerika Årsberättelse för Verksamhetsåret 1930–1931, till årsmötet i Chicago, Ill. Den 17–21 Juni 1931. Chicago: Missionsförbundets Expedition, 1931.

Swanson, Edgar E. "Missionary Peter Matson." *Our Covenant* 18 (1943) 33–35.

Swenson, Victor E. "Notes on Kikungshan." *The Chinese Recorder* 50 (1919) 276–77.

Syrdal, Rolf A. "American Lutheran Mission Work in China." Ph.D. diss., Drew Theological Seminary, 1942.

Tsu, Y. Y. "The Christian Service at Dr. Sun Yat-sen's Funeral March 18, 1925." *The Chinese Recorder* 62 (1931) 88–90.

Wang, Hwai-chen. "Labors and Results." In *Half a Century of Covenant Foreign Missions*, edited by P. Matson et al., 166–68. Chicago: Evangelical Mission Covenant Church of America, 1940.

Wu, Teng-yung. "The Mustard Seed." In *Half a Century of Covenant Foreign Missions*, edited by P. Matson et al., 172–73. Chicago: Evangelical Mission Covenant Church of America, 1940.

Yuen, Peh-yung. "Nanchang Items." In *Half a Century of Covenant Foreign Missions*, edited by P. Matson et al., 170–72. Chicago: Evangelical Mission Covenant Church of America, 1940.

———. "They Did Not Die in Vain." *The Covenant Weekly* (June 18, 1948) 3.

Yung Cheng. "The Martyrdom at T'ai-yuen-fu on the 9th of July." *The Chinese Recorder* 32 (1901) 210–11.

For additional bibliography, see Jack R. Lundbom, "Covenant Mission in Mainland China: An Annotated Bibliography." Available at the F. M. Johnson Archives and Special Collections, Brandel Library, North Park University, Chicago; also online at www.northpark.edu/archives.

Name Index